Every Chart-Topper Tells a Story:
The Sixties

A native of East Sussex, Sharon Davis was a devoted admirer of black American music from an early age, particularly that emanating from Motown Records in Detroit. Early in her career she worked for EMI Records, running the British Motown fan club in her spare time. She then became publicity manager for three American labels, followed this by working at Motown Records and then spearheaded her own press and promotion company, Eyes and Ears. She has written for several publications, including the prestigious *Blues and Soul* magazine where she is currently a features writer. Her previous books include *Marvin Gaye, Motown: The History* and *I Heard It through the Grapevine*. She worked with Diana Ross on the writing of Diana's autobiography, *Secrets of a Sparrow*, and penned, among others, the CD sleeve notes for the successful series 'Early Classics', released by Spectrum Records, and the forthcoming Britannia mail order series and 'Master Series' to be issued by Phonograph Records. *Every Chart-Topper Tells a Story: The Sixties* is the first in a series which also includes *The Seventies*. *The Fifties* and *The Eighties* will later be incorporated into the 'Chart-Topper' series, as will books on soul and dance music covering the same decades.

Every Chart-Topper Tells a Story
THE SIXTIES

SHARON DAVIS

MAINSTREAM
PUBLISHING

EDINBURGH AND LONDON

First published in Great Britain in 1997 by
MAINSTREAM PUBLISHING COMPANY (EDINBURGH) LTD
7 Albany Street
Edinburgh EH1 3UG

ISBN 1 85158 836 1

A catalogue record for this book is available from the British Library

Typeset in 11 on 13pt Plantin
Printed and bound in Finland by WSOY

This book is dedicated to the memory
of my new friend

Sandy Van Leer

BRITISH No. I SINGLES

1960–69

CONTENTS

CONTENTS

CONTENTS

INTRODUCTION

Ah! The glorious sixties, when the word 'free' applied to almost anything. It was the decade of the young and rebellious, who lived life to the full, usually through a marijuana haze.

The sixties offered an escape route from the drab fifties with technicolour music, sexual liberation and cultural freedom. When the musical residue of the previous decade was replaced by the likes of The Beatles and The Rolling Stones, and closely cropped hair gave way to shoulder-length, free-flowing locks, when sharp suits were discarded for denim and cotton, the decade got off into full swing.

The British music scene had never been so exciting, dangerous and versatile – British beat, American R. & B. with the Stax and Motown labels, straight pop, and Flower Power which gave way to commercial blues and pseudo-psychedelia. It was the decade of change and decadence. It was also a decade of new birth for acts whose popularity reigned true into the seventies and beyond. Others, of course, fell into the one-hit wonder category, to return to everyday life. And they're all here, starting with Emile Ford and 'What Do You Want to Make Those Eyes at Me For' in January 1960, through to December 1969 with The Archies' 'Sugar Sugar'. Ford was Britain's first black pop star, while The Archies were a non-existent American musical unit. Yep, a decade of changes indeed!

During the years in between, the Americans held their own on British soil with artists like Elvis Presley, Del Shannon, The Righteous Brothers and Frank and Nancy Sinatra. Scott McKenzie then carried his basket of flowers across the Atlantic, leaving the soul element of black America to the likes of The Supremes, the Four Tops, Ray Charles and Marvin Gaye, among others.

In all honesty, though, it was the British artists who injected a vitality, perhaps a danger, into the resurrection of a tired music scene. For example, The Beatles exploded to turn our lives inside out; The Rolling Stones transformed respectability into villainy, with music to match. Other groups, like Gerry and the Pacemakers, The Shadows

13

and The Tremeloes calmed the often frenetic musical pace, while the girls, led, of course, by Dusty Springfield, reigned and then rose again – Cilla Black, Sandie Shaw and Helen Shapiro are still household names three decades later. Of the British males, well, who else but Cliff Richard, Adam Faith, Tom Jones and Engelbert Humperdinck, crooning and reeling their way through 'The Young Ones', 'Poor Me', 'Green Green Grass of Home' and 'The Last Waltz'. We loved 'em all!

In this decade of limited media exposure for pop music, thank the Lord for the Friday night live television show *Ready, Steady, Go!* The programme epitomised all that was happening in the music and fashion scene. It was *the* show to be seen on, and watched. 'The weekend starts here . . .' Remember? BBC radio programmes were designed to cater for young taste; or were they? No, indeed not! Thankfully, pirate stations were born to replace the staid, ancient BBC policy, offering music for the cult followers, trendies and undecided. Pirates certainly projected a competitive, enlightening element to the airwaves, which were great fun while they lasted.

As the title suggests, this book is devoted to the No. 1 singles (chart-toppers) of the sixties. When more than one single reached the top during a particular month, the most topical has been included. This is also the case when, say, The Beatles had a consecutive run of chart-toppers. Other artists' singles have been included to break the (possible) monotony of writing and reading about the same act. For information, the chart-topping singles herein have been 'mixed 'n' matched' from listings printed in the weekly music papers of the decade, including among others the *New Musical Express, Blues and Soul, Melody Maker, Disc and Music Echo* and *Record Mirror*.

To help me achieve this mammoth task – it started as a dream and practically turned into a nightmare! – I must have rifled through what seemed like a million press clippings from British and American magazines, newspapers and so on, that included *Record Collector, Disc, Melody Maker,* the *New Musical Express* (as it was known during the sixties), *Billboard, Cashbox* and *Rolling Stone*. I read what appeared to be hundreds of credible artist biographies, both in book and article form, and consulted thousands of reference books, including a very tatty but invaluable *British Hit Singles – Volume 9* published by Guinness and compiled by Paul Gambaccini, Jonathan Rice and Tim Rice.

Other publications of particular help and which I've referred to in the text, were: *Step Inside* – Cilla Black; *Scott Walker: A Deep Shade of Blue* – Mike Watkinson and Pete Anderson; *The Elvis Presley Scrapbooks*

– Peter Haining; *Elvis: Murdered by the Mob* – John Parker; *Off the Record: An Oral History of Popular Music* – Joe Smith; *The Billboard Book of Number One Hits: Third Edition* – Fred Bronson; *Rock 'n' Roll Babylon* – Gary Herman; *Shout* – Philip Norman; *Radio Luxembourg Record Stars No. 4* and *Cliff Richard: The Complete Chronicle* – Mike Read, Nigel Goodall and Peter Lewry. Super reading, and my sincere thanks to all and everyone.

My mostest thanks, however, go to this project's co-ordinator and researcher, Gerry Constable, without whom none of this would have been possible. Her ability to discover information is second to none, and her tidy mind is enviable. Her expertise also spans my two sister books, *Every Chart-Topper Tells a Story: The Seventies* and *Every Chart-Topper Tells a Story: The Eighties*. Other researchers to thank are Tina Llewellyn, Julie Rough and Chris Williams.

Last but certainly not least, it's good to be hand-in-hand with the guys at Mainstream Publishing again. Thanks for believing in the project, Bill!

Nothing more to say, except hope you get as much fun from reading this trip through the sixties as I did writing it. Enjoy!

Sharon Davis
1997

EMILE FORD

What Do You Want to Make Those Eyes at Me For

In a musical climate that had been dominated by white British and American acts, Emile Ford forged a name for himself as Britain's first black pop star.

As the fifties closed, the best-selling names of the decade included Buddy Holly, Russ Conway, Bobby Darin, Ricky Nelson and, of course, Elvis Presley – and Britain's own Cliff Richard. Tough competition indeed! Also, a new musical style was starting to break ground: Traditional Jazz. It would never take a stranglehold on the charts although Chris Barber made considerable inroads.

Emile Ford's career was short; four hit singles with 'What Do You Want to Make Those Eyes at Me For' his only No. 1. Incidentally, twenty- seven years after its initial release, British rock 'n' roller Shakin' Stevens took his version to No. 5 in the chart.

Born Emile Sweetman on 16 October 1937 in St Lucia, Windward Islands, Emile Ford emigrated to London during the fifties. His family insisted he finish his education in London, but after studying at Paddington's Technical College and Tottenham's Polytechnic, the young man's interest turned to music. By early 1959, Ford headed his own group, The Checkmates, featuring his brother George and college friend Ken Street. The trio hit the popular Soho skiffle circuit of coffee bars and clubs and before 1959 was out had won a Soho Fair talent contest. A recording contract with Pye Records followed. Two additions were subsequently made to The Checkmates' line-up, namely, keyboardist Alan Hawkshaw and John Cutley on drums.

During October 1959, the group recorded a beaty version of the 1916 show tune 'What Do You Want to Make Those Eyes at Me For'. Success was instant; the single raced to the top of the British chart in January 1960, staying there for six weeks, earning Emile Ford his first gold disc for sales in excess of one million – an incredible feat for an unknown singer with his debut recording.

After much deliberation, his second single was issued in 1960. Another cover version, but older in years, 'On a Slow Boat to China' was written by Frank Loesser in 1948. It missed the top spot to settle at No. 3. Nonetheless the success proved Emile Ford wasn't a one-hit wonder, but the going was to get tougher.

For some reason, Ford opted on a change of musical direction for his third single, 'You'll Never Know What You're Missing', reported to be lifted from a Ricky Nelson album at Ford's request. Despite its catchiness, the record stalled outside the Top Ten. Hasty plans were made for its follow-up. This time he chose Billie Holliday's jazz standard, 'Them There Eyes'. Not a wise move, as it barely crept into the Top Twenty. Also, The Checkmates didn't provide back-up on this track. Pye Records decided to use the Johnny Keating Orchestra instead which, naturally enough, caused an immediate rift between Ford and the record company. It was not a prime time for arguments as Emile Ford now appeared to be struggling for chart power. However, help was at hand.

'Counting Teardrops', penned by Howard Greenfield and Barry Mann, returned the flagging singer to the British Top Five, restoring his status in the music market. But once more the impetus was short-lived, and with the next single the decline in Ford's career began.

In March 1961, the aptly named 'What Am I Gonna Do' written by Neil Sedaka and previously recorded by Jimmy Clanton, struggled into the British Top Forty, and in an attempt to alleviate further declining sales, Ford reverted to his familiar sound to revive 'I Wonder Who's Kissing Her Now'. Remarkably, even this failed to dent the Top Forty and represented his last chart entry.

The star had fallen, and by 1963 The Checkmates abandoned him. Their own recording career was nondescript and after five singles flopped, they disbanded, leaving John Cutley to work with the Climax Blues Band, George Ford to record and tour with Cockney Rebel, and Ken Street to turn to management to look after the British group, Love Affair.

There was only one option left for Emile Ford and that was clubland again. But this time he combined his public appearances with his work as a studio sound engineer, and by 1988, had opened his own electronics company. He now lives in America where he still performs.

Also a No. 1 single in January 1960: 'Starry Eyed' by Michael Holliday

February 1960

ANTHONY NEWLEY

Why

To be a successful actor, singer and composer was beyond Anthony Newley's wildest dreams when he was a budding child star. Yet he established himself in all three fields, and still performs today, winning critical acclaim for his excellent character roles.

Born in London on 24 September 1931, Anthony Newley was a successful child actor after attending the Italia Conti Stage School. He starred in movies like *The Little Ballerina*, and in 1948 played his much-remembered role of the Artful Dodger in David Lean's *Oliver*. This led to his stage debut in London in *Cranks*, and further character roles in over twenty adventure films during the fifties.

At the end of the decade, Newley established himself as a singer, playing the role of Jeep Jackson, a rock 'n' roll star, in *Idle on Parade*. He recorded the theme song which he took into the British Top Thirty. The Jerry Lordan ballad, 'I've Waited So Long', also lifted from the movie, soared to No. 3 in the British chart. Thus Anthony Newley, actor, had embarked upon a recording career whether he liked it or not! Decca Records had released his recorded output to date and, impressed by his sales, signed him to a recording deal proper, which lasted through to 1962 when he returned to acting.

Meanwhile, in June 1959, Newley's next single, 'Personality', a No. 6 hit, paved the way for his first British chart-topper, 'Why', during February 1960. And this, in turn, led to his second British No. 1 single, 'Do You Mind', written by Lionel Bart. Although not possessing a powerful, true voice – rather, a shaky, whispery style – he continued to enjoy three further Top Ten singles, namely, 'If She Should Come to You', the standard 'Strawberry Fair' and 'And the Heavens Cried'. During June 1961, the most unusual choice of 'Pop Goes the Weasel'/'Bee Bom' missed the Top Ten by two places. Interestingly, a 'green' David Bowie swiped sections from these last two titles during 1973 to include on his 'The Laughing Gnome' single.

It was in 1961 that Anthony Newley excelled as a singer with a track from *Stop the World – I Want to Get off*. Titled 'What Kind of Fool Am I?' it surprisingly faltered at No. 36 in the British chart, yet went on to become one of the most famous of standards in the history of music. *Stop the World – I Want to Get off* was, in fact, Newley's first musical, written with Leslie Bricusse. It went on to be hailed as one of the best musicals of the decade. A film version was released during 1966 and such was its longevity that it was filmed a second time under the title *Sammy Stops the World* during 1978. Ten years on from this, the musical was staged in London.

The composing couple then moved into the world of James Bond to write lyrics to the John Barry score for *Goldfinger*. Shirley Bassey sang the film's theme to enjoy a Top Twenty hit during October 1964.

Newley and Bricusse followed *Stop the World – I Want to Get off* with *The Roar of the Greasepaint – the Smell of the Crowd* during 1965. The show, starring Norman Wisdom, toured Britain successfully but inexplicably never made the London stage. From this musical another powerful song was lifted, namely, 'Who Can I Turn to?' which Tony Bennett took into the American chart. The song was subsequently re-recorded countless times by the world's top vocalists. When the musical travelled Stateside, Anthony Newley co-starred with Cyril Richard. It was an immediate hit with the critics and public alike.

Anthony Newley's last chart entrants were in 1962. The first was 'D-Darling' in January which reached No. 25; the other 'That Noise' in July, a No. 34 hit. Composing consumed his time now, either alone or with Leslie Bricusse. When Bricusse wrote the film score for *Doctor Doolittle*, Newley had a co-starring role with Rex Harrison. *Goodbye Mr Chips* and *Scrooge* followed.

Meantime, as a soloist, Newley survived a box-office flop with *Can Hieronymus Merkin Ever Forget Mercy Humpe and Find True Happiness?* during 1969, to regain success two years on with Roald Dahl's *Willy Wonka and the Chocolate Factory* when he wrote the score with Bricusse. 'The Candy Man' was lifted as a single by Sammy Davis Jr, who sold in excess of one million copies in America. And in 1971, they scored an adaptation of *Peter Pan* starring Danny Kaye and Mia Farrow for the American NBC-TV station, before returning to musicals to write *The Good Old Bad Old Days*. This was their last musical of note.

Years on, and now living in California, Newley hosted his own revue, *Once upon a Song*, in Miami, and enjoyed a lucrative cabaret career. In 1989, *Stop the World – I Want to Get off* was revived in London with Newley performing, but it was closed after two months. In the same year, he wrote the musical *Sherlock Holmes*.

More recently, in 1994, Anthony Newley toured Britain in a revival of the musical *Scrooge* when critics once more waxed lyrical over his extraordinary talent.

March 1960

ADAM FAITH

Poor Me

Of all the artists 'discovered' during the fifties in London's Soho coffee bars, Adam Faith and Cliff Richard probably became the most successful. At one time the two were competitors, but it was Richard who had the staying power. However, Adam Faith enjoyed a remarkable career as a pop singer and, unlike many, he had other talents that sustained him when the singing stopped.

Adam Faith, born Terence Nelhams in Acton, London, on 23 June 1940, left school with the sole ambition of joining the movie business. After securing a job with Rank Screen Services as a messenger, he was promoted to assistant film editor. Then his interest turned to music, notably skiffle, which was spreading through Britain. While still employed at Rank, he teamed up with colleagues to perform as The Worried Men. Like most at the time, they found their way to Soho, and the 2I's coffee shop, the heart of skiffle and rock 'n' roll.

In 1957 Jack Good's BBC TV music show *6.5 Special* was filmed from the 2I's coffee shop where the young Nelhams happened to be playing. Jack Good believed he would make a better soloist than group member, but before any plans could be made a name change was imperative. Hence, Adam Faith was born after searching through a children's name book.

Before 1958 was out, Adam Faith had recorded and released his debut single '(Got a) Heartsick Feeling' for EMI Records' HMV label. His second attempt was issued in November 1958. Titled 'Country Music Holiday', written by Burt Bacharach and Hal David, it was Faith's second bomber. HMV dropped him from its artists' roster, leaving a dissatisfied singer to return to Rank.

It was a temporary move, for early in 1959, Adam Faith was offered a residency on a new BBC TV music programme, *Drumbeat*. His stay ran into six months where he sang cover versions of American rock 'n' roll classics, like 'C'mon Everybody'. One song, 'Ah! Poor Little Baby', was chosen for release as a single on the Top Rank label. Another flop. Nonetheless, it sufficiently impressed his future manager, Eve Taylor.

While working on the *Drumbeat* series, Faith met and worked with composer Johnny Worth (aka Les Vandyke). He had written 'What Do You Want' with John Barry in the style of Buddy Holly's 'It Doesn't Matter Any More'. They wanted Faith to record it, and to this end encouraged John Burgess, producer for the Parlophone label (a subsidiary of EMI Records) to record him.

'What Do You Want' was issued late in 1959. It soared to the top of the British chart within three weeks from its release, giving the Parlophone label its first chart-topper, eventually selling in the region of 600,000 copies. The song's attractions (and indeed that of further Faith singles) were his pronunciation of the word 'baby' – he accentuated it to 'boy bee' – and his emulation of Buddy Holly's 'jerky' vocal style.

'Poor Me', the follow-up in March 1960, was no different. A diluted version of its predecessor and again written by Worth and Barry, it likewise shot to the top of the British chart. 'Someone Else's Baby' was next, a No. 2 hit.

Now a name of value, Adam Faith was in demand, particularly on the package tours. Fans flocked to see this slight figure perform a series of songs that vaguely sounded alike. Yet such was the sudden momentum of his popularity that he was second only to Britain's top soloist, Cliff Richard. And like Richard, Faith became an actor, although his movie debut wasn't a lightweight role but rather a risqué one. In April 1960 he appeared with co-star Shirley Ann Field in the X-rated *Beat Girl*, a tale of teenage revolution. One track, 'Made You', was lifted from the movie as a single, but due to the content of the lyrics (considered to be too explicit) it was banned by BBC Radio. The B-side, 'When Johnny Comes Marching Home', received the airplay instead to become a No. 5 hit. The soundtrack from *Beat Girl* notched up sufficient sales to reach the Top Twenty in the album chart. His second film, *Never Let Go*, starred Peter Sellers and Richard Todd, and was also considered unsuitable for family viewing.

To round off 1960, Adam Faith issued 'How About That' and to cash in on Christmas sales 'Lonely Pup (in a Christmas Shop)'. They both peaked at No. 4 in the chart. Faith's selling power was now consistent, so his first album, *Adam*, was finally released to peak at No. 6, although it stayed a Top Twenty album for nearly nine months.

'Who Am I' was the first 1961 disc, a Top Five hit, followed by a pair of No. 12 hits – 'Easy Going Me', written by Lionel Bart, and 'Don't You Know It'. During October, Faith appeared in his third movie, a comedy this time, *What a Whopper*. The plot concerned the mysteries of the Loch Ness monster. A month later, 'The Time Has Come' was lifted from the movie's soundtrack to reach the Top Five.

A change of musical direction brought in the New Year of 1962, with a ballad 'Lonesome'. The title crept to No. 12. Presumably his public was a little unsure of this new-sounding Faith, but how long could he continue to 'boy bee' his way through soundalike singles? To date, John Barry had worked with him, but as his success grew, he became increasingly in demand. This meant his collaborations with Faith were fewer, and when 'As You Like It' was issued in May 1962, it marked the last time the two would work together. The single hit the Top Five.

During September, the singer once again turned actor. This time he starred with Donald Sinden and Anne Baxter in *Mix Me a Person*. Faith played an innocent man imprisoned for murder. He admitted acting was as important to him as singing, and was lucky to be in a position to succeed at both.

Johnny Keating worked with Faith on his next single, 'Don't That Beat All'. Another departure from the Adam Faith sound, it nonetheless reached No. 8. In December 1962, 'Baby Take a Bow' stalled at No. 22, marking an end to a consecutive run of Top Twenty singles.

By now The Beatles were making their presence felt and Adam Faith felt the pinch. Soloists were becoming obsolete; the groups were taking over. Midway through 1963, he decided to join them and recruited a backing group. Known as The Roulettes, they gave the singer a new lease of life, as his material struck a musical edge previously unheard of from the 'boy bee' boy. With composer/singer Chris Andrews, also represented by manager Eve Taylor, Adam Faith and The Roulettes released 'The First Time'. The mix worked, the single returned him to the Top Five.

For the next two years Faith stayed with Chris Andrews (who also recorded as a soloist), and experimented with other composers like Burt Bacharach and Hal David. He recorded their 'Message to Martha' which became a No. 12 British hit in December 1964. It was at this time that Faith discovered Sandie Shaw, whom he persuaded Eve Taylor to manage. She recorded Bacharach and David's '(There's) Always Something There to Remind Me', which became her first chart-topper.

During the early part of 1965, Adam Faith joined the British invasion of America when he enjoyed a Top Forty hit there titled 'I Love Being in Love with You'. Regrettably, by April 1965, the American success ended with the poor-showing 'Talk about Love'. In Britain, he also suffered when 'Hand Me Down Things' notched up another flop (the previous one being the ballad 'Only One Such As You' in September 1964).

Luckily, Chris Andrews re-established him in the Top Forty with the Bacharach/David-styled 'Someone's Taken Maria Away'. The success was short-lived. After a trio of flops in 1966, his last chart entrant was 'Cheryl's Goin' Home', a remake of the Bob Lind original. Released in October, it clawed its way into the Top Fifty. A year later, Adam Faith recorded his final single, 'To Hell with Love', retired from live performances and abandoned the record industry entirely. He intended to seriously pursue his acting career, and to this end, joined a touring repertory company to star in *Billy Liar* and *Twelfth Night*.

During 1971, Adam Faith's name cropped up on the opening credits of a new television series, *Budgie*. He was hugely successful in his portrayal of a small-time 'wheeler-dealer', who wandered from one incident to another. A year on, he returned to the music business, not as an artist but as manager to newcomer Leo Sayer, who became a top-selling act.

Following a life-threatening car accident which left him with a slight limp, Faith returned to the movie world to star with David Essex in *Stardust*, the sequel to *That'll Be the Day*, also starring Essex, and Ringo Starr. In turn, this led to Faith's return to the recording studios after a seven-year break to record the *I Survive* album. When that bombed, he relied on his other talents – producing, managing and acting.

In 1979 he played a team manager in a football movie titled *Yesterday's Hero*. Ian McShane co-starred. A year on, he starred with Roger Daltrey in *McVicar*, the true story of John McVicar. With the turn of the decade, Faith once more became a small-screen star when he brought *Love Hurts* into the nation's homes. On the back of this remarkable success, he recorded and released the album *Midnight Postcards* which, due to the loyalty of his viewing public, peaked in the Top Fifty.

Adam Faith was a survivor of the sixties. Being a high-ranking actor helped him sustain his popularity. Many fail to associate the man of the nineties with the young, shy singer of the late fifties and early sixties. He also proved to the adult world that despite popular belief at the time, he was a pop singer with a brain, and not a member of the mindless moron syndrome associated with sixties' pop music.

Also a No. 1 single in March 1960: 'Running Bear' by Johnny Preston

April 1960

LONNIE DONEGAN

My Old Man's a Dustman

Often regarded as a forerunner of the skiffle movement in Britain, Lonnie Donegan was in fact a jazzman by nature. For a time skiffle was treated as 'fun' music, as musicians played improvised instruments like the washboard and broom-handle bass, inspired, incidentally, by the black Americans who had previously used them decades before. However, Lonnie Donegan's influence transformed skiffle into a legitimate musical form. To many he was the king!

Lonnie Donegan was born Anthony Donegan in Glasgow on 29 April 1931, and he spent most of his early life in Scotland. He was raised in a musical family as his father played the violin with the Scottish National Orchestra, while the radio regularly blared fifties' music. As his interest in music grew, Donegan began memorising the lyrics to traditional songs, and by the time he was seventeen years old he had mastered the guitar and drums. This led to him joining a local group during 1948 but his stay was short-lived because he was called up to join the Army.

During his two-year stay, Donegan developed his jazz skills by playing drums for the Wolverines Jazz Band. When he was demobbed he made London his home and became a follower of, and player for, Ken Colyer, who specialised in mixing New Orleans jazz with skiffle.

Donegan moved from Colyer's band to work with Alexis Korner, and in 1951 formed his own outfit, Tony Donegan and His Skiffle Group. However, after playing with Lonnie Johnson, Donegan not only adopted his first name, but abandoned his own group to join another, headed by Chris Barber. Together they were a powerful force during the early fifties, attracting a huge audience. Because of their popularity, hundreds of skiffle groups were born and by the end of the decade clubland was saturated with skiffle bands of various shapes and sizes. And the sales of guitars had quadrupled!

Record companies, however, were surprisingly slow to pay attention to this musical explosion, but eventually, Chris Barber and Lonnie Donegan did sign a recording contract with Decca Records, whereupon their debut album, *New Orleans' Joys* was issued during 1955. 'Rock Island Line', Donegan's interpretation of a blues original, was lifted as a single to crash into the British Top Ten, where it peaked at No. 8 in January 1956. Three weeks later, it made a re-entry to reach No. 16, and in May re-entered for the second time to peak at No. 19! It also became Donegan's first American hit, and went on to earn him a gold disc during 1961.

Lonnie Donegan's name was now synonymous with the skiffle boom. But he needed to establish himself as a soloist. In 1956 he moved from Decca to Pye Records for a reputed £10,000, where his first single, 'Stewball', became a Top Thirty hit for one week. Its B-side, 'Lost John', took over to soar to No. 2. In 1956, Donegan scored three further chart records – 'Skiffle Session' EP (he was the first soloist to place an EP on the British singles chart), 'Bring a Little Water, Sylvie' and *Lonnie Donegan Showcase*, which was an album!

Six further hits dominated 1957 – a re-entry of 'Bring a Little Water, Sylvie', followed by 'Don't You Rock Me Daddy-O', 'Cumberland Gap' and 'Gamblin' Man' (both chart-toppers), 'My Dixie Darling' and 'Jack o' Diamonds'. The remainder reached the Top Twenty.

Alongside his recorded output, Donegan excelled as a performer: whether playing in a pantomime, in his first movie role, an appearance in the first Royal Command Variety Performance in 1958, or his own television series, *Putting on the Donegan*. His last hit of 1958 was a version of The Kingston Trio's 'Tom Dooley', a British Top Three hit and a million-seller.

During February 1959, 'Does your Chewing Gum Lose its Flavour' likewise shot to No. 3, selling a million copies. Donegan actually discovered this song in an old Boy Scout handbook, one of his sources for unusual, catchy singles. This was followed by versions of Johnny Horton's 'Battle of New Orleans' and the traditional tune 'Sal's Got a Sugar Lip', No. 2 and No. 13 respectively in the British chart.

Through to the start of 1960, he was a top-selling artist in Europe and was rarely out of the British Top Twenty. In March 1960 when 'My Old Man's a Dustman' became a chart-topper, it was Donegan's first since 'Gamblin' Man' in June 1957. He had adapted this track from a rude Liverpudlian song 'My Old Man's a Fireman on the Elder-Dempster Line'. It was to be his last No. 1 single. This and 'Does your Chewing Gum Lose its Flavour' were issued in America on the Dot label, which also released a series of his albums beginning with the 1959 *Lonnie Donegan*.

By now, Donegan had opened his own music publishing company to protect the copyright in his original compositions and his additional or new lyrics to traditional songs and folk ditties. For example, in 1961, he recorded 'Have a Drink on Me' which was originally known as 'Have a Whiff on Me'. By doing this he also had another source of income when one of his songs was re-recorded.

Another four hits were released during 1960: 'I Wanna Go Home', 'Lorelei', 'Lively' and 'Virgin Mary'. Two more followed in 1961, the aforementioned 'Have a Drink on Me' and 'Michael Row the Boat', while 1962 marked the last year he would enjoy Top Twenty success with 'The Comancheros', 'The Party's Over' and 'Pick a Bale of Cotton'. Skiffle music began to move underground as popular music in general changed. The Merseybeat explosion was pending and artists like Lonnie Donegan felt the pinch. And like others, he relied on the cabaret circuit to earn a living.

During 1978 Lonnie Donegan returned to the studios to record the *Puttin' on the Style* album, produced by Adam Faith. Other featured artists were Leo Sayer, Elton John and Ringo Starr (who, like the rest of The Beatles, was heavily influenced by Donegan). Two years later, Donegan and Doug Kershaw recorded a country album titled *Sundown*. Although critically acclaimed it bombed, leaving Donegan no choice but to return to the lucrative world of cabaret.

May/June 1960

THE EVERLY BROTHERS

Cathy's Clown

The Everly Brothers were the world's No. 1 vocal group, whose popularity was second to Elvis Presley in the rock 'n' roll stakes. Their sound was partly country and folk but fast-lane rock was their business, and with their brotherly affection, good looks and smart American image, they were accepted by both kids and parents. Unlike Presley, of course!

Born Isaac Donald Everly on 1 February 1937 in Brownie, Kentucky, Don wasn't the twin of Phil, as so many believed. Phil was, in fact, born on 19 January 1939 in Chicago, Illinois. Also, the story of The Everly Brothers did not actually begin with these youngsters because their father Ike had performed with his two brothers using the same name.

When the two boys were living in Shenandoah, Iowa, their parents, both performers, introduced them to listeners on their Earl May radio show. Don was eight years old, Phil six, and they were known to listeners as Little Donnie and Baby Boy Phil. When their radio shows ended, the family group dispersed, but Don and Phil had music in their veins and wanted to continue in the business.

Family friend Chet Atkins helped the brothers reach a deal with a music publisher for a song they'd written, 'Thou Shalt Not Steal'. Kitty Wells recorded it, and Don and Phil received a cheque for $600. This led to a recording deal with Columbia Records. Phil Everly told author Joe Smith, 'We auditioned up in a hotel room and this lady was there and she said, "Oh, they're so cute." And we were signed!' They recorded four tracks at the Old Tulane Hotel's studios in Nashville during November 1955. Two were released on a single, namely, 'Keep A-Lovin' Me' and 'The Sun Keeps Shining' early in 1956. The record bombed. So Columbia Records canned the remaining tracks and dropped the brothers. Phil Everly: 'We hung around, borderline broke, for the next two years. We auditioned for every label in the United States, were turned down at least ten times.'

Once more Chet Atkins came to the rescue. He secured them positions as staff writers for a publishing outfit headed by Roy Acuff and Wesley Rose. And it was during 1957, when Archie Bleyer expressed interest in signing a country and western act to Cadence Records, based in New York, that Wesley Rose suggested The Everly Brothers. They were given the Felice and Boudleaux Bryant composition 'Bye Bye Love' to record despite thirty acts already rejecting it. The song was recorded at RCA's studios in Nashville but the result was far removed from the country and western style. Instead, it featured acoustic rock 'n' roll against sharp harmonies which would later become known as The Everly Brothers' 'sound'. The much-rejected track brought the duo instant success when it shot straight to No. 2 in the American chart, with sales in excess of one million copies. It also crossed over into both the R. & B. and country and western listings, while becoming a No. 6 British hit via London Records.

The brothers were unaware of the single's monumental American popularity until they performed in Buffalo. According to Phil Everly, 'A jock there started playing the record at a sock hop. All the kids would sing along. So the jock recorded his version with 2,000 kids singing it, and he played it over the air. That's when it hit me how big the record had become.'

American television viewers regularly saw Don and Phil on variety programmes, thanks to the unprecedented enthusiasm shown towards 'Bye Bye Love'. But the time soon arrived when the all-important follow-up needed to be considered. In the end who better to provide it than Felice and Boudleaux Bryant? They delivered another gem, 'Wake Up Little Susie', but Archie Bleyer was unhappy about the lyrics, claiming they intimated that the couple had been sleeping together. His objection was overruled and the single was released. Nonetheless, several American radio stations refused to air it because they shared Bleyer's opinion. Perhaps it was this that guaranteed the single a place at the top of the American chart, earning The Everly Brothers their second million-seller! The single soared to No. 2 in Britain where radio stations held no such qualms over the song's content!

By the close of 1958 The Everly Brothers' partnership with the Bryants had produced four million-sellers. 'All I Have to Do Is Dream' dominated the American top position for four weeks, becoming their biggest-ever selling single. It also became the duo's debut No. 1 single in Britain, holding on to that position for a staggering seven weeks. Incidentally, the Bryants claim to have written this song in fifteen minutes. Easy money indeed, when considering it has been an American chart entrant in the decades following its initial release. In 1963 Richard Chamberlain took his version into the Top Twenty; in 1970 Glen Campbell and Bobbie Gentry enjoyed a Top Thirty hit with it (No. 3 in Britain), and in 1981, Victoria Principal struggled into the Top Sixty.

A slight change of style came with 'Bird Dog', but the public cared not. Another American chart-topper, it came one place lower in Britain. And, to round off the Bryants' quartet, 'Problems', which stalled just outside the top spot in America and reached No. 6 in Britain.

After The Everly Brothers had headlined the Alan Freed *Christmas Rock 'n' Roll Spectacular* held at Loen's State Theater in Manhattan, New York, they flew to London to receive The World's No. 1 Vocal Group award, following the latest readers' poll in the *New Musical Express*. They also appeared on the *Cool for Cats* music television show. The trip lasted one day!

Their next two outings, recorded in stereo, marked a further musical change. The first, 'Poor Jenny' released in May 1959, struggled into the American Top Thirty and the Top Twenty in Britain. '('Til) I Kissed You', penned by Don Everly and featuring The Crickets (Buddy Holly's back-up group) as support, reached the American Top Five and the British No. 2 spot.

The Everly Brothers then announced that they were unhappy at Cadence Records due to royalty mismanagement and a difference of musical opinion, and intended to shop around for a new deal. In 1960 they found one with the major record company Warner Brothers, while 'Let It Be Me', an interpretation of 'J'Appartiens' with full string accompaniment, was issued by Cadence. It stalled at No. 7 in America; No. 13 in Britain. For a singing duo who expected top chart placings, this showing was abysmal, particularly as Warner Brothers were waiting.

The brothers knew the crossroads had been reached. When the time came to choose the next single, and debut, for Warner Brothers, nothing they had stockpiled seemed appropriate. Don Everly wrote the melody to 'Cathy's Clown'; Phil, the lyrics. Such was Warners' enthusiasm, the single was released within a week. During May 1960, it began a five-week stay at the top of the American chart, with Britain following, except the domination was eight weeks! 'Cathy's Clown' gave the British outlet of Warner Brothers its very first chart-topper with its first release!

It was the new Everly's sound – triple harmonising from an echo chamber, and a sound that would surely guarantee a successful career with Warner Brothers. Or would it?

Also see: 'Walk Right Back'/'Ebony Eyes', March 1961

Also a No. 1 single in June 1960: 'Three Steps to Heaven' by Eddie Cochran

July 1960

JIMMY JONES

Good Timin'

Jimmy Jones rose from the ranks of doo-wop to touch on a commercial recording career that spanned four minor British hits and one chart-topper in just over one year. He made his mark, although the public was hard pushed to remember his name three decades later. Such is the sorry side of the music business.

Born in Birmingham, Alabama, on 2 June 1937, Jimmy Jones joined the Army before moving to New York where, in the mid-fifties, he joined The Sparks of Rhythm. While he was a member of the group, they recorded the first version of 'Handy Man' for Apollo Records. In 1956 he formed his own outfit, The Savoys, later renamed The Pretenders, specialising in doo-wop. They went on to record for the Rama and Whirlin' Disc labels but success was limited to the New Jersey area and airplay support from the local radio stations.

Dumping The Pretenders, Jones embarked upon a solo career to sign first with Arrow Records, later Epic. Then he re-recorded 'Handy Man' which interested Otis Blackwell enough for him to sign the singer to Cub Records, the R. & B. subsidiary of MGM, in 1959. 'Handy Man' became Jones's debut single, which soared to No. 2 in the American chart while topping the R. & B. listing and peaking at No. 3 in Britain.

The follow-up was 'Good Timin'', written by Clint Ballard and Fred Tobias. It was another R. & B. and mainstream hit in America and, surprisingly, crashed into the British chart to reach No. 1 in July 1960. Two months later 'Handy Man' re-entered the chart to settle into the Top Forty. Both songs were catchy – 'ticka ticka timin'' – and annoyingly memorable due to Jones's high-pitched voice.

'That's When I Cried' was next and faltered in the American Top Ninety, while 'I Just Go for You', the follow-up to his chart-topper, became a Top Forty British hit during the September. 'Ready for Love' was issued a month later to reach the Top Fifty. And his last hit, 'I Told You So', which likewise struggled into the American Top Ninety, fared better in Britain, peaking at No. 33 during March 1961.

Also during 1961, Jones switched record companies to Vee Jay, and later Roulette, where his career disintegrated, the novelty of his voice now worn thin. It's ironic, but Del Shannon's cover version of 'Handy Man', in 1964, when it reached the British Top Forty, is better known than Jimmy Jones's original release.

CLIFF RICHARD

Please Don't Tease

'In the beginning all we did was copy American music. America is still the fatherland of rock 'n' roll [but] it belongs to the world now.' – Cliff Richard

Cliff Richard was born Harry Rodger Webb in Lucknow, India, on 14 October 1940 to Rodger and Dorothy. One sister, Donella, was born three years later, and another, Jacqueline, in 1948. That same year the family boarded the troopship SS *Ranghi* and emigrated to Britain with £5 between them. They moved into a room in Carshalton, Surrey, where Webb attended the Stanley Park Road primary school. During this time his father was unemployed, so times were hard. In 1950 his luck changed when he was hired by Ferguson's Radio in Enfield, Middlesex, while his wife found factory work in Broxbourne. This meant the family had to move house to Waltham Cross, Hertfordshire; switching Webb to the King's Road primary school in 1950, the same year as his youngest sister, Joan, was born.

When Webb failed his eleven-plus examination he was forced to attend the Chestnut Secondary Modern school, and for the third time the family moved home, this time into a council house in Chestnut. Webb's school life was consumed with amateur dramatics and rock 'n' roll: in fact, he often played truant to watch touring shows by American artists.

In 1957 Webb left school with one GCE 'O' Level in English and a skiffle group The Quintones which he formed with school friends. However, the group was forced to disband when the three female members moved on to secretarial college on a full-time basis.

For his first job, Webb worked at Atlas Lamps, Enfield, as a credit control clerk. During his spare time he joined Terry Smart and others in the Dick Teague Skiffle Group. Eventually, Webb and Teague left to form the rock 'n' roll group The Drifters, whereupon they came to the attention of John Foster who offered to manage them. The first problem to overcome was the name – Harry Webb and The Drifters held little magic for prospective booking agents. After much discussion John Foster chose Cliff Richard.

In the summer of 1958, with money lent by Foster's parents, Cliff Richard recorded his first demo record at HMV Records Store, Oxford Street, London. He chose two cover versions, Jerry Lee Lewis's 'Breathless' and Lloyd Price's 'Lawdy Miss Clawdy'. After regular gigs at the 2I's coffee shop in Soho and a spot in a talent show held at the Gaumont Theatre, Edmonton, entrepreneur George Ganjou took Richard's demo tape to Norrie Paramor, A. & R. manager for the Columbia record label, owned by EMI Records.

Suitably impressed, Paramor took Richard and The Drifters into Abbey Road Studios to record a handful of tracks. The first single was intended to be a version of Bobby Helms's 'Schoolboy Crush' but the public supported the B-side, 'Move It', penned by Ian Samwell, to push it to No. 2 in the British chart during November 1958. The record label on the initial pressings read Cliff Richards and this mis-spelling of his surname by EMI Records (a company who should have known better) has dogged him ever since.

In September, the group debuted on national television on Jack Good's popular *Oh Boy* music show. With the line-up of Bruce Welch, born Bruce Cripps in Bognor Regis, Sussex, on 2 November 1941, and Hank Marvin, born Brian Rankin in Newcastle, Tyne and Wear, on 28 October 1941, Ian Samwell and Terry Stuart, they toured Britain during October with The Most Brothers and The Kalin Twins. During this tour Richard met bass guitarist Jet Harris, born Terence Harris in Kingsbury, London, on 6 July 1939, and before it ended he had replaced Ian Samwell (who was becoming more involved in composing and production), while his friend, Tony Meehan, born Daniel Meehan in London on 2 March 1943, replaced Terry Stuart.

In December 1958 their second single, another Samwell composition, 'High Class Baby', was issued. It peaked at No. 7 in the British chart. Early the next year, with two hit singles to their credit, Richard and The Drifters embarked upon their first British headlining tour with Jimmy Tarbuck and Wee Willie Harris as support acts. Part-way through the tour Richard lost his voice, so Wee Willie Harris sang from backstage while Richard lipsynched front of house!

'Livin' Lovin' Doll', featuring Jet Harris, Hank Marvin and Bruce Welch for the first time on record, was their third single. It peaked at No. 20 in January 1959, while The Drifters issued their debut release 'Feelin' Fine'. A month on, Richard won the Best New Singer section in the annual *New Musical Express* readers' poll. Meanwhile, to support the release of their first album and their next single, 'Mean Streak', which became a Top Ten hit, Cliff Richard and The Drifters toured Britain once more, this time with The Dallas Boys and Des O'Connor, among others.

During May, cinema-goers saw Cliff Richard in his first full-length movie, *Serious Charge,* also starring Anthony Quayle and Sarah Churchill. Richard was cast as a young amateur rock 'n' roll singer, Curly Thompson. For the role, Richard curled his hair with hot tongs each morning before shooting began, and sang three songs, 'No Turning Back', 'Mad about You' and 'Living Doll', while The Drifters performed 'Chinchilla'. 'Living Doll' was lifted from the movie soundtrack as a single in July 1959. Written by Lionel Bart, it sold in excess of 500,000 copies to top the British chart for five weeks, earning Richard his first gold disc. It was also at this juncture that The Drifters became The Shadows to avoid confusion with the American soul group who had been using the name for considerably longer than Richard's backing band.

Filming started on Richard's second movie in September 1959. Titled *Expresso Bongo,* he played 'Bongo' Herbert, a rock 'n' roll artist waiting for stardom. Laurence Harvey played his manager, whose interest lay more in his percentage than his protégé. Sylvia Sims played Harvey's girlfriend who lent the sympathetic ear in the inevitable lovers' triangle! *Expresso Bongo* was premiered at London's Carlton Cinema on 20 December 1959.

Meanwhile, 'Travellin' Light' and its flipside 'Dynamite' began their upward chart climb. The latter stalled at No. 16, while the former topped the British chart in October 1959 where it stayed for five weeks. It became a Top Thirty American hit, prompting Richard and The Shadows to undertake a five-week tour there early in 1960. In their absence, 'A Voice in the Wilderness' (the last single to be issued in the 78 rpm format) was lifted from the *Expresso Bongo* movie soundtrack to soar to No. 2 in the British chart during January 1960, while the *Expresso Bongo* EP peaked in the Top Twenty.

Cliff Richard's rise to fame was extraordinary. His career appeared to follow that of his idol Elvis Presley inasmuch as both turned from singer to actor; they both combined ballads and rock in their repertoire and both had the support of strong management. Richard was quick to credit Presley as his inspiration from the curling of the lip to the sexual gyrations on stage. Indeed such was the similarity that Richard was later dubbed 'The British Presley'. Alongside the stardom came the fans. Uncontrollable and hysterical, they were whipped to a frenzy at sold-out concerts. Merchandising bore the singer's name and likeness in a range of unofficial jewellery and photographs.

With the close of the decade, Cliff Richard had won most of the prestigious industry awards ranging from silver and gold discs to Ivor Novello awards. He was voted Best British Male Vocalist on countless occasions and had appeared regularly on stage and television. He was now as popular on the small screen as he was on the cinema circuit, and in the singing stakes he could do little wrong.

The Cliff Richard phenomenon was to grow during the sixties. In the early part of the decade he topped the bill on television's prime entertainment show, *Sunday Night at the London Palladium*, before an estimated 19 million viewers, the biggest audience (then) in British television's history. As 'Fall in Love with You'/'Willie and the Hand Jive' soared to No. 2 in the British chart during March 1960, Richard moved himself and his family to a semi-detached house in Winchmore Hill. In the May he joined a star-studded cast that included Diana Dors, Adam Faith and Max Bygraves at the Royal Variety Performance before The Queen at the Victoria Theatre, London.

Recording sessions, British tours and media spots continued to ensure Cliff Richard and his Shadows worked non-stop, as typified in mid-1960 when they opened a season titled *Stars in your Eyes* at the London Palladium and a month on starred in a Sunday night series for Radio Luxembourg titled *Me and my Shadows*. The 15-minute shows ran for thirteen consecutive weeks.

At this juncture, Richard's management made the unorthodox move of asking the singer's fan club members to choose his next single. Eighty youngsters were asked to vote on twenty songs recorded a month earlier. 'Please Don't Tease', penned by Bruce Welch, was chosen. A wise decision. The single soared to the top of the British chart during August 1960, a position it held for four weeks before being displaced by The Shadows' 'Apache'!

The fan club members' runner-up choice, 'Nine Times out of Ten', quickly followed the chart-topper. Indeed, while 'Please Don't Tease' descended the chart, the new single leap-frogged it into the Top Ten to peak at No. 3 during September. This was Cliff Richard's tenth single, and broke the record for advance sales with an estimated 180,000 copies!

In the first two years of his career, Cliff Richard sold a staggering 5.5 million singles, and the best was yet to come.

Also see: 'The Young Ones', February 1962; 'The Next Time', January 1963; 'Summer Holiday', March 1963

Also a No. 1 single in August 1960: 'Shakin' All Over' by Johnny Kidd and the Pirates

September 1960

THE SHADOWS

Apache

Without doubt this slick and sharp group were Britain's premier instrumentalists. Their success was doublefold because they were successful in their own right and as back-up group for another of Britain's finest, Cliff Richard.

Hank Marvin, born Brian Rankin on 28 October 1941 in Newcastle, and Bruce Welch, born Bruce Cripps on 2 November 1941 in Bognor Regis, Sussex, formed the skiffle group The Railroaders while at school in Newcastle. In 1958, with their education behind them, they travelled to London to perform in a national talent contest. When they came third, the group disbanded. However, Hank Marvin and Bruce Welch didn't give up that easily. They stayed on in London, where they later formed The Five Chesternuts, which featured Pete Chester (son of comedian Charlie Chester) on drums, and two others.

In August 1958, with this line-up, they recorded and released 'Teenage Love' for the Columbia label, a subsidiary of EMI Records. This single ensured them a spot on the television music show *6.5 Special*, but unfortunately didn't ensure them a hit! Columbia dropped them.

To earn a living, Marvin and Welch worked in Soho's 2I's coffee bar, where in their spare time they performed as The Geordie Boys. During September 1958, following a stint with The Vipers, Hank Marvin was spotted by John Foster, Cliff Richard's manager. Richard was due to tour Britain as support act to The Kalin Twins, but his back-up group The Drifters needed a guitarist to replace the recently departed Ken Pavey. John Foster hired Hank Marvin, who insisted Bruce Welch also be given a job. Foster agreed.

During October 1958, The Drifters with Welch on rhythm guitar; Marvin on lead guitar; Terry Stuart on drums and Ian Samwell on bass, toured with Cliff Richard. But by the end of the tour, Jet Harris had replaced Ian Samwell, because of the latter's ineffective guitar playing, among other things. It was a logical move as Harris had

36

regularly played from the stage wings to strengthen Samwell's guitar inadequacies. And when Terry Stuart later left, another ex-coffee bar player, Tony Meehan, stepped in. (Jet Harris was born Terence Harris on 6 July 1939 in Kingsbury, London; Tony Meehan was born Daniel Meehan in London on 2 March 1943.)

It was this line-up that continued to work with Cliff Richard on stage, and that went into the Abbey Road recording studios in 1959 to back him on several tracks including 'Livin' Lovin' Doll'. Being impressed with their studio work, Norrie Paramor, producer for the Columbia label, auditioned The Drifters, and offered them a recording deal in their own right. The vocal track 'Feelin' Fine' penned by Ian Samwell (who by this time was also their manager) was their first release. 'Don't Be a Fool (with Love)' written by Hank Marvin and Pete Chester was the B-side. Following this, they recorded their first instrumental, 'Chinchilla', for the soundtrack of Cliff Richard's film *Serious Charge*. The second Drifters' single was Jet Harris's 'Jet Black'; it was their second flop.

When 'Feelin' Fine' was issued in America it was immediately withdrawn when The Drifters, a soul group of considerable standing, issued an injunction to prevent the British Drifters from using the name. After much discussion about a replacement, which they all agreed would be used worldwide, and not solely in America, Jet Harris suggested 'The Shadows'.

'Saturday Dance', issued during December 1959, became the first to bear The Shadows' name on the record label. It was another vocal track, written by Hank Marvin and Pete Chester – and another bomber!

Over the Christmas period in 1959, The Shadows joined Cliff Richard in Stockton-on-Tees, Cleveland, where he was performing in the pantomime *Babes in the Wood*. During the season, Jet Harris and Hank Marvin were involved in a car accident; both were injured, and learner-driver Harris was fined for not being accompanied by a qualified driver and not displaying the obligatory L-plates.

Early in 1960 when The Shadows toured North America with Cliff Richard, they met Jerry Lordan who offered them his self-penned 'Apache'. It was a sharp-edged instrumental, and when in August 1960 The Shadows recorded it, with Richard playing the bongos, it gave them their first British chart-topper. Ironically, it replaced Cliff Richard's 'Please Don't Tease' at the top, and remained there for six weeks. In America, the group lost out to Jorgen Ingmann, a Danish guitarist who was unaware The Shadows had recorded the number.

'Apache' was later voted Record of the Year by the readers of the *New Musical Express*, and went on to sell one million copies, earning the group their first gold disc.

Before 1960 was out, 'Man of Mystery' was issued as the follow-up. This was a reworking of the theme from Edgar Wallace's film, and was another hard-hitting instrumental. It peaked at No. 6 in the British chart.

Naturally enough, live work was now prolific. The Shadows were a working unit on their own, although they made it clear they intended to continue working with Cliff Richard. Being instrumentalists meant there was no prime focal point in the group; in fact, most guitarists were static in concert. To break the monotony, The Shadows adopted their own walk. A simple step, side to side, back to front, with a high kick for the finale. This enabled them to continue playing their guitars, yet move about the stage. In time, the bespectacled Hank Marvin would dominate much of the spotlight due to his extraordinary expertise on lead guitar, and his off-beat sense of humour!

The first single of 1961, 'FBI', a Shadows composition, shot into the British Top Five, while their first tour of the year included concerts in the Far East and Australasia. And as their next single, 'The Frightened City', was issued, the quartet was filming Cliff Richard's next movie *The Young Ones* in Elstree Studios. The film's title track raced to the top of the British chart, without stopping on the way, staying there for eight weeks, while the movie itself became the year's second-biggest box-office hit next to the war epic *The Guns of Navarone*.

By October 1961, The Shadows held the top single spot with 'Kon-Tiki', the No. 1 album slot with their eponymous debut, and the top EP, *The Shadows to the Fore*. Certainly their success was staggering, which made Tony Meehan's decision to leave the group to take an A. & R. position with Decca Records a little bewildering. His absence wasn't noticed because Bruce Welch immediately asked Brian Bennett, another ex-coffee bar player, who was supporting Tommy Steele on tour at the time, to join them.

'The Savage' was The Shadows' last hit of 1961. The group had forged their own identity, and their hit run of soft rock tunes with strong melodies had established their own unique sound, largely thanks to Hank Marvin's guitar work. He was the master of the lead guitar and was, undoubtedly, an inspiration to many a young musician.

Also see: 'Wonderful Land', April 1962

RICKY VALANCE

Tell Laura I Love Her

One 'sick' hit from a Welshman whose name would be confused with the American rock 'n' roller Ritchie Valens, who died with Buddy Holly and The Big Bopper in a plane crash during February 1959, wasn't much of a recording career. But it was all Ricky Valance had.

Ricky Valance was born David Spencer in 1939 in Ynytsdou, South Wales. He served his singing apprenticeship in his local clubs for several years before he was brought to the attention of a talent scout from EMI Records. Valance was offered a recording deal and worked with producer Norrie Paramor. Their very first session produced 'Tell Laura I Love Her', originally an American hit for Ray Peterson.

It was classed a 'sick' song because it typified, and glorified, death. Such singles attracted a lot of media and public attention ensuring healthy record sales. 'Tell Laura I Love Her' was no exception. Though it was banned by BBC radio because of its content, Radio Luxembourg afforded it maximum airplay. This pushed the single to the top of the British chart where it held off Cliff Richard ('Nine Times out of Ten') and Adam Faith ('How about That').

Regrettably, Ricky Valance was a true one-hit wonder. None of his follow-ups dented the charts, but happily he was able to maintain a career on the club and cabaret circuit. Today, thanks to his solitary chart-topper, he is a regular contributor to the revival packages that tour Britain.

November/December 1960

ELVIS PRESLEY

It's Now or Never

'Elvis Presley is a God-loving, jelly-kneed kid who has taken rock 'n' roll out of the category of race or R. & B. music and made it into pop.

Elvis is still a country boy at heart and he's not fixin' to change,' Colonel Tom Parker told the *San Francisco News* in 1956.

Born Elvis Aaron Presley on 8 January 1935 in East Tupelo, Mississippi, one of twin sons (Jesse died at birth) of Vernon and Gladys, he grew up in an impoverished neighbourhood said to be 'the poorest place that white folks could live'. It was only singing together at gospel revivals and being members of the congregation of the First Assembly of God church that helped the family survive.

While he attended the Lawhon Grammar School, his teacher, Mrs Grimes, encouraged the young Presley to enter the annual music festival, the 'Mississippi-Alabama Fair and Dairy Show' held in Tupelo. Ten-year-old Presley won the runner-up prize singing 'Old Shep', a sad tale about the relationship between a boy and his dog.

During 1948, Presley and his family moved one hundred miles to Memphis where his mother worked as a nurse's aide while his father joined the United Paint Company. Outside school hours, Presley contributed to the family finances by gardening for the neighbours, and managed to save $12.95 to buy his first guitar, enabling him to emulate the country and western and R. & B. music that was so much a part of his adolescence. In time, the family was rehoused to 185 Winchester Street in the Lauderdale Courts and Presley graduated from Humes High School.

Presley said, 'My upbringing was pretty quiet. I was never out of my mother's sight until I was sixteen. All the kids would go swimming in the creek but my mother wouldn't let me go . . . When I was fifteen I got crazy about football, but my folks thought it was too dangerous and tried to stop me. After school the white boys would team up against the coloured boys and they'd all come home with their clothes torn . . . I was always taught the difference between right and wrong. I remember once when I was five, I took two empty Coke bottles from a neighbour's porch, and got a spanking from my dad.'

With no academic qualifications, Presley worked as a truck driver for the Crown Electric Company. While driving around he would often visit the Memphis Recording Service (which guaranteed it could record anything anytime). It was located at 706 Union Avenue, and it cost $4 to record a private track. Sam Phillips, who owned the company and its offshoot Sun Records, regularly saw Presley using the facilities but took little notice of him. Yet, for some reason, his office manager, Marion Keisker, secreted a tape of Presley singing 'My Happiness' and 'That's When your Heartaches Begin' which he played to Phillips. The next time Presley visited the studio, Phillips asked him to record with a couple of musicians. The original material Phillips had prepared was discarded when Presley sang 'That's All Right, Mama'. This track, with 'Blue Moon of Kentucky', became Presley's debut single on the Sun label. Within days, DJ Dewey Phillips on WHBQ, Memphis' premier radio station, aired 'That's All Right, Mama' and before the track had finished the station's switchboard was jammed by callers wanting to purchase the disc. Within a week, Sam Phillips was desperately trying to press records to fulfil the 6,000 advanced orders! Within a month, Elvis Presley was invited to participate in Nashville's Grand Ole Opry, where he performed 'Blue Moon of Kentucky'.

During July 1954, Presley signed a recording contract with Sun Records and returned to the studio to cut his next single, 'Good Rockin' Tonight', released during September. His third release, 'Milkcow Blues Boogie', followed early in 1955. It was at this juncture that Colonel Tom Parker entered Elvis Presley's life. He recognised a raw, crude talent in the young singer and Presley's father, Vernon, asked him to manage his son. Parker, quoted in John Parker's *Elvis: Murdered by the Mob*, said, 'I agreed a deal with Elvis and his father to become his manager and promoter, promising to handle his record contracts, tours, personal appearances and to try to get him into motion pictures.' Originally, Parker received 25 per cent of all Presley's income; later other deals, including merchandising, ensured he received a staggering half of Presley's earnings. His percentage, Parker said, depended on the type of deal he negotiated; in time, he became the richest manager in the history of the music business.

Parker's first move was to interest a major record company in his protégé. RCA Records were sufficiently impressed that they paid Sam Phillips $35,000 to release Presley from his contract with him. This money helped Phillips to promote other artists' careers.

In January 1956 Presley recorded his debut single for RCA Records. Titled 'Heartbreak Hotel', it was written by Parker's public relations officer, Mae Axton, and Tommy Durden, who conceived the song after reading of a suicide victim's note: 'I walk a lonely street.' It was released on 27 January to coincide with the singer's television debut on *Stage Show*, hosted by Tommy and Jimmy Dorsey. He appeared on the show five times during the next two months. In April Presley sang the single on NBC's *The Milton Berle Show*, televised from the aircraft carrier USS *Hancock* moored in San Diego before an estimated one quarter of the American viewing population. Within three weeks, 'Heartbreak Hotel' dominated the American chart, selling in excess of

41

one million copies. During May 1956 it peaked in the British chart at No. 2.

On Presley's second performance on *The Milton Berle Show* during June (and his first with his backing group The Jordanaires) he sang 'I Want You, I Need You, I Love You' and 'Hound Dog', causing uproar with the viewing public who instantly lodged complaints with the television company about his provocative hip-shaking and vulgar leers. It was the singer's last performance on the show for over ten years! The more certain sectors of the public continued to express their outrage at Presley's 'bumps and grinds', the more in demand he became. However, when he appeared on *The Steve Allen Show* during July 1956, he took on board the criticism to restrainedly perform 'Hound Dog'! This in turn prompted Ed Sullivan, Allen's greatest rival, to invite Presley to perform on his equally high-ranking show only if he would agree to be shown from the waist up. Presley conceded – and was criticised by *The New York Times* for making lewd movements with his tongue!

As Presley's eponymous album dominated the American chart, following advance orders of 350,000, 'Blue Suede Shoes' reached the American Top Forty, and in June 1956 it peaked at No. 9 in Britain.

Behind the scenes, Colonel Tom Parker beavered away ensuring his client received maximum media attention. Not a difficult task, because television, radio and press were only too willing to serve the public's growing demand for Presley. In between the promotion bandwagon schedules, Presley released his second American million-seller 'I Want You, I Need You, I Love You' which soared to No. 3, while in Britain it stalled in the Top Twenty.

With Presley's recording career now progressing according to Parker's master-plan, it was time to approach the film world. To this end the singer did a screen test for Hal Wallis at Paramount Pictures who told the media he possessed 'the same power, virility and sexual drive on screen as the Young Errol Flynn' and signed him to a seven-year contract. By August 1956, Presley-the-actor was loaned to 20th Century Fox to star as Clint Reno in *The Reno Brothers*, a Civil War western. So strong was Presley's ballad, 'Love Me Tender', in the movie, that the film's title was changed. Critics were mixed in their opinion – some believed him to be the rightful successor to James Dean, while others felt he should stick to singing. *Love Me Tender* was premiered at the Paramount Theater, New York, in November 1956, and despite the critics, the movie recouped $1 million of its costs within one week. The 'Love Me Tender' single, written by Ken Darby, soared to the top of the American chart and, following the film's British premiere in London, peaked at No. 11 in the chart during December 1956.

Presley mania continued to grip America: his brand of rock 'n' roll caused uncontrollable hysteria among the young and disgust among the mature. The frenzy, the unprecedented furore and excitement that was Presley was translated into countless hit singles including those which charted in Britain, like 'All Shook Up', 'Jailhouse Rock', 'King Creole', 'A Fool Such As I' and 'Stuck on You'. From the proceeds of his success Presley bought Graceland, a two-storey mansion, for $102,500, which had originally been built by S.E. Toof who named it after his daughter.

Following the release of 'Don't' (his first ballad since 'Love Me Tender') in March 1958, which sold in excess of two million copies to dominate the American chart, Presley was drafted into the Army. The military actually did not expect the singer to undertake the two-year term and indeed had encouraged him to fulfil his commitment in the Special Services which would have allowed him to continue with his career. Presley agreed to this, but Parker and RCA Records' executives demanded he serve his country as a private, a move, they said, that would benefit his career in the long run.

The Army granted Presley a postponement of call-up to enable him to complete his fourth film, *King Creole*, but on 24 March 1958, a very reluctant singer reported for duty at the Memphis draft board, amid a huge publicity hype organised by Parker, who said Presley's stint in the Army would cost America $500,000 a year in lost taxes! When Presley was shipped to Fort Hood in Texas, his family followed. This would have been the first time Presley and his mother Gladys had been parted since he was born. However, such was her grief that she died on 14 August 1958 from heart and liver failure shortly before Presley was due to be shipped to Germany.

Army life bored him; the daily drudge left him eager to enjoy his social pursuits. To this end he rented a three-storey house in Bad Neuheim, in which he installed his father and grandmother. Most nights the house was crammed with Presley, select Army colleagues and hordes of young girls, one of whom was fourteen-year-old Priscilla Ann, stepdaughter of Captain Joseph Paul Beaulieu.

On 2 March 1960, GI 53310761, Sergeant Elvis Presley, left the Army. Prior to leaving Germany, and dressed in the khaki green uniform of the Third Armoured Division, he held a press conference in Friedberg where he said, 'The Army has been a great experience for me. I wouldn't have missed it.' His flight to America was interrupted when the plane made an hour-long refuelling stopover at Prestwick Airport, Scotland. This was to be the first and only time Elvis Presley stood on British soil.

Once back in America, Presley was quick to see music had changed in his absence. His image needed remoulding from rock 'n' roller to balladeer, and this was exactly what Colonel Parker had in mind. To spearhead the change, and to impress upon the American public that Presley was an ideal citizen, he arranged for him to appear on *The Frank Sinatra Spectacular*, a nationwide television special filmed in Miami. By the time viewers saw Presley arm-in-arm with Sinatra, he had already cut six tracks during an eleven-hour recording session in Nashville. From this, 'It's Now or Never' was chosen as his first single to be released since he had left the Army. (The tracks issued during his two-year stay of duty had been recorded prior to his departure.)

'It's Now or Never' buried Presley's rock 'n' roll past by becoming the first in a series of adult ballads. It was adapted by Wally Gold and Aaron Schroeder for commercial release from the Italian original 'O Sole Mio' written by Eduardo di Capua and G. Capurro in 1901 and previously recorded by Enrico Caruso. However, the adaptation very nearly missed its British outing because the song was banned from release due to copyright restrictions in Britain. It was thought that RCA Records would have to wait seven years to release it. America, on the other hand, had no such restriction. Hasty discussions ensued between RCA executives and the Italian song publishers until agreement was reached.

'It's Now or Never' topped the American chart for five weeks following its release in August 1960. Due to the publishing hassles which prevented immediate British release, the single entered the chart at No. 1 during November 1960, holding that position for a remarkable nine weeks. Its sales were the fastest recorded anywhere in the world; selling in excess of 750,000 copies in two weeks.

Presleymania had crossed the Atlantic to grip Britain. Record stores were jammed with customers wanting to buy the single. One shop that had queues outside only admitted those who wanted to purchase Presley's single, while another reported it was selling twelve copies of 'It's Now or Never' to one by any other act.

Naturally enough, these sales earned Presley his first British gold disc which was presented to him by DJ Jimmy Saville on the Hollywood set of *Wild in the Country*, Presley's next movie. Saville wrote in the *New Musical Express*, 'I knew that he already had thirty-four gold discs, so another one might not make any difference to him. I was wrong. He danced around the set, clutching his latest trophy in his hands and showing it to everyone.'

Also see: 'Are You Lonesome Tonight', February 1961: 'Wooden Heart', April 1961; 'Surrender', June 1961; 'Rock a Hula Baby'/ 'Can't Help Falling in Love', March 1962; 'Good Luck Charm', June 1962; 'She's Not You', September 1962; '(You're the) Devil in Disguise', August 1963; 'Crying in the Chapel', July 1965

January 1961

JOHNNY TILLOTSON

Poetry in Motion

'Poetry in Motion' was the blending of a country music sound with a beaty ballad, a style that was synonymous with American male soloists during this decade. Bobby Vee and Glen Campbell are good examples, and perhaps Elvis Presley who was, after all, the master of the ballad. The songs were inspired by love and girl/boy relationships and the singers were typical of America's current style – they had short-cut hair, good looks, and a cute, sharp appearance.

Johnny Tillotson was no different. Born in Jacksonville, Florida, on 20 April 1939, Johnny Tillotson was a teenage contributor on Radio W-WPF and on the television show *Toby Dowdy*, both local stations. He had mastered the guitar and ukulele by the time he attended the University of Florida. His musical ambitions soon overtook his studies when in 1958 he was lured to Cadence Records, based in New York and owned by Archie Bleyer. The company released Tillotson's debut, the double A-sided disc 'Well I'm your Man' and 'Dreamy Eyes', which became No. 87 and No. 63 American hits respectively.

Through 1959, 'True True Happiness' made the Top Sixty; likewise 'Why Do I Love You So?'. Following a stab at R. & B., Tillotson recorded the evergreen 'Poetry in Motion', penned by Mike Anthony and Paul Kaufman. The song, born in Nashville and completed in a New York studio, soared to No. 2 in America during 1960, but reached the top spot in Britain in January 1961, where it stayed for two weeks. All told, 'Poetry in Motion' sold in excess of 1.5 million copies worldwide.

In March 'Jimmy's Girl' was issued, a Top Thirty American hit but a disappointing No. 43 in Britain. 'Without You', its follow-up, bombed but hit No. 7 across the Atlantic.

Prior to joining the US Army for six months at Fort Jackson, South Carolina, Tillotson released his self-penned 'It Keeps Right On a Hurtin''. This re-established him in the American Top Three, selling a million copies on the way. The song stalled at No. 31 in Britain.

When the singer left the Army he instantly embarked upon a promotional American tour to capitalise on his recent success. The tour also cemented his future. Late 1962, following another international charter, 'Send Me the Pillow You Dream on', Tillotson re-recorded Hank Williams' 'I Can't Help It (if I'm Still in Love with You)', a British Top Forty entrant but a No. 21 American hit.

A year later and after a cameo appearance singing 'Judy Judy Judy' in the movie *Just for Fun*, Tillotson's British chart run ended with 'Out of my Mind'. He continued to enjoy American success although he switched record companies. In November 1963 he recorded his last hit for Cadence Records, namely 'Funny How Time Slips Away', a cover of the Willie Nelson original, before joining MGM Records.

A country-flavoured 'Talk Back Trembling Lips' was his first release under MGM's banner. It shot into the American Top Ten, and through 1964 and 1965 a succession of songs, mostly ballads, kept his chart career alive. Titles included 'I Rise I Fall', 'Angel' (from the movie *The Calloways*), a version of Guy Mitchell's 'Heartaches by the Number', and his last hit, in December 1965, 'Our World'.

Undeterred at the slide in his career, Tillotson adopted a change of image to drop his teen appeal. After presenting his new, mature act at the Copacabana in New York, he was in demand as a performer in Las Vegas and Miami Beach, and further afield in countries like Germany, Sweden and Japan, where he enjoyed a staunch following.

When Tillotson moved to California in 1968, he joined the acting profession with bit parts in movies and television specials. A further recording deal in 1970 with Ampex Records produced the *Tears on my Pillow* album, and a later contract with Buddah Records resulted in the *Johnny Tillotson* album. Both flopped.

ELVIS PRESLEY

Are You Lonesome Tonight

'Mr Presley should stay off celluloid and get back to the groove where he belongs.' – *Daily Mirror*, 1958

By now Elvis Presley had starred in six movies. His seventh, *Wild in the Country*, in which he played Glenn Tyler, co-starred Tuesday Weld. Shooting began in November 1960.

His film debut was in *Love Me Tender*, followed by *Loving You* (which started life on the storyboard as *The Lonesome Cowboy*), where Presley played Deke Rivers opposite Lizabeth Scott. *Jailhouse Rock* was next in which the singer played an accidental killer reclaimed for the world of music by the love of a devoted woman. However, before the movie could make headline news, Judy Tyler, who had co-starred with Presley, was killed in a car accident in Wyoming in bizarre circumstances. British censors threatened to edit the film sequences where Presley was flogged by a prison warden. Eventually, they remained untouched as did the frames showing Presley participating in a bar-room brawl and getting punched on the chin!

His last movie before being drafted into the Army during 1958 was *King Creole*, about which one critic wrote: 'The city streets are slick with rain. Flick knives glint in the shadows. With two shootings, a back alley stabbing and sundry beatings-up, it brings the Wild Ones back to town. But are they welcome? . . . It is a classic case of a bad film made well.'

When Presley left the Army it seemed appropriate to star him as Tulsa McLean in *GI Blues*. The plot more or less portrayed his actual stay with the military and co-starred Juliet Prowse. In 1960 he returned to the western with *Flaming Star*. Playing a role rejected by Marlon Brando, Presley was a half-breed Indian named Pacer Burton. This time his co-stars were Barbara Eden and Steve Forrest.

It was as *Wild in the Country* was on the production line that 'Are You Lonesome Tonight' was issued as a single. Like 'It's Now or Never' before it, the song was another adult-listening ballad, originally recorded by Al Jolson during the twenties, and a 1959 hit for Jaye P.

Morgan. Released during December 1960, Presley's version shot to the top of the American chart where it stayed for six weeks, selling in excess of two million copies. Upon its release in Britain in February 1961, and with 500,000 advance orders, it entered the chart at No. 2 before dominating the top spot for four weeks. Part of the song's attraction, though, was the spoken middle section – although not everyone agreed. Pete Murray, radio DJ during the sixties: 'As for that dramatic little speech Elvis gives; I thought it was sickening, but what a fabulous gimmick . . . I bet 75 per cent of women who buy a disc with a title like this are frustrated!'

All didn't go according to Presley's plan either, because hundreds of singles were returned to record stores. British record buyers believed the single was faulty because the stylus jumped on the vinyl. In actual fact, the track was pressed with too much bass, and a worn stylus could not cope with the heavy sound, so it skipped across the disc. Re-pressings were hastily arranged with a lower bass level!

Inevitably 'Are You Lonesome Tonight' posed a question that other artists just couldn't resist answering. Countless 'reply' singles were released, notably, 'Yes, I'm Lonesome Tonight' recorded by five separate vocalists including Linda Lee and Dodie Stevens. Others included country and western, comedy and instrumental responses.

As 'Are You Lonesome Tonight' dominated the British chart, the singer was guest of honour at 'Elvis Presley Day' in Memphis, where he was made 'Honorary Colonel' for putting Memphis on the map.

Also see: 'It's Now or Never', November/December 1960; 'Wooden Heart', April 1961; 'Surrender', June 1961; 'Rock a Hula Baby'/'Can't Help Falling in Love', March 1962; 'Good Luck Charm', June 1962; 'She's Not You', September 1962; '(You're the) Devil in Disguise', August 1963; 'Crying in the Chapel', July 1965

March 1961

THE EVERLY BROTHERS

Walk Right Back/Ebony Eyes

With a string of million-selling singles behind them, the future of The Everly Brothers seemed assured. Professionally speaking it was, but when discord hit their personal lives their downfall was predicted. The duo who inspired generations of rock acts and laid the ground rules for close harmonising was destined to fall apart.

The Everly Brothers' first hit of 1961, 'Like Strangers', was quickly followed by 'Walk Right Back', written by Sonny Curtis of The Crickets, with whom the brothers had previously worked. It was coupled with 'Ebony Eyes', penned by John D. Loudermilk, and became the brothers' most successful double-sided disc. The top side peaked at the top of the British charts in March 1961 where it stayed for four weeks, also reaching No. 7 in America, while its flipside, 'Ebony Eyes', charted in its own right – No. 17 and No. 8 respectively.

Two months on from this success, the duo opened their own record label, Calliope, to cater for new artists. Meantime, their own career continued its upward spiral. During June they released their version of the Bing Crosby original, 'Temptation'. It was a magnificent track, eerie and haunting, with a mass of shrill female vocals as padding. It became an immediate British chart-topper for two weeks in July 1961.

After the release of their next single, 'Muskrat', in November, The Everly Brothers joined the US Marine Corps Reserves for six months' active service, working as artillery men. In February 1962, they were allowed leave of absence to appear (wearing their uniforms) on *The Ed Sullivan Show* to promote their new single, 'Crying in the Rain' written by Carole King. With the Marines behind them, 'How Can I Meet Her?' staggered into the American Top Seventy-five, while 'That's Old Fashioned (That's the Way Love Should Be)' fared better, reaching the Top Ten, and the Top Twenty in Britain.

Their career flowed at a healthy pace on both sides of the Atlantic. They were described as the world's richest music duo and were regular headliners on British tours. During one such tour in 1962 Don Everly was admitted to hospital twice in one day. The media was told he had collapsed from nervous exhaustion. In reality, he had overdosed on speed and was eventually flown home. Phil Everly completed the tour alone. Nonetheless, their public image stayed undamaged as they hosted their own American television shows, and were generally regarded as the All-American dream. However, before long it became apparent they were in personal conflict. They led separate lives except when on stage, hired separate managers and lawyers, travelled alone and stayed in different hotels. Then the crunch came when Don Everly divorced his second wife and wanted to re-marry. He declared he wanted to retire from the act altogether. The brothers continued to record as a duo for a time, while Don also released his own eponymous album for the Ode label. The American dream then turned into a public nightmare when an audience witnessed a showdown between the brothers.

In June 1973, during a performance at the John Wayne Theater, Knott's Berry Farm, Hollywood, Phil smashed his guitar before storming from the stage, leaving Don to tell a stunned audience that The Everly Brothers were finished. Phil Everly: 'When Donald and I split up, I did basically nothing for the next ten years. During that period, people would ask me what was wrong with me and I'd say I was suffering from an acute case of stupidity. You get at odds, and Donald and I were both very opinionated . . . it was nothing you could really lay your finger on.'

Various compilations of the brothers' best work kept them in the public eye, until March 1983 when Phil Everly duetted with Cliff Richard on 'She Means Nothing to Me', a No. 9 British hit. This success had a knock-on effect because in the following June, it was announced that The Everly Brothers had healed their ten-year-old differences and would host a concert at London's Royal Albert Hall on 23 September 1983. Many claimed it to be the event of the decade, while others believed it was simply two old men reluctantly chirping away at golden oldie songs. Nonetheless, the concert was filmed for future screening, and recorded for *The Everly Brothers Reunion Concert*, issued during January 1984. It reached No. 47 and was their first album to chart for twenty-two years. In America, it stalled at No. 162 following a fourteen-year absence.

According to Phil Everly, 'If I had it all to do over again, if I had known Donald and I were going to last, I would have laughed . . . and probably had a better time.'

Also see: 'Cathy's Clown', May/June 1960

April 1961

ELVIS PRESLEY

Wooden Heart

'Elvis is the warmest, nicest, most attractive man I've met in ages. He has everything a girl finds desirable in a man.' – Ann-Margret

'I like Elvis very much. I met him in Germany and became very fond of him. I think he's a very fine young man.' – Priscilla Beaulieu's mother

'Wooden Heart', lifted from the soundtrack of the movie *GI Blues*, was released as a single throughout the world except America. The simply constructed song shot to the top of the British chart during April 1961 where it stayed for a staggering six weeks. In America, meanwhile, 'Come Back to Sorrento (Torna a Sorrento)' topped the chart for two weeks, under the title 'Surrender'.

By this time, Elvis Presley's girlfriend, Priscilla Beaulieu, had with her parents' consent visited him at Graceland several times. She would eventually move in permanently under Vernon Presley's guardianship, and attend the Immaculate Conception High School. Her presence in Graceland was kept secret from the media; indeed Presley's own staff were sworn to keep tight-lipped on the threat of losing their jobs. Child brides were a sour topic in America following Jerry Lee Lewis's marriage to his thirteen-year-old cousin, Myra. When the public ostracised him, he plunged headlong into the depths of heavy drugs. Chuck Berry, on the other hand, was jailed and fined for associating with a fourteen-year-old girl.

To steer attention away from his home life, Presley publicised an affair with actress Ann-Margret, who believed he would marry her. In turn, his life away from young Priscilla was likewise secret, particularly his night-time frolics with other women. On occasion, Beaulieu would join Presley and his entourage on their night excursions but these were usually to the cinema or bowling alley which the singer would hire. These expeditions left the teenager exhausted, unable to stay awake in the classroom. Presley, on the other hand, would sleep a drug-induced sleep until late afternoon, when a further intake of drugs would prepare him for the next evening's entertainment.

Elvis Presley did not accept he was a junkie. The reasoning behind his constant pill popping was simple – he took medication to enable him to cope with his erratic and stressful lifestyle. All the pills he took were prescribed for him by a variety of doctors who were paid handsomely to do so. Therefore, his reasoning was correct, despite the fact that the vast quantity of medications he took were classed as street drugs. All the while, Elvis Presley's public image of 'a very fine young man' remained intact.

Also see: 'It's Now or Never', November/December 1960; 'Are You Lonesome Tonight', February 1961; 'Surrender', June 1961; 'Rock a Hula Baby'/'Can't Help Falling in Love', March 1962; 'Good Luck

Charm', June 1962; 'She's Not You', September 1962; '(You're the) Devil in Disguise', August 1963; 'Crying in the Chapel', July 1965

May 1961

THE MARCELS

Blue Moon

When the idea of 'Blue Moon' was first conceived by Rodgers and Hart, it was a ballad of beauty. When The Marcels recorded it, the composers would hardly have recognised their original!

'Blue Moon' was Richard Rodgers and Lorenz Hart's only song not to have been written for a musical. It started its life as 'Make Me a Star' for a Jean Harlow movie, but both song and star were later dropped from the project. The composing duo decided to rework the tune. It became 'The Bad in Every Man' and was a contender for MGM's *Manhattan Melodrama*. The film company wasn't happy with it, so asked the composers to rewrite the lyrics. It was then that the evergreen 'Blue Moon' was finally born!

The song was a movie favourite and was heard in *East Side, West Side* during 1950, and *With a Song in my Heart* two years later. During the mid-fifties Elvis Presley's impassioned interpretation reached the British Top Ten.

The Marcels were a multi-racial group formed in Pittsburgh, Pennsylvania. They chose their name from a hairstyle popular at the time. They comprised Cornelius Harp as lead vocalist; Fred Johnson, bass singer; Ronald Mundy and Gene Bricker, tenors; and Dick Knauss, baritone. They were regular club performers with an act that was devoted to doo-wop and R. & B. cover versions.

When Stu Phillips from Colpix Records in New York was searching for a new act he remembered a demo tape sent to him by The Marcels. As he was the only one with faith in the quintet, Phillips booked a recording studio at Colpix's expense but without anyone's knowledge, where The Marcels recorded three songs. When it became apparent there was time left for another, 'Blue Moon' was chosen as the best available. Through trial and error they recorded the track, altering sequences and adding slices, like Johnson's deep bass introduction, with lashings of doo-wop that practically suffocated Rodgers and Hart's original.

When DJ Murray the K, at New York's WINS radio station, heard the studio tape he became so addicted to the song that he afforded it maximum airplay. Stu Phillips was subsequently summoned by his Colpix boss to explain how 'Blue Moon' carried his company's logo, and, more to the point, where it had come from. Public demand forced Colpix to issue it.

When 'Blue Moon' was commercially released it shot straight to the top of the American chart where it stayed for three weeks, notching up sales of one million copies. The track was licensed to Pye Records for British release in May 1961, where it was issued immediately to dominate the chart for two weeks. An album named after the single quickly followed.

The chart-topper's follow-up was a version of George Gershwin's 'Summertime', during June 1961. But, by comparison, it failed, struggling to reach No. 78 in America, and No. 46 in Britain. Their third single, 'You Are my Sunshine', fared worse. It bombed.

Before 1961 closed, 'Heartaches', a cover version of Ted Weems' forties' original soared into the American Top Ten. But in Britain the story was the same, it flopped.

With a change of line-up and an appearance in the *Rock around the Clock* movie with Chubby Checker, The Marcels' first single of 1962 was the 'Blue Moon' soundalike, 'Melancholy Baby'. It crept into the American Top Sixty. In truth the group realised their booming doo-wop charm was fading. Indeed, 'Melancholy Baby' turned out to be their last hit, while their last single for Colpix was 'I Wanna Be the Leader'. A subsequent one-off single, 'How Deep Is the Ocean', was their last release on the Kyra label. That likewise bombed. With no hits, The Marcels disbanded.

During the seventies, they regrouped to perform on a series of American nostalgia shows, and in the eighties their 1961 chart-topper 'Blue Moon' was heard in the closing sequence of the movie *An American Werewolf in London*. Bobby Vinton's version opened the film.

Also No. 1 singles in May 1961: 'On the Rebound' by Floyd Cramer; 'You're Driving Me Crazy' by The Temperance Seven

ELVIS PRESLEY

Surrender

'God gave me a voice. If I turned against God I'd be ruined.' – Elvis Presley

It was inevitable that following the runaway success of 'It's Now or Never', Presley would at some time turn once more to Italy for a single. This time he chose the B.G. de Curtis and Ernesto composition, written during 1911, titled 'Torna a Sorrento'. Mort Shuman and Doc Pomus translated the lyrics into English and Presley recorded it at RCA's Nashville studios. 'Surrender' was one of two secular songs from a session that spawned sufficient gospel tracks for the *His Hand in Mine* album. The second song was reputedly 'Crying in the Chapel', held back for future release.

'Surrender' shot to the top of the American chart, his fifteenth chart-topper, where it stayed for two weeks. When it was released in Britain, during June 1961, it soared to No. 1, dominating that position for four weeks.

As the single rode high, Presley was filming *Blue Hawaii*, originally titled 'Hawaii Beach Boy', co-starring Angela Lansbury, and had raised $50,000 from his charity performance staged at Pearl Harbor for the USS *Arizona* Memorial Fund. (The *Arizona* was sunk by Japanese aircraft in 1941 with over 1,000 men on board.)

Minnie Pearl, his co-star, said, 'The reception Elvis got in Hawaii – both on and off stage – was fantastic. I seriously worried for [his] safety as the fans surged from all sides to try and get to him from the moment he landed on the island . . . There was an estimated 3,000 fans at the airport, plus the ones lining the streets as we drove to the hotel, where another 500 nearly mobbed him . . . Elvis was at his best that night and the crowd gave him one encore after another. He wore a gold lamé jacket, heavily sequinned, and among the numbers he sang were "Such a Night", "Somethin' Blue", and he climaxed the show with that all-out rocker "Hound Dog".'

It was Presley's last concert for at least seven years.

Also see: 'It's Now or Never', November/December 1960; 'Are You

Lonesome Tonight', February 1961; 'Wooden Heart', April 1961; 'Rock a Hula Baby'/'Can't Help Falling in Love', March 1962; 'Good Luck Charm', June 1962; 'She's Not You', September 1962; '(You're the) Devil in Disguise', August 1963; 'Crying in the Chapel', July 1965

July 1961

DEL SHANNON

Runaway

Del Shannon said 'Runaway' was born from his ambition to be one. In fact he believed the single was so popular because everyone at one time or another wanted to run away. Judging by the record's sales, he might have had a point.

Born Charles Westover in Coopersville, Michigan, on 30 December 1939, he learned to play the bazoo, ukulele and, eventually, the guitar. Shannon sang and played his way through high school, his heart set on being a country singer.

From high school he was drafted into the Special Services where he entertained the troops until he was discharged. He moved to Battle Creek in Michigan where his daytime job was selling carpets and where, at night, he was a regular replacement for a nightclub act, Doug Dermont, who rifled Elvis Presley's music catalogue for his act. In time, Del Shannon became more established and worked under the name Charlie Johnson and the Big Little Show Band, with a residency at the Hi-Lo Club.

Still known as Charles Westover, he worked with Max Crook, the group's pianist, writing and experimenting with music. Ollie McLaughlin, a DJ for the WGRV radio station, heard their work and passed it on to Harry Balk and Irving Micahnik of Embee Productions. They, in turn, negotiated a recording deal with Big Top Records.

Now known as Del Shannon (the first name taken from the owner of the carpet store where he worked, 'Shannon' a suggestion from a fan of the Big Little Show Band), he was shipped to New York to record, with disappointing results. He and Max Crook decided they could do no worse and worked again on their own material. Within three hours they had formulated the idea for 'Runaway', and others including 'Jodie' (its future flipside). In actual fact, 'Runaway' was born from an accident. Del Shannon told Joe Smith: 'It all started at the Hi-Lo Club one night when Max and I were on stage. Max hit an A minor on his piano, and then went to G . . . All we were doing was C, A Minor, F and G chords. And then I said, "Play that again and follow me." And I just played the chords and sang any words I could think of.' The singer wrote the song's lyrics proper at work the following day, and while performing that next evening, he taped Crook's instrumental version of the song.

Unsure of Big Top Records' reaction to 'Runaway', Shannon continued to include it in his stage act for a time before he and Crook returned to New York to record it. One of the song's attractions was Crook's contribution on the musitron which perfectly complemented Shannon's voice. 'Runaway' was issued as a single in America, and sold a million copies on its way to the top of the chart in April 1961. It enjoyed a four-week stay. Subsequently, Del Shannon dumped his carpet selling to concentrate on promoting the single; one of his first performances was in Brooklyn where he earned his annual daytime wage in one evening.

When 'Runaway' was released in Britain, it sold in excess of half a million copies and raced to the top of the chart during July 1961, where it also stayed for four weeks.

In August 1961, 'Hats off to Larry', the chart-topper's clone, was issued. Another compulsive number, it soared to No. 5 in the American chart and a position lower in Britain, where it was Shannon's last single of the year.

Early in 1962, 'Hey! Little Girl' became a No. 2 British hit after an abysmal American showing in the Top Forty. This was followed by the minor hit 'Cry Myself to Sleep', one of several tracks recorded in Nashville with back-up support from The Jordanaires. However, this was only a hiccup; when another track from those sessions was issued, namely 'Swiss Maid', complete with Shannon's yodelling, it returned him to No. 2 in the British chart, with a poor showing in the American Top Seventy.

Del Shannon's first single of 1963 was 'Little Town Flirt', another infectious slice of three minutes. Again, it was a bigger hit, at No. 4, in Britain; in America it reached No. 12. By May, his second single of the year, 'Two Kinds of Teardrops', reached the British Top Five, but only managed the American Top Fifty.

As 'Two Kinds of Teardrops' peaked, Del Shannon toured Britain with Johnny Tillotson and Dusty Springfield, before supporting The

Beatles at London's Royal Albert Hall. It was at this time that Shannon told the Fab Four he intended to record a cover version of their 'From Me to You'. Despite objection from John Lennon, who realised Shannon could deny them an American hit, Shannon went ahead and recorded the song in London prior to returning to the States. His version was released simultaneously with The Beatles' original, holding off their American chart entry for six months. Hence, Del Shannon was the first artist to chart a Lennon/McCartney composition in America. 'From Me to You' was flipped over for British release. 'Two Silhouettes' became the A-side and reached the Top Thirty.

Del Shannon admitted at this point in his career that he had a tough time coping with his success; his fear almost crippled him. He turned to alcohol – 'that made it easier'. It was a short-term solution because it made him unable to cope with a series of disagreements with Embee Productions which led to him leaving to open his own label, Berlee Records. His debut single was 'Sue's Gotta Be Mine', a minor hit on both sides of the Atlantic. Likewise 'Mary Jane', its follow-up.

In August 1964, following a new deal with Amy Records, Shannon's star began to rise again with a revival of Jimmy Jones's 'Handy Man', a Top Thirty British hit; Top Forty in America. His career plodded on sufficiently for him to join Liberty Records during 1967 where his only chart single was 'The Big Hurt'. Two years on, singer and record company had parted, whereupon Shannon shrugged off his own career to produce other artists like Brian Hyland.

Eventually, the pull of the spotlight returned him to the recording studios during the late seventies/early eighties but with little success. However, he went on to earn a living performing on the lucrative nostalgia packages that toured Britain and America. But that wasn't enough. Del Shannon was unable to accept the role he now played, that of a 'golden oldie'.

At the height of his depression he killed himself with a .22 calibre rifle at his Santa Clarita home in California on 8 February 1990. Del Shannon had run away for the last time.

EDEN KANE

Well I Ask You

As solo artists came and went during the early sixties, Eden Kane was one of the breed whose success was immediate – and short. He came from The Allisons and John Leyton mould, who, to all intents and purposes, were overnight sensations releasing 'throwaway' singles. Their image was unruffled, extremely acceptable and their talent debatable.

He was born Richard Sarstedt on 29 March 1942 in Delhi, India, and his family moved to Britain in the mid-fifties. While at school, Richard Sarstedt and his brothers, Peter and Robin, formed their own skiffle group. But it was as a solo artist that Richard found success. He won a 1960 talent contest and immediately joined forces with the management team of Philip Waddilove and Michael Barclay of Audio Enterprises. It was then that the name change to Eden Kane occurred, taken from the movie *Citizen Kane* and the biblical Garden of Eden.

Cadbury's, the chocolate conglomerate, sponsored Eden Kane's first single, 'Hot Chocolate Crazy', but despite the financial backing, it bombed. Nonetheless, it brought him to the attention of Decca Records who released his first commercial single, 'Well I Ask You', a play on a cliché at the time. Displaying more of a growl than a singing voice, the disc was a runaway hit and reached No. 1 within days during August 1961. In much the same vein, 'Get Lost' followed, but it stalled at No. 10.

To start 1962, 'Forget Me Not' bolted to No. 3, followed by his self-named album, while the last release of the year, 'I Don't Know Why', was his final hit for two years.

The start of his decline happened when Audio Enterprises went into liquidation. Manager Vic Billings (who also represented Dusty Springfield with whom Kane was later reputedly romantically involved) added him to his books. He arranged for Kane to meet Jack Baverstock, A. & R. manager at Fontana Records, and the two went on to work on Kane's return as a chart artist. During January 1964 he did just that. 'Boys Cry' shot into the British Top Ten. Unfortunately, the return was short-lived. This was to be his only success under his new management, and by the end of the year Eden Kane had emigrated to Australia, later to America.

Eden Kane's two brothers, Robin and Peter Sarstedt, also enjoyed a short recording career in their own right. They did, however, all join forces during 1973 to record the *World's Apart Together* album.

Like so many acts from the early sixties, Eden Kane has found renewed public interest in his singles from the expanding revival touring packages.

September 1961

JOHN LEYTON

Johnny Remember Me

Independent British record producer Joe Meek was responsible for John Leyton's success. With composer Geoff Goddard, he produced four eerie, echo-filled singles which turned Leyton into a short-lived chart artist.

Born in Frinton-on-Sea, Essex, on 17 February 1939, John Leyton started his professional life in the television series *Biggles*. His recording career began when he signed a contract with Top Rank Records even though his voice wasn't the attraction; rather his smooth good looks and blond hair. Nevertheless, Leyton had the experienced back-up of manager Robert Stigwood and, of course, the dedicated talents of Joe Meek.

'Tell Laura I Love Her' was Leyton's debut single but he lost the battle of the hits when Ricky Valance took his version to the top of the British chart during 1960. 'Girl on the Floor Above' was Leyton's next: that too bombed. A change of composer, though, brought a change of luck.

Geoff Goddard wrote 'Johnny Remember Me', a haunting song that captured the public's imagination. The single swept to No. 1 in Britain in September 1961. Much of the song's success, however, was attributed to the singer's then current television series, *Harpers, West One* where his role was one of a singer named Johnny St Cyr, who regularly sang 'Johnny Remember Me'.

Another Goddard composition followed, 'Wild Wind', which was in a similar style to the chart-topper. It gave Leyton a No. 2 British hit in October 1961. His last of the year, 'Son This Is She', reached the Top Twenty and marked his first release on the HMV record label.

During 1962 Leyton enjoyed two Top Forty hits – 'Lone Rider' and 'Down the River Nile' – and one Top Twenty entrant, 'Lonely City'. By 1963 he could manage only one Top Thirty disc, 'Cupboard Love', while 'I'll Cut your Tail Off' struggled into the Top Fifty, and upon re-entry into the Top Forty. Leyton's recording career was sliding, and in 1964 he issued his last chart single, 'Make Love to Me', which peaked at No. 49 in the British chart.

However, all was not lost because singing had been a sideline since 1963 when he decided to move into film work. To this end, he appeared in *The Great Escape* with Steve McQueen among the star-studded cast, and in 1965 starred in another war epic, *Von Ryan's Express* with Frank Sinatra. Three years later he had a role in *Krakatoa*, followed by *Schizo* in 1977.

It took ten years before John Leyton returned to the studios to record an eponymous album, produced by Kenny Young. Since that time, his name has been kept alive via compilation albums, until the man behind the name took to the stage once more to perform on nostalgia package tours.

His most recent tour, in 1996, was a nationwide trek promoted by Flying Music with fellow sixties artists, Marty Wilde and Eden Kane.

Also a No. 1 single in September 1961: 'Reach for the Stars'/'Climb Ev'ry Mountain' by Shirley Bassey

October 1961

THE HIGHWAYMEN

Michael Row the Boat

'Michael Row the Boat' was a song of many colours. Originally it was sung by slaves in Georgia in the nineteenth century, and years later was adapted easily to different styles. For example, soul fans will know it after watching The Supremes sing it during a 1967 *Tarzan* show. Pop followers have The Springfields' album version, while followers of skiffle will remember Lonnie Donegan's Top Twenty hit because it was issued more or less at the same time as this chart-topper.

Featuring members Bobby Burnett, Steve Trott, Chan Daniels,

Steve Butts and Dave Fisher, The Highwaymen were formed at Wesleyan University, Middletown, Connecticut. Local support encouraged them to pursue a musical career, and by enlarging their repertoire to sing in several tongues including French and Hebrew, The Highwaymen became a big attraction on the local circuit.

Although the group members really wanted to continue with their studies, they did concede to public pressure to contact music impresario Ken Greengrass in New York during 1961. He took over their management and arranged an audition with United Artists Records.

The first release was the group's eponymous album from which 'Michael Row the Boat' was lifted. The single floated for several months until a radio DJ at WORC in Massachusetts gave it concentrated airplay. The mellow folk sound shot to the top of the American and British charts in 1961, but as The Highwaymen never intended to be fully fledged professionals they rejected most offers of live work that accompany a No. 1 disc.

Late in 1961 'Gypsy Rover' was issued in Britain, stalling at No. 41, and when it re-entered in January 1962 it stopped two rungs lower. In America, meantime, The Highwaymen enjoyed one further hit with 'Cottonfields' and released their second album, *Standing Room Only*.

When Steve Trott and Bobby Burnett left in 1962, The Highwaymen continued with one replacement until Burnett returned a year later, whereupon the album *Hootenanny with The Highwaymen* was released. Burnett's stay was, unfortunately, short-lived because the group split up in 1964. ABC Records purchased the rights to the name to form a totally new group.

During 1970 the original line-up reworked 'Michael Row the Boat' but it bombed. The members, with the exception of Dave Fisher and Chan Daniels, moved into other professions, leaving their musical career behind them as the hobby it was meant to be.

November 1961

HELEN SHAPIRO

Walkin' Back to Happiness

'Wup-pah oh yeh yeh . . . !'

Helen Shapiro was the first British act to release two Top Ten singles while still at school, namely 'Walkin' Back to Happiness' and 'You

Don't Know'. She was the teenager with the mature voice and her recording success was instant but brief.

Born in Bethnal Green, London, on 28 September 1946, Helen Shapiro took vocal classes at the Maurice Berman Academy while still attending school. EMI Records' producer, John Schroeder, chanced to be at one of the classes and was greatly impressed with such a strong voice soaring from a slip of a girl, barely in her teens. Schroeder arranged for her to audition for Norrie Paramor, from EMI's Columbia label. Like Schroeder before him, Paramor refused to believe his eyes and ears. Nonetheless, he signed Shapiro as a recording artist, leaving Schroeder to compose her debut release, 'Don't Treat Me like a Child'. A full promotional schedule backed this release, including television and radio spots, which helped push the single to No. 3 in the British chart during May 1961.

By contrast, the follow-up, also penned by John Schroeder (with Mike Hawker) titled 'You Don't Know' was a smooth ballad which, under other circumstances, would be alien to teenage interpretation. The combination worked perfectly. Selling in excess of 40,000 copies daily, the single raced to the top of the British chart where it stayed for two weeks. International sales soared above one million by the end of 1961, as it became a top-seller in most European countries.

Helen Shapiro celebrated her fifteenth birthday on 28 September 1961. She left school and was free to concentrate fully on her career and fulfil her performing itinerary that included a season at the London Palladium.

'Walkin' Back to Happiness', again written by Schroeder and Hawker, with advance orders of 300,000 entered the Top Ten immediately. And while 'You Don't Know' descended, the new release rose to the top, a position it occupied for four weeks. Readers of the *New Musical Express* subsequently voted her Top UK Female Singer.

To date, the young songstress had been totally reliant on her composers' choice of material and indeed it had been entirely compatible with her vocal ability and range. But Shapiro had ideas of her own, as exemplified by a four-song EP comprising standard material that included 'Goody Goody', which elevated the disc into the EP chart.

During March 1962, after Helen Shapiro had toured Britain for the first time, 'Tell Me What He Said' was issued. Written by Jeff Barry, it soared to No. 2 thus denying Shapiro the distinction of enjoying three consecutive chart-toppers with her first three singles!

As if to push her preference for established tunes further, her debut album, *Tops with Me*, released during April 1962, featured her versions of several, including 'Lipstick on your Collar', previously recorded by Connie Francis who enjoyed a British No. 3 hit with it during July 1959.

From recording artist, Shapiro turned to actress to secure the starring role in *It's Trad, Dad*, a British pop music movie. 'Let's Talk about Love' was lifted from the soundtrack to stall outside the Top Twenty, a dismal result from a young lady who was more familiar with the top end of the chart than the bottom. In fact, unbeknown to her, this poor showing signified the start of the decline, beginning in August 1962 when 'Little Miss Lonely' peaked at No. 8. Despite being written by her hit-making duo Schroeder and Hawker, this would mark Helen Shapiro's last Top Twenty hit.

Due to her previous success on the big screen, Shapiro was included, albeit as a cameo appearance, in *Play It Cool*, a movie starring Billy Fury. Her contribution was two songs, 'But I Don't Care' and 'Cry my Heart Out'; neither was issued as a single. Instead, the Bacharach/Hilliard composition 'Keep Away from Other Girls' was released. Originally recorded by the American vocalist Babs Tino, it faltered in the Top Forty for Shapiro.

During February 1963, she once more headlined a British tour. This time her support act was The Beatles who gave her 'Misery', a composition written with her style in mind. Norrie Paramor turned it down, preferring 'Queen for Tonight' as the next single. Once again, Shapiro watched a single stagger into the Top Forty. In May 1963, following a recording session in Nashville, Tennessee, 'Woe Is Me' was issued, another staller in the Top Forty. Yet, with the proper guidance, Helen Shapiro could have been reinstated as a Top Ten artist because she recorded the original version of 'It's my Party'. American teenager Lesley Gore took her version to No. 9 in the British chart during June 1963, and topped the American chart after sales of one million copies.

The second of Shapiro's Nashville sessions was issued in July 1963. Titled 'Not Responsible', it was her first single not to receive a British chart placing. And when the *Helen in Nashville* album itself was issued in October, that too bombed.

Another track was taken early in 1964. Shapiro covered the Peggy Lee classic 'Fever'. This almost desperate move to save her career only reached the Top Forty. It was her last British hit, and to all intents and purposes, her recording career was over.

The remainder of 1964 was spent touring abroad, particularly in the Far East. In the spring of 1965 Shapiro performed 'Here in my Arms' in the British Song Festival held in Brighton, East Sussex. That flopped. Nothing her management planned could rescue her from the decline, so in 1967 she moved to the stage to appear in *I'll Get my Man*.

The Columbia label dropped her when her recording contract expired, and in 1968 she struck a deal with Pye Records in the hope that that company could save her flagging recording career. While there, she worked again with John Schroeder, recording 'Today Has Been Cancelled', but the hit-making magic had worn off. Shapiro turned to the stage once again, this time as a straight actress and singer. Taking up her recording career once more, she made a series of singles for countless labels, before joining Charlie Gillett's Oval Records in 1983. While there, she recorded her first album in two decades titled *Straighten Up and Fly Right*. Although welcomed by critics, it failed to sell.

Two years on, Helen Shapiro joined Humphrey Lyttelton and his band on the Duke Ellington tribute album *Echoes of the Duke*, and watched in the sidelines as compilations of her best material were issued, including *The Helen Shapiro 25th Anniversary Album*, in 1986.

With the start of the nineties, she participated in several gospel shows, including one with Cliff Richard. Shapiro continues to perform today, mostly as a jazz singer. Her demise as a recording artist was attributed to the success of the new female brigade like Dusty Springfield and Cilla Black. But, Helen Shapiro was lucky. She had her day.

December 1961

BOBBY VEE

Take Good Care of my Baby

As a teenager, Bobby Vee, born Robert Thomas Velline on 30 April 1943 in Fargo, North Dakota, was obsessed with Buddy Holly. When it was announced that Holly and The Crickets were due to perform in his home town, Bobby Vee hastily formed a high school group with his brother Bob and three others. Calling themselves The Shadows they slavishly copied Buddy Holly's material. And as macabre as it sounds now, Buddy Holly's sudden death on 3 February 1959 gave The Shadows their first professional break.

Buddy Holly and The Crickets were due to perform at the Winter Dance Party in Fargo when their plane crashed killing him, Ritchie Valens, The Big Bopper and J.P. Richardson. The Shadows stepped in to fill their spot on the show after answering an appeal from their local radio station.

And it was from this performance that Bobby Vee's Shadows moved on to regular gigs, before financing their recording session at Soma Records' studio in Minneapolis. 'Suzy Baby', written by Bobby Vee, in Holly's style of course, was the result. When the single was issued it naturally became a local hit. Then Liberty Records purchased the master recording to release it on a national basis. It debuted in the American chart at No. 77, at which point the record company offered the group two deals. One for The Shadows, the other for Bobby Vee as a soloist.

Early in 1960, after working with respected producer Snuff Garrett, Bobby Vee, emulating Holly, recorded 'What Do You Want?' (covered by Adam Faith who had the British hit in 1959). It struggled into the American Top One Hundred. After much persuasion by Garrett, Vee recorded 'Devil or Angel', previously a hit for The Clovers. Despite Vee's reservations, the single stormed up the American charts to an impressive No. 6.

But it was in 1961 that the young singer really made his mark when he recorded 'Rubber Ball', an infectious yet childish song written by Gene Pitney and Aaron Schroeder. It was Vee's first million-seller. Within weeks, 'Rubber Ball' also gave Vee his debut British hit at No. 4, beating rock 'n' roller Marty Wilde's version which stalled at No. 9.

'More Than I Can Say', originally the B-side of the American hit 'Stayin' in', likewise reached No. 4, but it was his fourth single that finally elevated Bobby Vee to the No. 1 position. Snuff Garrett was searching for suitable songs and went to various publishers including Aldon Music. There he heard a demo of 'Take Good Care of my Baby' written by Carole King. He was told the song wasn't available as Dion had already recorded it, although it was doubtful it would be issued. Garrett persuaded Carole King to modify the song to suit Vee. 'Take Good Care of my Baby' was the perfect pop song, bursting with the writer's innate ability to compose a strong, flowing melody. It blended perfectly with Vee's voice and topped the charts on both sides of the Atlantic, selling a million copies in each country. Dion did later release his version on the *Runaround Sue* album and Bobby Vee himself re-recorded it at a slower pace for his 1972 album *Nothin' Like a Sunny Day*, released under his real name.

The follow-up, 'Run to Him' was equally impressive, although it faltered at No. 6 in Britain, while the album *Take Good Care of my Baby* reached the Top Ten.

To cash in on his British success, Bobby Vee, with his all-American clean-cut image, toured the country, fitting in television spots when he could. 'Please Don't Ask about Barbara' became a No. 29 hit, and in July 1962 'Sharing You' peaked at No. 10.

After releasing the inevitable *Bobby Vee Meets The Crickets* album which figured as his best-selling album in Britain, the singer actually toured with Buddy Holly's group. Following this and before 1962 was out 'A Forever Kind of Love' reached the Top Twenty. Recorded in Britain, with Norrie Paramor as producer, it was another slice of Bobby Vee magic. A strong melody against his warm voice. It couldn't fail.

To start 1963 'The Night Has a Thousand Eyes' lifted from the *Just for Fun* movie soared into the Top Three in both Britain and America. Yet despite the conveyor belt of hits, Bobby Vee's final British entrant was imminent. Titled 'Bobby Tomorrow' it stalled outside the Top Twenty at the end of 1963. Although his British recording career was finished, Vee continued to work with Snuff Garrett until 1965. None of his singles reached the Top Twenty in America until 1967 when he recorded 'Come Back When You Grow Up' with The Strangers, which hit the Top Three.

Bobby Vee remained a recording artist until 1972 but his past success evaded him. All attempts to leave his 'sound' behind and to experiment with different styles like lightweight country and western didn't work.

Following the release of the compilation *The Bobby Vee Singles Album*, the singer was a regular contributor to the oldies but goldies packages. His last British tour was as recent as 1995.

Also No. 1 singles in December 1961: 'Tower of Strength' by Frankie Vaughan, 'Moon River' by Danny Williams

ACKER BILK

Stranger on the Shore

When Acker Bilk originally wrote 'Stranger on the Shore' he called it 'Jenny' after one of his children. In stepped BBC TV who wanted him to write the theme for a new children's series titled . . . 'Stranger on the Shore'. It was released as a single during 1962 and rose to remarkable heights. Not only did it top the British chart but it was the first British single to hit No. 1 in America – twenty months before The Beatles headed the British invasion. Without doubt, it was a tremendous achievement for a jazz musician.

Acker Bilk was born Bernard Stanley Bilk on 28 January 1929 in Pensford, Somerset. His father was a Methodist preacher and church organist, but this didn't inspire Bilk to take up music because when he left school he trained as a blacksmith. In the late forties Bilk was called up by the Armed Forces. It was in unusual circumstances that he learned to play the clarinet. In 1947 Acker Bilk was posted to Egypt and during a stint on guard duty he fell asleep. His punishment was three months in jail. To relieve the boredom of his incarceration Bilk was given a clarinet. By the time he was freed, he had mastered the instrument.

Upon his discharge from the Armed Forces, Bilk decided to stick with music and drifted from band to band, earning a solid reputation in the Bristol area. His first break was in 1954 when he worked with Ken Colyer, a stylist of New Orleans jazz. This gave Bilk the confidence to form The Paramount Jazz Band during 1955. From Bristol, Bilk moved to Germany where he spent much time performing. When he returned to Britain, and known as 'Mr' Acker Bilk, he met Dennis Preston from Record Supervision. The two worked together, with Preston as producer.

Acker Bilk's first hit from this relationship was 'Summer Set' which raced to No. 5 in the British chart during 1959. This single brought the clarinettist and The Paramount Jazz Band to a much wider audience than jazz factions had previously enjoyed. Three further hits during 1960 proved Bilk's growing popularity: 'Goodnight Sweet Prince', 'White Cliffs of Dover' and 'Buona Sera'. The first two were Top Fifty hits, while the third crashed into the Top Ten.

Following two further hits in 1961, namely 'That's my Home' and 'Stars and Stripes Forever', 'Stranger on the Shore' was issued. Backed by The Leon Young String Chorale, it stayed in the British chart for a staggering 55 weeks, sold approximately 2.5 million copies worldwide and was voted the Best Instrumental of 1961. Such now was Acker Bilk's status that he was invited to perform at the Royal Variety Show in 1961.

The clarinettist and his band were constantly in demand both on television and for live performances. Wearing their trademark stage outfits of striped waistcoats and bowler hats, they toured America and Europe, while upholding their chart standing at home. In 1962 Bilk enjoyed three British hits with 'Frankie and Johnny', 'Gotta See my Baby Tonight' and 'Lonely'. But the run was coming to an end due to the increasing popularity of pop music; the beat boom was tightening its stranglehold on the charts, freezing out jazz artists on the way. 'A Taste of Honey' was Acker Bilk's last hit, in January 1963. It peaked at No. 16 but at least he bowed out honourably.

Nevertheless, hits or not, the demand for Acker Bilk's live performances remained constant. He even returned to the British charts in 1976 with 'Aria' which soared into the Top Five. This unexpected success was capitalised upon with the release of *The Very Best of Acker Bilk*. Other albums followed: *Sheer Magic* and *The Best of Acker Bilk – Volume Two*, both in 1979, and *Mellow Music* a year later.

Mr Acker Bilk and The Paramount Jazz Band were successful because they combined their love of jazz with material that had catchy melodies, or recorded versions of established tunes already known to the public. If the pop invasion hadn't happened, who knows what heights they would have reached?

February 1962

CLIFF RICHARD

The Young Ones

With his greased look and leather jackets replaced by sharp suits and naturally waved hair, a more boyish Cliff Richard was presented to the public. During May 1961 Cliff Richard announced that he planned to star in his third movie, *The Young Ones*. His co-stars were Carole Grey, Robert Morley, Melvyn Hayes, Richard O'Sullivan and, of course, The

Shadows. Richard played Nicki, leader of a youth club situated in a rundown area of London. His father, a property owner, intended to purchase the land for redevelopment, and the storyline developed around the arguments between the two. The finale was a concert which raised £2,000 to save the youth club. Produced by Kenneth Harper and directed by Sidney J. Furie, it was a musical for the family to enjoy and certainly the finest teenage entertainment to emanate from Britain in a long time.

'When the Girl in your Arms Is the Girl in your Heart'/'I Got a Funny Feeling' were the first tracks lifted from the film soundtrack. It was Richard's fifteenth single and peaked at No. 3 during October 1961. Two months on, *The Young Ones* was premiered at the Warner Theatre, London, whereupon the soundtrack album was issued to displace Elvis Presley's own soundtrack, *Blue Hawaii*, from the top of the album chart.

During January 1962 *The Young Ones* opened in various cinemas around Britain to eventually become the second box-office hit of the year behind the war epic *The Guns of Navarone*. With advance orders in excess of one million copies, 'The Young Ones' single, written by Sid Tepper and Roy C. Bennett, was issued. Norrie Paramor produced it: 'Some people said that when I dubbed on the strings it "made" the record. I don't agree. They added to the effect by all means, and they probably made it sound much nicer.' The single entered the British chart at No. 1, a position it held for a staggering six weeks, earning the singer a gold disc. It was Cliff Richard's biggest-selling single to date.

As Richard and The Shadows were touring Britain, he was voted the Top British Male Singer in the *New Musical Express* readers' poll for the second year running, received the Showbusiness Personality of the Year Award from the Variety Club of Great Britain, and was the recipient of a Special Award at the annual Ivor Novello Awards ceremony held at the BBC Television Centre, London.

Before 1962 closed, two further singles were issued: both were hits, Peggy Lee's 'I'm Looking out the Window'/'Do You Wanna Dance', originally recorded by Bobby Freeman, and Jerry Lee Lewis's 'It'll Be Me'.

And still there were no signs of Cliff Richard and The Shadows' popularity waning. In truth, the success story was still formulating.

Also see: 'Please Don't Tease', August 1960; 'The Next Time', January 1963; 'Summer Holiday', March 1963

ELVIS PRESLEY

Rock a Hula Baby/Can't Help Falling in Love

Blue Hawaii was the most successful of Elvis Presley's movies, although critics were quick to fault its poor storyline. Nonetheless, it grossed $30 million. Following its release during November 1961, the soundtrack album topped the American chart for an unbelievable twenty weeks, selling in excess of two million copies. It also became a British chart-topper.

Two tracks from this album were lifted for single release early in 1962, namely, 'Rock a Hula Baby' which reached No. 23 in the American chart, and 'Can't Help Falling In Love' which soared to No. 2. Released as a double A-sided single in Britain, it sped to the top of the chart in March 1962. 'Rock a Hula Baby' was a swinging, uptempo track that brought alive the spectacular scenery of the Hawaiian locations used in the movie; the vivid colour and glorious sandy beaches under a deep blue sky; while 'Can't Help Falling in Love' was one of Presley's finest emotional ballads.

Hawaii was still very much on Presley's mind, as his next movie, *Girls! Girls! Girls!*, was to be filmed there. In fact, shooting began while he dominated the British chart. This romantic movie also featured Stella Stevens and Jeremy Slate, and was another conveyor-belt production to placate public and film company demand. Film producer Hal Wallis still believed in Presley's viability as an actor: 'It was the look of him, the eyes – with flickers of Rudolph Valentino – the way he moved. There was just an excitement about him. There was never a problem with him on the set,' he added. Presley was always on time, had learned his lines and was polite to everyone, especially his co-stars.

Yet even these attributes failed to compensate for the lightweight storylines which were based more or less on the same theme of boy-gets-girl. Despite the excitement generated from his first roles as a rebellious young man, Presley had slowly transformed into the acceptable all-American boy as the scripts he was expected to work on turned from boiling hot to lukewarm. There was nothing he could do, trapped by contracts that still had time to run. However, the conveyor belt would stop, and suddenly; in the meantime, singer and manager continued to rake in the profits.

During his movie years, Presley purchased houses in Palm Springs and Bel Air, and as he loathed 'showbiz parties', he hosted his own, inviting the ever-expanding entourage he attracted. Young Priscilla Beaulieu rarely joined him while he was on location, although by now she wasn't excluded from his medication habit because she would take the same drugs purely to keep up with Presley's lifestyle.

Also see: 'It's Now or Never', November/December 1960; 'Are You Lonesome Tonight', February 1961; 'Wooden Heart', April 1961; 'Surrender', June 1961; 'Good Luck Charm', June 1962; 'She's Not You', September 1962; '(You're the) Devil in Disguise', August 1963; 'Crying in the Chapel', July 1965

April 1962

THE SHADOWS

Wonderful Land

Now established as one of Britain's most successful instrumental groups, The Shadows moved from strength to strength until their own career left them little time to work with Cliff Richard. They combined the two until 1968 when they performed for the last time together at the London Palladium.

Written by Jerry Lordan, 'Wonderful Land' marked a change of ideas. The Shadows' basic guitar work, which had already given them two British chart-toppers with 'Apache' in 1960 and 'Kon-Tiki' in 1961, was now padded by a studio orchestra. The result was smooth, melodic, and the public flocked to buy this softer sound, pushing the single to the top of the British chart in April 1962 where it stayed for eight weeks.

Shortly after this latest success, and following their appearance at the *New Musical Express* Poll Winners' concert, Jet Harris walked away from the group, having tired of differences of opinion with Bruce Welch. While Harris pursued a solo career, Brian Locking, an ex-Krew-Kats member, replaced him. His debut appearance as a Shadow was in May 1962 at a charity function in London's West End. Also that month, The Shadows flew to Greece to film *Summer Holiday* with Cliff

Richard. The movie's title track was written by Brian Bennett and Bruce Welch, and went on to become a 1963 chart-topper for Richard.

The Shadows then performed a two-week stint in Paris and upon their return added the final touches to their *Out of the Shadows* album which held the No. 1 position for three weeks. As 1962 closed, *The Boys* EP, from the movie of the same name, soared to the top of the EP listing, and The Shadows performed with Cliff Richard at the Royal Variety Show.

The Avons' composition, 'Dance On', was the group's first chart-topper for 1963, followed by their last No. 1 single, 'Foot Tapper', in March. This single, lifted from the soundtrack of *Summer Holiday*, replaced Cliff Richard's own 'Summer Holiday' single at the top position. And following the release of 'Atlantis' in June and 'Shindig' in October, both Top Ten hits, Bruce Welch seriously considered leaving The Shadows through ill-health. However, with the help of medication he was able to postpone his decision until a later date. The group's last single of the year, 'Geronimo', failed to reach the British Top Ten, peaking at No. 11, and also marked the leaving-point for Brian Locking, a recent convert to the Jehovah's Witness faith. John Rostill, an ex-member of The Interns, born in Birmingham on 16 June 1942, replaced him. Before the dust settled, he and the group were involved in shooting *Wonderful Life*, a movie with Cliff Richard.

During 1964, The Shadows continued with their hit run – 'Theme for Young Lovers', No. 12; 'The Rise and Fall of Flingel Bunt', No. 5, and 'Rhythm and Greens', No. 22. They also toured Europe, appeared in their own musical comedy, *Rhythm and Greens*, which was the B-film on the cinema circuit to *King and Country*, and they wrote and performed in the pantomime *Aladdin and his Wonderful Lamp* with Cliff Richard. The Shadows also penned the score for *Babes in the Wood* starring Frank Ifield.

'Mary Anne', released in March 1965, was The Shadows' first single to feature vocals since 'Feelin' Fine' in 1959. It peaked at No. 17 in the British chart, and was followed by the second vocal single of the year, 'Don't Make my Baby Blue', a Top Ten British hit. The year ended with the Top Twenty instrumental, 'War Lord', the title track from the movie of the same name, featuring Charlton Heston.

For the next two years the group recorded as a unit, backed Cliff Richard, wrote and performed in a further pantomine, *Cinderella*, and toured the world. They also released their first bomber – 'Tomorrow's Cancelled' – in September 1967, four months after Bruce Welch left his wife for singer Olivia Newton-John.

During October 1968, Cliff Richard and The Shadows celebrated their tenth anniversary in the music business by releasing a joint album, *Established 1958*. The occasion was marred when both Hank Marvin and Bruce Welch disclosed their intention to leave the group. In the end, only Welch left, following a performance at the London Palladium. The departure had a knock-on effect, because by the end of the year The Shadows disbanded, citing lack of creativity and exhaustion as the reasons.

Hank Marvin went on to record 'Goodnight Dick' as a soloist, before duetting with Cliff Richard on the Top Ten hit 'Throw Down a Line' during September 1969. By October, The Shadows had temporarily reformed for a Japanese tour, unable to resist the purse. Early in 1970, Hank Marvin and Richard duetted for a second time on 'Joy of Living', the theme from Richard's weekly television series. It reached No. 25 in the British chart.

After a year's absence, Bruce Welch returned to a new line-up, that of a trio featuring Hank Marvin and John Farrar, and by 1971 they had returned to touring Europe, supported by Brian Bennett on drums and Dave Richmond on guitar. Meanwhile, the *Marvin, Welch and Farrar* album became a Top Thirty hit.

During the next three years, The Shadows were reborn and killed off several times. *Rockin' with Curly Leads*, featuring Welch, Marvin and Farrar with newcomer Alan Tarney on bass guitar, became a No. 45 album hit in April 1974. Six months later, The Shadows were born again to perform at a charity event at the London Palladium. From here, Bill Cotton, head of BBC TV, requested they represent Britain in the Eurovision Song Contest the following year. 'Let Me Be the One' was the public's choice and when The Shadows performed it in Stockholm, Sweden, they had to content themselves with the runner-up position. Teach-In, a Dutch outfit, won with 'Ding-a-Dong'. Nevertheless, The Shadows enjoyed renewed singles success with a No. 12 British hit. This prompted interest once more in their music, and the group was persuaded to perform in Paris where their show was taped for release as the *Live at the Paris Olympia* album in November 1975. It was The Shadows' last performance.

In 1976, Bruce Welch produced 'Miss You Nights' and 'Devil Woman' for Cliff Richard, while John Farrar moved to America to work with Olivia Newton-John. In February 1978, The Shadows reformed to perform several concerts with Cliff Richard at the London Palladium in celebration of their twentieth anniversary in the music business. Typically, compilations of The Shadows' singles were issued

73

alongside new albums from Hank Marvin and Brian Bennett. The Shadows also enjoyed renewed chart success with 'Don't Cry for Me Argentina', No. 5, and 'Theme from The Deer Hunter (Cavatina)', No. 9.

The year 1983 marked twenty-five years in showbusiness, and by way of honouring this achievement The Shadows were presented with a special Ivor Novello award, after which they released a celebratory album titled *XXV.*

To date, Hank Marvin appears to be the only Shadow to remain working in the public eye. Although he relocated to Australia, he performs regularly in Britain. His last hit single, 'We Are the Champions', with Queen guitarist Brian May, reached the British Top Sixty in October 1992, while his last album (to date) titled *Hank Plays Cliff* reached the Top Twenty in 1995.

Like Cliff Richard, The Shadows are part of Britain's musical heritage, and with Hank Marvin's continued presence their unique sound will never die.

Also see: 'Apache', September 1960

May 1962

B. BUMBLE AND THE STINGERS

Nut Rocker

'Bum bababa bum bum ba bum ba' taken at breakneck speed had needles bouncing on vinyl and dancers gyrating like creatures possessed. Yes, it was an unrecognisable stab at Tchaikovsky's 'Nutcracker Suite' according to B. Bumble and the Stingers.

Comprising (at any one time) B. Bumble (real name R.C. Gamble); Don Orr, on drums; Terry Anderson and Jimmy King on guitars, this American outfit was conceived by the wizard of pop music, Kim Fowley, who was signed as a composer/producer to Rendezvous Records at the time.

Born in the Philippines, Fowley was to American music what Jonathan King was to British 'pop' when it came to the subject of novelty records. Raised in Hollywood, he was a member of The Jayhawks during the mid-fifties, and The Sleepwalkers, which also featured Phil Spector at some point.

Fowley moved on to produce Paul Revere and The Raiders prior to moving to Los Angeles to record one-hit wonders. 'Alley-Oop' by The Hollywood Argyles was one in 1960, and The Rivingtons' 'Papa-Oom-Mow-Mow' was another two years later.

With lead pianist Ernie Freeman, Kim Fowley created B. Bumble and The Stingers. Their first single, in 1961, was 'Bumble Boogie'. This was a fantasy version of Rimsky-Korsakov's 'Flight of the Bumble Bee'. It flew into the American Top Twenty. The follow-up was 'Nut Rocker', featuring Lincoln Mayorga on keyboards, which zoomed to the top of the British chart in May 1962. This compulsive 'rocker' released on the Top Rank label, tore shreds off Tchaikovsky's classic piece and was one of the best sellers of the year. It was one of that rare breed of singles – a one-off that couldn't be matched and one that ultimately wouldn't die.

Ten years after its original release, 'Nut Rocker' was re-issued on the Stateside label to become a British Top Twenty hit in June 1972.

During the seventies, Kim Fowley turned his attention to Britain where he produced records for The Rockin' Berries and Cat Stevens, among others, and worked as choreographer for P.J. Proby. Back in America he worked with Frank Zappa on the Mother of Inventions album *Freak Out* before moving on to liaise with Jonathan Richman.

He then went on to create The Runaways, an all-girl outfit, from which Joan Jett embarked upon a successful career with The Blackhearts.

Kim Fowley has now retired from the music business, but 'Nut Rocker' lives on.

June 1962

ELVIS PRESLEY

Good Luck Charm

Elvis Presley continued to outsell and outshine all competitors. His spate of movies, almost three a year, continued to generate millions of dollars for those concerned, while his record sales maintained their staggering proportions. 'I was lucky,' he once said. 'I came along when there was no trend in music and people were looking for one.' Within four years, everything connected to Presley was due to change.

When 'Good Luck Charm' topped the American chart in April

1962, it became his sixteenth chart-topper. Between 1956 and 1962 he notched up a No. 1 per year, a record he held until The Beatles broke loose in America. Indeed, it was to be the Fab Four and the music they represented that inadvertently heralded Presley's decline, something he would avenge.

When 'Good Luck Charm' dominated the American chart, Presley's latest movie, *Follow that Dream*, opened. His co-star this time was Anne Helm who said he was 'wonderful to get on with' on set. 'I've always studied acting myself, but Elvis doesn't bother. It just seems to come instinctively to him. It's the same with his singing. He hasn't had vocal lessons but the results are pretty fine.'

'Good Luck Charm' sped to the top of the British chart in June 1962, where it stayed for five weeks. Hot on its heels was the *Follow that Dream* EP which peaked in the Top Twenty. The Presley magic showed no signs of declining in Britain, but like America, it would finally happen almost overnight.

As the single descended the chart, Presley was already engrossed in *It Happened at the World's Fair*, which was being filmed at the MGM studios in Culver City. And as he worked on this, *Kid Galahad* was premiered in America during August 1962. Presley's role was one of a boxer, with co-stars Charles Bronson and Gig Young. The singer refused to use a stand-in during the fight scenes and his expertise in the ring led Colonel Tom Parker to boast to the media that, 'Boxing promoters have been calling me every day offering figures for Elvis since stories have leaked out about his personal prowess in the ring. One guy in New York is offering $200,000 for one fight.'

Did anyone actually believe these stories except, perhaps, the Colonel himself?

Also see: 'It's Now or Never', November/December 1960; 'Are You Lonesome Tonight', February 1961; 'Wooden Heart', April 1961; 'Surrender', June 1961; 'Rock a Hula Baby'/'Can't Help Falling in Love', March 1962; 'She's Not You', September 1962; '(You're the) Devil in Disguise', August 1963; 'Crying in the Chapel', July 1965

Also a No. 1 single in June 1962: 'Come Outside' by Mike Sarne with Wendy Richard

RAY CHARLES

I Can't Stop Loving You

He was born in poverty and overcame his blindness to become a musical genius as a pianist, composer and singer. Although Ray Charles believes that being called a genius is the highest compliment, he insists he never 'wanted to create a fuss'. Nonetheless, his fans christened him with the title thirty years ago – and it stuck.

Born Ray Charles Robinson in Albany, Georgia, on 23 September 1930, he was raised in Greenville, Florida. His mother was a washerwoman, his father a handyman. Life was hard, and it would get more cruel. Ray Charles was blinded at the age of seven from glaucoma. His younger brother drowned in a washtub in their family home. His father died in 1940, his mother five years later.

As a youngster, Charles sang in the Shiloh Baptist Church, studied clarinet and classical music at a school for the deaf and blind in Orlando, but became obsessed with secular music. Moving to Jacksonville, Florida, he joined The Honeydippers, and three years on relocated to Seattle.

After winning a talent contest, Charles secured a residency at The Elks Club with his newly formed group The McSon Trio, playing Nat King Cole styled material. During 1949, the trio recorded and released 'Confession Blues' on Downbeat Records. Further singles included 'See See Rider', but Ray Charles pined to be a soloist. In time he made the move, and with guidance from Jack Lauderdale, owner of Downbeat Records, later to become Swingtime Records, he spent two years in Los Angeles working with music director Lowell Fulson.

Following a couple of R. & B. hits with The McSon Trio during 1951, namely 'Baby Let Me Hold your Hand' and 'Kiss-a-Me Baby', Atlantic Records purchased Ray Charles's recording contract from Swingtime for a reputed $3,000. By late 1952, he was in the recording studios working with Jesse Stone. From that session some of the finest R. & B. sounds of the late fifties were issued including his first Atlantic single, 'Mess Around', in May. It was written by Ahmet Ertegun, owner of the record company (who would oversee Charles's future recordings) and produced by Jerry Wexler.

During the next four years Ray Charles regularly hit the R. & B. chart. 'It Should Have Been Me' in 1954, later 'Don't You Know' and 'This Little Girl of Mine' are prime examples. But that crossover hit failed to happen until November 1957 with 'Swanee River Rock (Talkin' 'bout that River)' which stormed into the American Top Forty. In 1958, Atlantic recorded Ray Charles's performance at the Newport Jazz Festival to release as an album at the end of the year. His appearance at Atlanta's Herndon Stadium was likewise recorded for future release. Meantime, he was becoming a stronger chart contender in both the American R. & B. and pop listenings.

His first major recording achievement was his self-penned 'What'd I Say'. In August 1959 it topped the R. & B. chart for two weeks, and reached No. 6 in the pop chart. The song became his first million-seller.

At the close of 1959, Ray Charles switched record companies to ABC Paramount because Atlantic were unable to meet his financial demands. His debut single in August 1960 was 'Sticks and Stones', a Top Forty hit, while Atlantic Records continued to issue his canned material. The follow-up, 'Georgia on my Mind', a version of Hoagy Carmichael's original, sold one million copies to become an American chart-topper. It was also his first British hit, charting in December 1960, at No. 47, and on re-entry at No. 24. The album from which this single was lifted, namely his ABC Records' debut *The Genius Hits the Road*, quickly followed to reach the American Top Ten album chart. 'Georgia on my Mind' went on to win Grammy Awards for the Best Performance by a Pop Single Artist and Best Vocal Performance – Single Record or Track, Male, while the album won Best Vocal Performance – Album, Male. The state of Georgia then adopted the song as its anthem.

'Hit the Road Jack', written by Percy Mayfield, was his third American million-seller, in October 1961. While it sat at the top of the chart, the single soared to No. 6 in Britain. It won Ray Charles a further Grammy Award for the Best R. & B. Recording. But in December, the artist hit the headlines. Not because of his music, rather his arrest for possession of heroin in an Indianapolis hotel.

Early in 1962 'Unchain my Heart' and its B-side 'But on the other Hand' became American hits, while Atlantic Records released *Do the Twist*, his best-selling album for that label. In June his album sales rocketed further when *Modern Sounds in Country and Western Music* sold a million copies and dominated the American album charts for a staggering fourteen weeks. It was from this mega-heavy album that 'I

78

Can't Stop Loving You' was lifted. Written and recorded by Don Gibson during 1959, Ray Charles first heard it four years later and decided to include it on his album, which many of his advisers felt was a foolhardy move because he was known as an R. & B. artist, not a country and western whiner. Charles retaliated, 'I'm not singing it country and western. I'm singing it me.'

'I Can't Stop Loving You' notched up unprecedented sales of two million, topped the American chart for five weeks and was later recognised as 1962's top-selling single. While it peaked across the Atlantic, it soared to the top of the British chart in July 1962, his one and only chart-topper. It won a Grammy Award for the Best R. & B. Recording. The mother album, meantime, became his first hit in the British Top Ten. The follow-up single, 'You Don't Know Me', was also taken from *Modern Sounds in Country and Western*, and reached No. 2 in America and No. 9 in Britain.

As the combination of Ray Charles and country and western gelled so well, and was, surprisingly, so successful, he recorded another album, *Modern Sounds in Country and Western, Volume Two*. This time the lifted single, 'Your Cheating Heart', stalled at No. 22 in America, but did better in Britain, reaching No. 13. The album likewise achieved high chart positions.

'Take these Chains from my Heart' was the second single from *Volume Two*, a No. 8 and No. 5 hit in America and Britain respectively. It was his last British Top Ten single, although he would continue to be a charting artist until 1968.

His seventeen years of drug addiction once more became public. In 1964 Ray Charles was arrested at Logan Airport in Atlanta for possession of heroin, and again in 1966 when he was fined $10,000 and given a suspended sentence on condition he kicked the habit. He said at the time, 'I didn't quit because the heroin was killing me but because it was going to bring down my family and maybe even cause me to rot away in some jail cell.'

Through to the seventies, Ray Charles's status grew; he was in demand as a performer, headlining jazz festivals, appearing with soul legends like Aretha Franklin, and cramming in European tours where he could. With Charles at the piano, and his orchestra and female back-ups The Raelettes on hand, his shows were impassioned, exciting and totally emotional. Such was the status of working with the Genius that when a member of The Raelettes wanted to leave, she was guaranteed a recording contract.

The Raelettes, previously known as The Cookies, were formed to give response vocals to Ray Charles. The group spawned numerous solo careers for members like Minnie Riperton, Merry Clayton and Mable John. They also recorded in their own right for Ray Charles's Tangerine label.

Ray Charles's albums like *A Man and his Soul* continued to sell countless millions of copies, while singles 'Crying Time' and two Beatles cover versions – 'Yesterday' and 'Eleanor Rigby' – kept Charles in the top-selling listings.

During the next decade, the artist was honoured with the most prestigious awards the music industry had to offer, including his induction into the Black Rock 'n' Roll Hall of Fame; being presented with a Lifetime Achievement Award by NARAS at the thirtieth annual Grammy Awards ceremony, and voted Chairman of the Rhythm and Blues Foundation, based in Washington DC. His restless nature ensured regular touring schedules, while his contribution to music continued, including his participation in USA For Africa's 'We Are the World' charity single in 1985.

In 1992, among other notable appearances, Ray Charles performed at 'Capital Radio Jazz Parade' at the Royal Festival Hall, London, and at Caesars Palace, Las Vegas. A year later, alongside other principal artists, he participated in President-elect Bill Clinton's inaugural ceremonies; was given the Hall of Fame Lifetime Achievement Award, and released the *My World* album, produced by Richard Perry, on the Warner Brothers label.

Ray Charles's career so far was summed up in 1988 when he received the NARAS Lifetime Achievement Award: 'He is the father of soul, whose unique and effervescent singing and piano-playing have personified the true essence of soul music in all his records and personal performances of basic blues, pop ballads, jazz tunes and even country music.'

There's no argument . . .

_____

August 1962

FRANK IFIELD

I Remember You

In a year when the Twist was the most popular dance – for those who could master it; when Berry Gordy's Motown company was finally making its presence felt in America, and when The Beach Boys were poised to take Britain by storm, along came yodelling Frank Ifield, a country and western singer. Who said music was dull?

Frank Ifield was born in Coventry, Warwickshire, on 30 November 1936. His family emigrated to Australia when he was still a lad, and as a teenager he became interested in the music business. The name of Frank Ifield first became known during 1957 when he recorded 'Whiplash' (a song devoted to the 1851 goldrush in Australia), which was the theme for an Australian television series of the same name.

The singer returned to his homeland following 'Whiplash', and was signed to EMI Records' Columbia label where he was assigned to Norrie Paramor. 'Lucky Devil', issued early in 1960, entered the British chart twice – in February when it peaked at No. 22, and two months later when it managed to climb into the Top Forty. Its follow-up was 'Gotta Get a Date', another minor hit in September of that year.

This love affair with the chart was to become more serious in August 1962 when 'I Remember You' sped to the top. It was the first-ever single to sell in excess of one million copies in Britain as it dominated the chart for an incredible seven weeks, holding off some of the strongest competition of the decade, like Cliff Richard, Pat Boone and Joe Brown.

'I Remember You' also crashed into the American chart, another momentous achievement for a lone British vocalist in the sixties. The song was easy to listen to, it swept and swayed, and was highlighted by an adventurous harmonica sequence. A typical middle-of-the-road song whose sales were obviously strengthened by adult buying on both sides of the Atlantic.

Frank Ifield said at the time, 'Being No. 1 in the charts was never really my ambition, but naturally the big jump was good for me. It improved my confidence, for a start. I plan to keep my career on an even level. Record buyers are always looking for something new.'

Also see: 'Lovesick Blues', December 1962

ELVIS PRESLEY

She's Not You

After an incredible run of American chart-toppers, Elvis Presley's recording career began its decline. His last No. 1 was 'Good Luck Charm', in April 1962, while in Britain he maintained his run until the following year.

'She's Not You' enjoyed a three-week stay at the top of the British chart beginning in September 1962. It sold one million copies in America, stalling in the Top Five. Its follow-up, 'Return to Sender', issued during November, fared better by reaching No. 2, while in Britain it sold in excess of 750,000 copies to dominate the chart for three weeks. It would be fair to say that Presley was unaware of his singles success as he was so engrossed in his acting career. He didn't even see royalty statements and cheques, as these were filtered through Colonel Tom Parker to Presley's father, Vernon, who was in charge of his son's finances, even to the extent of being in control of the daily expenses at the family home, Graceland. He also paid the bills for Elvis's escalating drug habit.

In between record releases, the movie *Girls! Girls! Girls!* opened across the world, while its soundtrack went on to earn Presley a gold disc. Where did he put them all?

With the movie treadmill working to plan, in April 1963 *It Happened at the World's Fair* premiered in Los Angeles, while Presley was working on the next, titled *Fun in Acapulco*. Six months later, he began filming *Viva Las Vegas*, later retitled *Love in Las Vegas*. The storylines grew weaker, until they were flimsy.

When Colonel Tom Parker was asked why Presley never objected to his movie scripts he replied, 'For the $500,000 a picture they're [the film company] paying him, plus $5,000 a day expenses, they're not going to offer Elvis a bad script!' Perhaps that should have been put to public vote.

Despite countless invitations for Presley to perform in Britain, none had so far been accepted. However, during 1962, hopes were raised when it was thought he would accept an invitation to appear on the Royal Variety Show before members of the Royal Family. In the end, the request was rejected because of movie commitments. Colonel Tom Parker went on to say, 'It is true we have not been able to make personal appearances in Britain, but it is also true we have not appeared elsewhere. Through a motion picture, millions see Elvis. Through a personal appearance, a very small fraction would see him. We are thinking in terms of the many rather than the few.'

Elvis Presley would never perform in Britain.

Also see: 'It's Now or Never', November/December 1960; 'Are You Lonesome Tonight', February 1961; 'Wooden Heart', April 1961; 'Surrender', June 1961; 'Rock a Hula Baby'/'Can't Help Falling in Love', March 1962; 'Good Luck Charm', June 1962; '(You're the) Devil in Disguise', August 1963; 'Crying in the Chapel', July 1965

October/November 1962

THE TORNADOS

Telstar

On 10 July 1962 America launched the world's first communications satellite whose purpose was to relay television signals between America and Europe. Before the year was out, an instrumental inspired by this man-made phenomenon was known to several million people. Both were titled 'Telstar' and in their own way were as famous as each other. In fact, it's believed one couldn't talk about the satellite without the tune coming to mind.

The group behind 'Telstar' the record was the Tornados, a London-based quintet of musicians – drummer Clem Cattini, born 28 August 1939 in London; Heinz Burt, bass guitarist, born 24 July 1942 in Hargin, West Germany; Roger Lavern on keyboards, born 11 November 1938 in Kidderminster; Alan Caddy, lead guitarist, born 2 February 1940 in London, and George Bellamy, rhythm guitarist, born 8 October 1941 in Sunderland. Producer/writer Joe Meek was responsible for this line-up, and would prove to be the mastermind behind their success.

Joe Meek's first love from childhood had been electronics and this stayed with him during his stint in the Royal Air Force where he was a radar technician. When demobbed, he became a sound engineer with IBC Studios in London before moving to the Landsdowne

Studios. While working behind scenes he wrote for Tommy Steele and with the royalties earned started Triumph, his own record label. The first single was 'Angela Jones' by Michael Cox, a British hit, while the first No. 1 was John Leyton's 'Johnny Remember Me'. What prompted the forming of The Tornados was Joe Meek's need for a session group in the studios to back his other artists. But instead, in April 1962, he cut their first release, 'Love and Fury', a play on words following the group's touring spell with soloist Billy Fury. The single was issued via Decca Records and died.

The next did far better. Not only did 'Telstar', with its supernatural, eerie mood enhanced by an easy melody that brought to mind pictures of objects that flew about in space, top the British chart for five weeks, eventually passing the one-million-sales mark, but it enjoyed similar success in America where it stayed for three weeks. This achievement made The Tornados the only British group to reach the No. 1 spot prior to The Beatles.

When the disc dropped from the charts, The Tornados lost Heinz Burt to a solo career. His replacement was ex-Outlaw Chas Hodges, who in turn was replaced by Tab Martin. The public was oblivious to the personnel changes; it was the follow-up that was important. And Joe Meek let no one down when, in early 1963, he wrote and released 'Globetrotter', a weaker version of 'Telstar' which, nonetheless, reached the Top Five. A month after its release, Brian Gregg, an ex-Pirate (the Pirates backed Johnny Kidd) stepped in for the departing Tab Martin who formed his own band The Saints, also produced by Joe Meek.

Retaining the mystique of the technological, 'Robot' was The Tornados' third outing. It stalled inside the Top Twenty, while the EP *Tornado Rock* that followed was devoted to rock tracks like 'Long Tall Sally', indicating their out-of-this-world sound belonged to the past.

Meanwhile, Heinz (he dropped Burt) released his debut solo single, 'Dreams Do Come True', taken from the movie *Farewell Performance*, but it was his tribute to the late Eddie Cochran titled 'Just Like Eddie', penned by Meek, that gave him his biggest hit at No. 6.

By 1964 The Tornados were struggling. Group members drifted in and out, their singles failed to chart. When in early 1965 Clem Cattini left to become a session drummer, the success story was over. And the man who gave them that success ended his life. On 3 February 1967 Joe Meek committed suicide. Nobody was absolutely sure of the circumstances. But the date was the eighth anniversary of Buddy Holly's death.

In 1975, as the final tribute to the American Space Programme by which 'Telstar' was inspired, The Tornados, with their original line-up, re-recorded their 1962 chart-topper. Regrettably, this time, it never left the launching pad.

December 1962

FRANK IFIELD

Lovesick Blues

Still reeling from his unexpected chart-topper 'I Remember You' in August 1962, Frank Ifield recorded another, again under the guidance of EMI Records producer Norrie Paramor.

Frank Ifield: 'Fashions go up and down, and the public latch on to you. You can get the impact, but you can drop and be old-fashioned if you carry on doing exactly the same. To sustain you must give out, get more scope and make more people like you.'

With 'Lovesick Blues', the follow-up to his first No. 1, Ifield returned to the top of the British chart in December 1962. This time he leaned more on his love of country and western, and interspersed this with touches of yodelling. The combination worked.

But it was his next single that engraved his name in the record books of the music industry. 'Wayward Wind' also bolted to No. 1 in March 1963, making Frank Ifield the first British soloist to achieve three consecutive chart-toppers!

'Nobody's Darlin' but Mine' was next and broke the run. It stalled at No. 4 during April 1963. The next, 'Confessin'', once more took him all the way to the top during June. If the release sequence had been different, Ifield's achievement would have been all the more spectacular.

Like other artists of his ilk, the singer was to suffer with the birth of The Beatles, although he continued to hold his own for a while. During 1964 he enjoyed one Top Ten entrant with 'Don't Blame Me' in January, and three Top Forty entrants – 'Angry at the Big Oak Tree', 'I Should Care', 'Summer Is Over' – before the year was ended.

Only 'Paradise' charted the following year, at No. 26, but his talent was ploughed into movies. He wrote eight songs with his road manager Mick Conlin for *Up Jumped a Swagman*. The soundtrack album, featuring their compositions among others, was issued in

1966, alongside two Top Thirty singles, namely 'No One Will Ever Know' and 'Call Her your Sweetheart'.

Prior to this, Ifield had found immediate acceptance playing Robin Hood in the pantomime *Babes in the Wood* at the London Palladium, where it became a box-office record-breaker. According to Ifield, 'I stand to gain a lot through this panto. Whereas I used to cater for only record buyers, now it has all expanded and my career is solid. With good exposure and good records my name will still be around in twenty years' time.'

Now a regular attraction on the flourishing cabaret circuit, Ifield returned to the British Top Forty in 1991 with 'The Yodelling Song' single, featuring The Backroom Boys.

Also see: 'I Remember You', August 1962

January 1963

CLIFF RICHARD

The Next Time

Towards the close of 1962, Cliff Richard and The Shadows appeared on *The Ed Sullivan Show* as part of a short promotional visit to America, but he was never able to crack the country as a popular singer, unlike most British acts during the 'Invasion' era.

Upon his return, he did what he was best at, performing before British audiences, a craft he had perfected during the early stages of his career. 'When you are standing on the stage before a vast audience, to the majority of the people out front, you are a comparatively tiny figure on a large stage. This means you've got to work darned hard to project yourself to everyone,' he said. And as his popularity grew, so did the size of the venues he played, and that meant he had to exaggerate stage movements. 'From the microphone amplification of the voice to broader facial expressions to body movements . . . the artist's technique has to take the place of binoculars to make the audience feel it's much nearer to them than it actually is.'

Always in demand as a performer, Richard, naturally, now spent much of his career on stage, a useful vehicle for testing out future releases. And this is what he did when, following a series of concerts at the London Palladium, he embarked on a fully fledged tour to discover audience reaction to his next single, the double A-sided 'The Next Time'/'Bachelor Boy', due to be his first 1963 release.

The combination of the ballad 'The Next Time' and the semi-paced 'Bachelor Boy' was a winning formula. The single sold in excess of 900,000 copies to soar to the top of the British chart in January 1963.

Richard typified the good in 'pop' music; he was a clean-cut, acceptable young man, and critics were hard pushed to unearth anything unsavoury about him, even when he publicly announced his intention to become a committed Christian and leave showbusiness to concentrate on teaching religion.

True, the singer did become actively involved in delivering Christian teachings but he did so within the limits of his career. By finding a middle road that he could live with, he combined the two, although rock 'n' roll was treated more cautiously. As author Gary Herman observed, 'Cliff Richard is the perfect example of a performer who has reconciled one of rock 'n' roll's central conflicts by learning how to be in two minds at once.'

Although Elvis Presley's influence on Richard's public image was well known by now, Richard did not fall into the trap of starring in bad movies with unoriginal lightweight storylines and music. Instead, he concentrated on quality; his next was a perfect example.

Also see: 'Please Don't Tease', August 1960; 'The Young Ones', February 1962; 'Summer Holiday', March 1963

February 1963

JET HARRIS AND TONY MEEHAN

Diamonds

When Cliff Richard and his group The Drifters toured Britain for the first time in October 1958 as support act to The Kalin Twins, Jet Harris (born Terence Harris in London on 6 July 1939) played his bass guitar from the wings to back up Ian Samwell's inadequate stage work. When the tour ended Harris had replaced Samwell as a member of The Drifters. Two months later, drummer Tony Meehan (born Daniel Meehan in London on 2 March 1943) joined the group to replace the departing Terry Stuart, who joined the Merchant Navy.

With the group line-up of Harris, Meehan, Bruce Welch and Hank

Marvin, The Drifters moved on to back Cliff Richard in the studios at Abbey Road, London, to record 'Livin' Lovin' Doll' early in 1959. The Drifters then became a recording act in their own right with their first single, 'Feelin' Fine', in February 1959.

'Chinchilla' followed that May, and 'Jet Black', written by Jet Harris, in July 1959. Harris and Meehan stayed with The Drifters, later re-named The Shadows, for a spectacular career until the success became tarnished beyond repair.

Tony Meehan left the group in October 1961, midway through a Blackpool residency with Cliff Richard. The last single he performed on was the chart-topper 'Kon-Tiki'. His replacement was Brian Bennett. Meehan joined Decca Records as an A. & R. man and producer. A year later, following the release of 'Wonderful Land' in 1962, the differences between Jet Harris and Bruce Welch finally came to a head, culminating in Harris leaving. He was replaced by Brian Locking. Jack Good became manager and signed him to Decca Records as a solo guitarist and vocalist.

Jet Harris's debut solo single 'Besame Mucho', on which he played bass, featured Tony Meehan on drums. Released during July 1962, it reached the Top Thirty. A month on, the ex-Shadow debuted on stage with his newly formed band, The Jet Blacks, in Torquay, Devon. Next was a version of 'Main Title Theme' from Frank Sinatra's 1950 movie *The Man with the Golden Arm*. That fared much better, shooting to No. 12 in September 1962.

In February 1963 Cliff Richard's 'The Next Time' was dethroned from the top of the British chart by 'Diamonds'. Written by Jerry Lordan, Harris and Meehan, the single enjoyed a three-week stay at the top of the British chart and for the first time the record label credited both ex-Shadows. As if to avenge himself, Cliff Richard knocked 'Diamonds' from the top with his 'Summer Holiday'!

Following the release of 'Scarlet O'Hara', which reached No. 2 in April 1963, and 'Apple Jack', which made the Top Five, the duo's future looked rosy. Almost overnight that prospect turned bleak. Jet Harris and his girlfriend, singer Billie Davis, were involved in a car accident. This left Harris with mental and physical scars. So much so that he walked out on Tony Meehan during a performance on television's music show *Ready, Steady, Go!*. Once home, Harris destroyed his collection of guitars.

As Harris was incapable of working, and as their recording contract had to be honoured, Meehan had no choice but to continue without him. Under the name The Tony Meehan Combo, he recorded 'Song of Mexico' early in 1964. It peaked at No. 39 and was his last hit. Jet Harris attempted to recapture past success with 'Big Bad Bass' but once again his career fell victim to personal problems.

Tony Meehan worked through the recording contract, then left the public spotlight behind him to concentrate on his production work.

March 1963

CLIFF RICHARD

Summer Holiday

'Someone suggested it's sissy to proclaim your Christian beliefs, but I don't think it is. I feel great all the time and know it's because of my beliefs.' – Cliff Richard

Midway through 1962 Cliff Richard started work on his next movie, *Summer Holiday*, with a supporting cast of Una Stubbs, Ron Moody, David Kossoff, Melvyn Hayes, Lauri Peters and The Shadows. The plot this time centred around a group of mechanics who updated a London Transport double-decker bus to drive through five European countries. Naturally, plans went awry. En route, the group met a young girl whose car had broken down on the way to Athens, while a young boy who stowed away on the bus turned out to be a girl. It transpired that she was a starlet on the run from her overpowering mother. The adventures the group subsequently encountered made the movie extremely enjoyable, with the inevitable ending of Richard falling in love with his co-star Lauri. 'I wouldn't have believed that such a first-class musical could have been made in this country,' one critic glowed.

The movie was premiered simultaneously in London and South Africa during January 1963, whereupon Richard and The Shadows embarked upon a South African tour that included dates in Durban and Johannesburg. Shortly before the release of the 'Summer Holiday' single, three of Richard's other singles from the film were in the chart, namely 'Bachelor Boy', 'The Next Time' and 'Dancing Shoes'. When 'Summer Holiday' charted he became the first artist to have four songs from one movie in the chart. Richard said, 'My last couple of singles were ready-made, in a sense they more or less selected themselves since they came straight from the film. We would never have released "Summer Holiday" as a single if it hadn't been featured in the film. Frankly, we didn't think it was good enough to stand up on its own.'

'Summer Holiday', Richard's twentieth single, did not stand at all, it raced to the top of the British chart during March 1963 where it stayed for two weeks. The soundtrack, meanwhile, dominated the album chart for an incredible fourteen weeks. During May 1963 the movie won the Ivor Novello Award for the Year's Outstanding Score of a musical.

'Lucky Lips' was the next single which peaked at No. 4 in Britain, while it became Richard's first American hit (in the Top Seventy) since 'Living Doll'. 'It's All in the Game', a cover version of the Tommy Edwards original, followed, reaching No. 2 in Britain, and following an appearance on *The Ed Sullivan Show*, it became Richard's biggest American hit, peaking in the Top Thirty.

In December 1963, Richard and The Shadows began shooting their next movie, *Wonderful Life*, in the Canary Islands. Co-starring with the singer this time were Susan Hampshire, Walter Slezak, Richard O'Sullivan, Una Stubbs and Melvyn Hayes. Cliff and The Shadows were the entertainment on a luxury Mediterranean cruise, but they lost their jobs. The ship's captain put them to sea on a raft, and they drifted to the Canary Islands where they became a distraction in the shooting of *Daughter of a Sheik*.

Wonderful Life was premiered in July 1964 at London's Leicester Square Empire Theatre. 'No one will be able to say they haven't had their money's worth, there's everything in it except the kitchen sink,' one critic wrote.

'On the Beach' was swiped from the movie's soundtrack for single release to become a No. 7 British hit during August 1964. It was the follow-up to 'Constantly', a No. 4 hit. The last two singles of the year were 'The Twelfth of Never' (previously recorded by Johnny Mathis) and 'I Could Easily Fall (in Love with You)', both Top Ten hits. The latter track, incidentally, was taken from Richard's pantomime *Aladdin and his Lamp* staged at the London Palladium, where advanced ticket bookings topped £100,000.

The first single of 1965, 'The Minute You're Gone', topped the British chart; 'On my Word' followed in July to reach No. 12; 'The Time In Between' faltered in the Top Thirty, while 'Wind Me Up (Let Me Go)' re-established him at No. 2. In between releases, Richard and The Shadows toured Britain and Europe.

Following their debut at the foremost cabaret nightspot, Talk of the

Town, in London during February 1966, Richard recorded and released the Mick Jagger/Keith Richard track 'Blue Turns to Grey'. It reached No. 15 in the British chart. Richard and The Shadows then went on to perform with Dusty Springfield and The Rolling Stones, among others, at the annual *New Musical Express* Poll Winners' concert at Wembley. A month later, Richard returned to the stage but for a different reason. He joined evangelist Billy Graham to talk of his newly found Christian faith. In December 1967, Richard was confirmed in the Church of England membership at St Paul's Church in Finchley, London.

On the film front, Richard had already completed *Two a Penny* which was premiered in London during June 1968. He played a young pedlar, Jamie Hopkins, who encountered the Christian faith through his girlfriend, Carol. Co-stars this time included Dora Bryan, Billy Graham (who produced the movie) and Ann Holloway. And, lurking in the wings, was another, *Finder's Keepers*, a musical comedy about a nuclear bomb lost off the coast of Spain.

Recording-wise, Richard's most significant release of 1968 was 'Congratulations', which he performed as Britain's entry in the Eurovision Song Contest held at London's Royal Albert Hall. It was runner-up to 'La La La', Spain's entry. Nonetheless, 'Congratulations' soared to the top of the British chart that April, where it stayed for two weeks. It was Richard's first chart-topper for three years and his last for seven. He had recorded the single in several languages, helping it to sell in excess of one million copies in Europe. Germany alone had an advance order of 150,000 copies.

From 1968 through to the start of the seventies, Richard was a regular name in the British chart with discs like 'Good Times (Better Times)', No. 12; 'Throw Down a Line' (a duet with The Shadows' Hank Marvin), No. 7; and 'With the Eyes of a Child', No. 20.

Early in 1970, Richard turned to television to host his own series, *Cliff*, then moved to the stage to appear as a straight actor in *Five Finger Exercise* in Bromley, Kent. A year later, he hosted his second television series, *It's Cliff Richard*, with fellow resident Hank Marvin. A further series was screened in 1972.

Once again, in 1973, the singer was asked to represent Britain in the Eurovision Song Contest, this time held at the Nouveau Theatre in Luxembourg. The British public chose 'Power to All our Friends' from several nominations, which came third in the contest. The single went on to become a No. 4 British hit during March 1973.

And so it was to continue, the Cliff Richard magic. He was

affectionately nicknamed 'The Peter Pan of Pop' because he maintained his youthful looks and young outlook on life. His singles charted every year, he appeared at the most important music business functions, collected awards and gold discs until his walls must have sagged, but, more importantly, he sustained a career that appealed both to those fans who grew up with him, and their children, the new generations. Richard also recorded with other artists, including Stevie Wonder, Phil Everly, and Olivia Newton-John, while his tours continued to guarantee packed houses in Britain and Europe. His charity work was endless from Christian-based concerts to Live Aid.

In 1986 he starred in Dave Clark's musical, *Time*, staged at London's Dominion Theatre, and more recently played Heathcliff, a childhood ambition.

With a career that has spanned four decades, Cliff Richard has succeeded where others failed by riding musical tastes and by guaranteeing a crystal clear image. He is Britain's most celebrated star.

Hank Marvin: 'Cliff has been the perfect ambassador of British show business wherever he has travelled.'

Also see: 'Please Don't Tease', August 1960; 'The Young Ones', February 1962; 'The Next Time', January 1963

April 1963

GERRY AND THE PACEMAKERS

How Do You Do It?

'A lot of people call me "The Grin". I don't mind, I like it. I like being happy. There are too many miseries walking around with long faces complaining. I can't stand moaners or people who won't enjoy themselves.' – Gerry Marsden

Born Gerard Marsden in Liverpool on 24 September 1942, he formed his first group with his brother Freddie, born 23 November 1940, also in Liverpool. It was a skiffle outfit named The Red Mountain Boys, and Gerry Marsden was fourteen years old. Les Chadwick was also recruited, born 11 May 1943 in Liverpool, and later, Arthur McMahon.

They changed their name to Mars Bars in the hope of securing sponsorship from the chocolate company but the ploy backfired; the company demanded the band change its name. Nonetheless, they performed publicly for the first time at Holyrock Hall, Liverpool, during 1959.

During the following year, Gerry and his renamed Pacemakers extended their performing experience by supporting Gene Vincent at the Liverpool Stadium, before co-starring with The Silver Beatles, until finally travelling to The Star Club in Hamburg where they stayed for a four-month season.

A line-up change occurred mid-1961 when Arthur McMahon left. Les Maguire, born 27 December 1941 in Wallasey, Lancs, joined as keyboardist, leaving Les Chadwick to play bass guitar instead of his previous lead. Freddie Marsden stayed with his drum kit.

According to Gerry Marsden, 'In those early days we were happy just making a bit of extra cash each week. We knew absolutely nothing about real show business, and never dreamed of recording.'

After performing with The Beatles (the 'Silver' had been dropped) through to 1962, Gerry and the Pacemakers signed a management deal with the Fab Four's mentor, Brian Epstein, in June 1962. They were his second group. Epstein then invited The Beatles' producer, George Martin, to watch his new act perform in Birkenhead. What particularly impressed Martin was their interpretation of 'How Do You Do It?', written by Mitch Murray for Adam Faith, and reluctantly recorded by The Beatles during September 1962. (The track wasn't issued as a single; The Beatles' own composition 'Love Me Do' replaced it.)

George Martin had no hesitation in signing Brian Epstein's new group to EMI Records' Columbia label, and during their first recording session that included their own compositions, they recorded the happy-go-lucky song 'How Do You Do It?'. It was considered to be the best, and was released as a single in April 1963. It went on to sell half a million copies, and dominated the top of the British chart for three weeks.

To capitalise on this extraordinary achievement, Gerry and the Pacemakers embarked upon an extensive British tour with Roy Orbison and The Beatles. Marsden said, 'My whole system rebelled at first. All the travelling up and down the country practically killed me. I used to stagger to bed every night swearing I would never get up again.'

This was only the beginning.

Also see: 'I Like It', July 1963; 'You'll Never Walk Alone', November 1963

THE BEATLES

From Me to You

No one could have predicted the effect four young men from Liverpool would have on the world. They turned the music industry inside out from their first EMI recording, and by the time they had finished music just wasn't the same any more. The quartet had been making their presence felt since 1957, but it wasn't until October 1962 that the potential of their full weight was heard with 'Love Me Do'.

The Beatles were here to stay – and how!

John Winston Lennon was born during a Liverpool air raid on 9 October 1940 to Julia and Freddy, but when his father 'disappeared' he was raised by his four sisters. Lennon's mother remarried, leaving him to be raised by his aunt Mimi and her husband George (who died tragically when John was still a teenager).

At the age of four, Lennon attended Dovedale Primary School, where he played with Peter Harrison, younger brother of George. Before Lennon was ten years old, he'd written his own books including one titled *Sport and Speed Illustrated*. From Dovedale Primary School he moved to Quarry Bank Grammar School where he was reported to have been a poor student as his talent for writing and sketching wasn't part of the school curriculum! By the time he was fifteen years old Lennon was a dedicated Teddy Boy with a passion for rock 'n' roll. The more Aunt Mimi insisted he concentrate on his studies, the more he rebelled. With his first guitar came his first skiffle group, The Quarry Men, with Pete Shotton and two others. As this was the age of Liverpool talent contests, The Quarry Men entered them all. Arguments within the group led to several line-up changes but nothing deterred John Lennon.

James Paul McCartney was born to Mary and Jim on 18 June 1942 and had one brother, Michael. Although born into a Catholic family, Paul and Michael went to Protestant schools, first to Stockton Road Primary, then Joseph Williams Primary in Gateacre. Unlike Lennon, Paul McCartney excelled in his studies to become accepted at the Liverpool Institute.

In 1955, a short time after the McCartney family moved from Speke to Allerton, in Liverpool, Paul's mother died from breast cancer. Family life continued as normally as possible, but like the other youngsters in the area, Paul was drawn to music, especially skiffle. His father bought him a guitar, then taught him to play it. It was a long process, until he realised his son could cope better playing the instrument left-handed.

In the summer of 1957, a garden party was organised in Woolton, and The Quarry Men were performing. Among the audience was a curious Paul McCartney who, after watching their show, was introduced to John Lennon. The two became friends when Lennon learned he knew the lyrics to all the current rock 'n' roll songs. In time, Pete Shotton left The Quarry Men, and Paul McCartney replaced him.

Also during 1957, Lennon left Quarry Bank Grammar School with few qualifications, yet won a place at the Hope Street Art College. Paul McCartney, meantime, continued his education at the Institute. However, outside school hours, Lennon and McCartney experimented as composers. They wanted to see if they could emulate their American rock 'n' roll heroes using their own material.

During one of The Quarry Men's concerts, McCartney introduced fourteen-year-old George Harrison to Lennon, believing another guitarist would benefit the group.

George Harrison was born on 24 February 1943, the third son and fourth child of Lousie and Harry. He attended Dovedale Primary School at the same time as John Lennon, and in 1954 moved to the Liverpool Institute alongside Paul McCartney. Studies bored him; all he wanted to be was a Teddy Boy and play the guitar. The former he already was, much to the disgust of his tutors, and the latter he would be when his mother bought him the instrument.

As George Harrison wasn't instantly recruited into The Quarry Men, despite his guitar skills, he contented himself with following them from gig to gig, and being a last-minute stand-in when a regular band member missed a date. The group agreed to this because George had insisted they use his home for rehearsals.

The Quarry Men floated on, going nowhere quickly. A name change to Johnny and the Moondogs likewise brought no success, although performing as The Silver Beatles before Liverpool promoter Allan Williams, at a specially organised talent contest, did. They were offered the job of backing Johnny Gentle on a tour of Scotland, and when that passed without incident Williams took over their management. The Silver Beatles enjoyed regular bookings, often alongside fellow group, Gerry and the Pacemakers.

In time, Williams established himself and his roster of artists with Herr Bruno Koschmider, owner of the Kaiserkeller Club, in Grosse Freiheit, Hamburg, Germany. After sending his more established (and experienced) acts like Rory Storm and the Hurricanes to play at the Hamburg club, Williams had little choice but to send The Beatles for a two-month stint. ('Silver' had been dropped because Lennon refused to accept the connotation of 'Long John Silver'.) The trip came to a sudden halt when George Harrison was deported for being under-age in a licensed venue. John and Paul, drummer Pete Best (born Randolph Peter Best on 24 November 1941 in India) and guitarist Stuart Sutcliffe (born in Scotland on 23 June 1940) had their work permits taken away, so they followed Harrison back to Liverpool. It took the boys a few weeks to regroup and search for work, having sacked Allan Williams as their manager.

In April 1961, The Beatles returned to Hamburg, this time to play at the Top Ten Club owned by Peter Eckhorn. Stuart Sutcliffe was reunited with his German girlfriend Astrid Kirchherr and his relationship with Paul McCartney gradually soured. (It was Astrid who was responsible for styling The Beatles' hair to give the 'mop-head' effect.) Sutcliffe's heart wasn't really in music; he preferred the arts, so left The Beatles to take up a studentship at the Hamburg State Art College.

During this second trip The Beatles met the West German orchestra leader Bert Kaempfert. He was also a producer for Polydor Records based in Germany and hired The Beatles (under the name 'The Beat Brothers') to back Tony Sheridan in the studios. They recorded 'My Bonnie', 'When the Saints Go Marching in', 'Ain't She Sweet' and 'Cry for a Shadow'. The first two titles were issued as a single in Germany, and could be bought on import in Britain.

In 1958, Harry Epstein had opened his first shop selling electrical appliances in Liverpool. His son Clive ran the household side while his older brother Brian looked after the record section. The shop was called NEMS (North End Road Music Store). With the profits from this store, a second shop was opened with a larger record department to cater for the public's growing demand. When Brian Epstein was regularly asked for 'My Bonnie', he was curious to see what the fuss was about. One visit to the nearby Cavern Club to see The Beatles perform answered the question.

In December 1961 Brian Epstein became The Beatles' manager, and as he was already familiar with record companies' workings through his retail business, he quickly set about securing a deal for his group.

After sending demo tapes to most of the major companies to no avail, he turned to the smaller outlets like EMI Records' two labels, Columbia and HMV. They too turned down the group. However, Epstein was successful in securing The Beatles an audition with Decca Records, but when ex-Shadows' drummer Tony Meehan refused to produce them, Decca dropped the offer.

Brian Epstein wasn't to be defeated. His enthusiasm and determination never wavered. Through a series of contacts he eventually met George Martin, A. & R. manager for Parlophone, another subsidiary label of EMI Records. George Martin felt the group had 'something' and agreed to produce a recording session with them in the Abbey Road Studios, North London. After listening to and guiding the nervous group through the session that included the Lennon/McCartney composition 'Love Me Do', he decided to work further with them on the understanding that Pete Best was dropped from the line-up.

The Beatles knew instantly who his replacement would be but what they hadn't bargained for was the public uproar following the sacking of Pete Best. Nevertheless, the drummer they had kept tabs on played in Rory Storm's Hurricanes.

Born Richard Starkey on 7 July 1940 to Elsie and Ritchie, Ringo Starr became The Beatles' new drummer. He had spent much of his childhood with his grandfather as both his parents worked. Not a child to enjoy good health, Starr was hospitalised with a burst appendix shortly after joining primary school. Following the operation, he was comatose for a time. It was this and other illnesses that prevented him from attending school regularly. A year after studying at Dingle Vale Secondary School, Starr was once again hospitalised with pleurisy which led to him spending two years at a children's sanitorium.

At fifteen, Ringo Starr left school and took a variety of jobs before becoming a joiner's apprentice. Working with him was Eddie Miles whose obsession in life was skiffle. He recruited Starr as a drummer in his makeshift group, later to be known as The Eddie Clayton Skiffle Group. By this time, Starr had acquired his own drum kit and could competently play most styles. From the skiffle group, he drummed for Rory Storm and the Hurricanes. At this point, the Ringo Starr nickname was born because he wore a handful of rings and 'Starr' was an abbreviation of 'Starkey'.

The Beatles first met him in Hamburg while he was playing with Rory Storm's group, and indeed, by this time, he had occasionally stood in for Pete Best. When Rory Storm's career tumbled, Ringo

Starr was hired by the Top Ten Club's owner, Peter Eckhorn, to play with his resident group, headed by Tony Sheridan. After a spell there, Ringo Starr was homesick and returned to Liverpool where Rory Storm and the Hurricanes' luck had changed. They were booked for a Butlin's season in Skegness. It was there that John Lennon reached him to ask if he would join The Beatles . . .

John, George, Paul and Ringo travelled to Abbey Road Studios during September 1962 for their first official recording session with George Martin. When he heard 'Love Me Do' he decided to record that as a single with 'PS I Love You' for the flipside. Newcomer Ringo Starr, untested by Martin, was replaced by seasoned drummer Andy White. (Martin had been expecting Pete Best still to be with the group and had taken the precaution of booking a replacement.) Subsequently, two versions of 'Love Me Do' were recorded, one featuring Starr, the other White. Both were practically identical although it's believed Ringo was featured on the single, leaving Andy's contribution to be included on *Please Please Me*, the album version.

'Love Me Do', written by Paul McCartney, and featuring John Lennon playing harmonica in a style swiped from Bruce Channel's 'Hey Baby', was issued in October 1962. Seven days later The Beatles were support act to Little Richard at the Tower Ballroom, New Brighton. As the general consensus among record companies appeared to be that the public preferred solo artists to groups, EMI Records put little promotion behind 'Love Me Do'. Despite this, the single reached a healthy No. 17, and topped the singles chart published in the music weekly *Melody Maker*. (At this time the four music weeklies – *Melody Maker*, *New Musical Express*, *Record Mirror* and *Disc and Music Echo* – each printed singles and albums charts. There was no one official sales listing used by the music industry.) By this time, The Beatles had left Britain for their last Hamburg season at the renovated Star Club, owned by Manfred Weissleden.

Upon their return and in between sessions at the Cavern Club and one-night gigs, The Beatles recorded their second single, 'Please Please Me', in November 1962. In actual fact, another song had already been earmarked for them, namely 'How Do You Do It?' penned by Mitch Murray. But this was rejected when the group insisted another Lennon/McCartney song be used. 'How Do You Do It?' later became Gerry and the Pacemaker's debut single and first No. 1 in April 1963.

The *New Musical Express* Readers' Poll was published and The Beatles were voted eighth in the British Small Group section (The

Springfields were the top group) and fifth in the British Vocal Group category. Within days of this result The Beatles were confirmed as support act to young singing sensation Helen Shapiro on a British package tour.

'Please Please Me' was issued in January 1963 and with a performance on the television music show *Thank your Lucky Stars* before a five-million plus audience, where leather jackets were replaced by matching suits, the single climbed to No. 1 in the *Melody Maker* chart. During the disc's life, the group had returned to the recording studios to work on their first album. The ten-hour recording session produced ten tracks for the *Please Please Me* album which was destined to spend thirty consecutive weeks at No. 1. It only dropped to make way for The Beatles' second album, *With The Beatles*.

And still Brian Epstein beavered away. With the British side of his operation running smoothly, he wanted to make the same impression on the Americans. He had been trying to persuade EMI Records' American company, Capitol, to release 'Please Please Me'. The response was negative, leaving Epstein little option but to place the track with a smaller company. Vee Jay Records released it, then lost it.

In April 1963, the third single, 'From Me to You', was released, the same month as a son, Julian, was born to John and Cynthia Lennon at Liverpool's Sefton General Hospital. The couple had first met in 1958 and had married in August 1962. On the professional front, Brian Epstein once again approached Capitol Records to issue a Beatles single, and again they declined. Vee Jay released it, but this time managed to promote it into the American Top One Hundred, only to be beaten back by Del Shannon's cover version. Shannon became the first artist to chart in America with a Lennon/McCartney composition.

By now, The Beatles were in constant demand on television, radio and for live dates. Brian Epstein worked them non-stop, obsessed with his ambition that the group would be bigger than Elvis Presley. He ensured that The Beatles were seen and heard in every corner of the British Isles. Together they were on the verge of changing British music for ever, and they needed the public behind them when they did. How The Beatles actually survived was a mystery, but survive they did. The heights they reached were unthinkable, often unbelievable, and their influence stretched from music into fashion into public behaviour.

'From Me to You' was only the start.

Also see: 'She Loves You', October 1963; 'I Want to Hold your Hand', December 1963; 'Can't Buy Me Love', April 1964; 'A Hard Day's Night', August 1964; 'I Feel Fine', January 1965; 'Ticket to Ride', May 1965; 'Help!', August 1965; 'We Can Work It Out'/'Day Tripper', January 1966; 'Paperback Writer', July 1966; 'Yellow Submarine'/ 'Eleanor Rigby', September 1966; 'All You Need Is Love', August 1967; 'Hello Goodbye', January 1968; 'Lady Madonna', April 1968; 'Get Back', May 1969; 'The Ballad of John and Yoko', July 1969

July 1963

GERRY AND THE PACEMAKERS

I Like It

'With success I found I needed to take things much easier, and cut out many of the things I used to do. Anyway, I was always so tired at nights that I doubt if I could have gone anywhere except bed. Now I have come to grips with all the odd hours, and can stand the pace better!' – Gerry Marsden

'I Like It' was the follow-up to the group's debut single and first chart-topper, 'How Do You Do It?'. Written by Mitch Murray with Gerry and the Pacemakers in mind, the song soared to No. 1 in Britain in July 1963 where it stayed for four weeks. Two chart-toppers with their first two singles was an incredible achievement for a new group.

The height of the Merseybeat explosion was approaching and Brian Epstein managed the top three names. In 1963 he showcased his finest at the Odeon Cinema in Romford, Essex, when Gerry and the Pacemakers, The Beatles and Billy J. Kramer and The Dakotas appeared on stage. Between them, they dominated the top three chart positions. Following this one-off, ITV screened a Merseybeat special, *Lucky Stars (Summer Spin)*, which included The Searchers and The Fourmost as support acts to the top three.

Gerry Marsden remained in awe of the success achieved so far. In fact, the volume of public acclaim worried him. He cited an instance when he was due to perform: 'I suddenly realised the audience was waiting to see the number one recording artist in the country, and I was supposed to go out there and prove that I was. I suddenly knew what it was like to be really worried.'

Also see: 'How Do You Do It?', April 1963; 'You'll Never Walk Alone', November 1963

August 1963

ELVIS PRESLEY

(You're the) Devil in Disguise

RCA Records were never short of Elvis Presley material because the majority of the singles and EPs issued were swiped from the constant stream of movie soundtracks. No single was recorded for a particular purpose, nor to follow a current trend. The record company had what was on offer and that was it. To date, however, this method had worked well; records sold, usually achieving chart-topper status, but that was to end. Public taste was changing, the British beat boom was imminent, young record-buyers demanded excitement. In other words, Presley was being left behind; his music rapidly becoming dated, and he was left to flounder.

But '(You're the) Devil in Disguise' became a British chart-topper, in August 1963. In America the single soared to No. 3. 'Crying in the Chapel' would be Presley's next British No. 1 single in 1965.

Meantime, Presley was so preoccupied with his movie schedules that he had little time for anything else. It is conceivable that his singles success remained a mystery to him because he never promoted any. Colonel Tom Parker had banned him from live appearances, and had now refused to let him appear on television, claiming fans could see all they wanted on the big screen. The age of the promotional film wasn't that far off, but it would, generally speaking, bypass Presley.

Following the release of '(You're the) Devil in Disguise', the singer started filming *Kissin' Cousins*, a slice of hillbilly humour where he played two roles – a mountain boy and an Air Force officer. When Colonel Parker realised this, he asked MGM to double Elvis's salary. On the other hand, the dual roles meant Presley had two leading ladies, Yvonne Craig and Pamela Austin.

Locked within a film set, Presley was oblivious to the real world, particularly the music business. He wouldn't have been totally aware of the impact The Beatles were making in 1964 when Beatlemania was gradually gripping the world. Indeed, the Fab Four had already toured America to riotous acclaim, reminiscent of Presley's early career, so

101

perhaps it was at this point he realised how they threatened his already precarious position as the world's top music name.

The two musical giants did actually meet at Presley's Beverly Hills home during August 1965; it was at the request of The Beatles because, of course, Presley was their hero. It transpired that neither were impressed and The Beatles were disappointed that their teen dream had been shattered.

Presley took his disappointment one step further. He went on to inform the FBI and the Bureau of Narcotics and Dangerous Drugs that John Lennon and Paul McCartney's compositions encouraged illegal drug use and that the group itself was 'the real force behind the growing anti-American spirit'. This was reputedly Presley's revenge – he blamed The Beatles for his inability to crack the top of the American chart. That his material might have contributed to this obviously did not enter his mind. However, more importantly, with Presley condemning The Beatles in this way to the American agencies – and later President Nixon himself – he took the heat off himself.

Whether the American agencies took The Beatles' drug involvement seriously or not is not known but John Lennon experienced countless visa and permit problems when visiting America, and even more legal entanglements when he decided to take up residence there with Yoko Ono. Was this due to Lennon's own drugs busts in Britain? Or some other reason?

Also see: 'It's Now or Never', November/December 1960; 'Are You Lonesome Tonight', February 1961; 'Wooden Heart', April 1961; 'Surrender', June 1961; 'Rock a Hula Baby'/'Can't Help Falling in Love', March 1962; 'Good Luck Charm', June 1962; 'She's Not You', September 1962; 'Crying in the Chapel', July 1965

September 1963

BILLY J. KRAMER AND THE DAKOTAS

Bad to Me

When Brian Epstein signed The Beatles to a management contract, he realised Liverpool was bursting with other talented singers. He was obviously selective; his artist roster expanded gradually, as he chose quality rather than quantity. Few, however, had the staying power of The Beatles, although most had a helping hand from them. Billy J. Kramer was no exception.

Born William Howard Ashton in Bootle, Merseyside, on 19 August 1943, Kramer left school to take 'a very dirty job' as an apprentice fitter for British Rail. At lunchtimes and during the evenings, he would race to The Cavern Club, the centre of Liverpool's young sound, to sing with The Coasters. With his mother supplementing his weekly wage, Kramer could indulge in his passion for buying clothes. 'Friday night would be the big night. I'd dash home, get cleaned up, put on a smart suit and go dancing or to a party. I used to feel real good then,' he said.

Billy J. Kramer had his own manager, Ted Knibbs, but when in 1963 Brian Epstein spotted the singer at The Cavern Club he too wanted to represent him. He bought Kramer's contract from Knibbs for £50 and signed him to a management deal with his NEMS company. The Coasters preferred their regular paying jobs to taking a chance in the music business, so kept their amateur status, playing with singer Chick Graham. Epstein realised Kramer needed a back-up group and after much searching hired The Dakotas.

The Dakotas were a Manchester-based quartet and comprised Mike Maxfield (born 23 February 1944 in Manchester) as lead guitarist; Robin MacDonald (born 18 July 1943 in Scotland) on rhythm guitar; Ray Jones (born 22 October 1939 in Greater Manchester) on bass guitar, and Tony Mansfield (born 28 May 1943 also in Greater Manchester) on drums.

Their career moved pretty quickly. By February 1963, they had perfected their stage act, performing at The Cavern before embarking on a season at The Star Club in Hamburg, Germany. A month later, Billy J. Kramer and the Dakotas had secured a recording contract with EMI Records' Parlophone label, and, like The Beatles before them, were assigned to George Martin. It appeared that any act Brian Epstein chose to represent would be guaranteed a recording contract, especially with EMI Records who, of course, had The Beatles under contract. Being represented by Epstein also meant access to any Beatles material superfluous to their needs.

Some of the first material offered to Billy J. Kramer was 'I'll Be on my Way' and 'Do You Want to Know a Secret' (a track from The Beatles' first album *Please Please Me*). The latter was chosen and Billy J. Kramer and the Dakotas released their version in June 1963 as their debut single. It soared to No. 2 in the British chart, unable to go all the way because The Beatles' 'From Me To You' was already there, and not yet ready to climb down.

Back in 1961, Dakota Mike Maxfield had written an instrumental which he called 'The Cruel Sea' after chancing to read a copy of Nicholas Monserrat's novel. The Dakotas finally recorded and released this track, which became a Top Twenty hit during August 1963.

Meanwhile, John Lennon had written 'Bad To Me' as the follow-up to and clone of 'Do You Want to Know a Secret'. In September 1963 it raced to the top of the British chart, a position it held for two weeks. The Beatles' 'She Loves You' replaced it.

In the wake of this success, Billy J. Kramer was voted Best British Newcomer by readers of *Melody Maker*.

Kramer said, 'We were lucky, of course, that our music was different, our records commercial and that the kids liked us. But then I had to emerge as a personality and establish myself. Clothes obviously were going to be important. I had a lot of ideas of my own, but I relied a lot on Brian Epstein's advice.'

Being one of the sharpest-dressed singers on the circuit was, many believed, a camouflage for his nervousness and lack of confidence while performing. Perhaps he felt his audience would look at his suit rather than his face. Whatever the reason, Kramer's performances were awkwardly presented.

A month after performing on the television variety gala *Sunday Night at the London Palladium*, the third single, 'I'll Keep You Satisfied', was issued in October 1963. Another Lennon/McCartney song, it reached No. 4, and before the year was over, the album *Listen – To Billy J. Kramer* had sold sufficiently to reach the Top Twenty.

Billy J. Kramer: 'I deliberately set out to create my own style, and always wanted to be an immaculate, well-dressed singer. For me it would be foolish to try anything different.'

Also see: 'Little Children', February 1964

THE BEATLES

She Loves You

Beatlemania was beginning to make its presence felt. At every concert, the group was greeted with screaming young fans hell-bent on pulling at their hair and clothes. During the shows themselves, The Beatles were barely audible over the noise from the audiences, and those who didn't become hysterical, fainted on the spot. Ambulances lined up with police vans outside theatres in preparation. These scenes were now regularly reported in the tabloids under misleading headlines, leaving parents shuddering at the effect this musical revolution would have on their children.

A whole new era had opened, soon dubbed the swinging sixties, and The Beatles would be leaders for the decade. The changing face of music was evident, and record companies climbed over themselves to sign up anyone remotely connected to the Liverpool quartet. Other stars were born while many failed, yet record companies collected vast amounts of money thanks to The Beatles.

As mayhem followed The Fab Four, business boomed. And that meant recording sessions. These were now slotted in between radio interviews, television spots and the never-ending concert schedule. Nevertheless, The Beatles thrived on it.

Early in July 1963 The Beatles recorded their fourth single, 'She Loves You', written by John Lennon and Paul McCartney three days prior to the actual recording session. Once more their producer George Martin (now referred to as the fifth Beatle) tidied up the song by suggesting the chorus of 'She loves you' followed by 'yeah, yeah, yeah' should start the song. This gave birth to the famous catchphrase that would haunt the group for years. With advance orders of half a million, the single shot to the top of the British chart two weeks after its release, and went on to sell in excess of 1.3 million copies, to become the top-selling single of the year.

Prior to its release, The Beatles' EP, titled *Twist and Shout*, had peaked at No. 2 in the chart.

For a third time Brian Epstein contacted Capitol Records in America to release The Beatles' current single and for the third time they refused. Vee Jay Records was passed over in favour of Swan Records, but they did no better. The third Beatles' single bombed in America and Brian Epstein was in a state of desperation. Someone, somewhere must want the group.

By this time he had tied up The Beatles' song publishing rights with Dick James. The company was later to become Northern Songs. He had also added to his artist roster acts like Billy J. Kramer and the Dakotas, and Cilla Black. Both recorded Lennon/McCartney songs, although the very first to record one was Kenny Lynch with 'Misery' in February 1963.

During November 1963 the second album, *With The Beatles*, with advance orders in the region of 300,000, knocked *Please Please Me* from the top of the chart. The album was worth its weight in gold because of monumental public demand. This was evidenced when 3,000 copies were stolen from an EMI delivery van in Reading. Security guards were assigned to accompany drivers on further deliveries. *With The Beatles* also had a knock-on effect on the group's singles. It pushed 'She Loves You' back up to No. 1 for a further two weeks. And as if to prove the overwhelming popularity of the group, while that single dominated the top spot, Billy J. Kramer and the Dakotas' 'I'll Keep You Satisfied' (written by Lennon/McCartney) was at No. 6, three Beatles EPs, namely *Twist and Shout*, *The Beatles Hits* and *Beatles No. 1* were at Nos. 14, 17 and 20 respectively, while The Rolling Stones' 'I Wanna Be your Man' (written by Lennon/McCartney) peaked at No. 30.

Before the year ended, The Beatles had embarked upon their first European tour. When they returned to Heathrow Airport it was under siege as hundreds of screaming fans greeted their idols. They had appeared on the popular variety show *Sunday Night at the London Palladium*, and at the Royal Command Performance where their act was best remembered for John Lennon's quip to the audience: 'Will the people in the cheaper seats clap your hands, while the rest of you just rattle your jewellery.' They had also collected the Top Vocal Group of the Year Award at a Variety Club luncheon in London, one of numerous awards and honours during the year.

Dora Bryan, one of Britain's most lovable actresses, recorded 'All I Want for Christmas Is a Beatle'. Whether or not her wish came true has never been disclosed.

Also see: 'From Me to You', May/June 1963; 'I Want to Hold your Hand', December 1963; 'Can't Buy Me Love', April 1964; 'A Hard

Day's Night', August 1964; 'I Feel Fine', January 1965; 'Ticket to Ride', May 1965; 'Help!', August 1965; 'We Can Work It Out'/'Day Tripper', January 1966; 'Paperback Writer', July 1966; 'Yellow Submarine'/'Eleanor Rigby', September 1966; 'All You Need Is Love', August 1967; 'Hello Goodbye', January 1968; 'Lady Madonna', April 1968; 'Get Back', May 1969; 'The Ballad of John and Yoko', July 1969

November 1963

GERRY AND THE PACEMAKERS

You'll Never Walk Alone

'Determined not to get in a rut, I made it a point to ensure each record was different from the last. At least no one will be able to criticise me for jumping on the bandwagon with the "Merseysound". People will realise I can do all styles of material. It worked too.' – Gerry Marsden

Selecting the follow-up to two British chart-toppers ('How Do You Do It?' and 'I Like It') must have been a living nightmare for Gerry Marsden. Late in 1963 the group recorded 'Hello Little Girl', penned with them in mind by Lennon and McCartney. But Marsden was unhappy with the result and passed on it, leaving The Fourmost to later enjoy a British No. 9 with their version.

Instead, Gerry Marsden turned to Rodgers and Hammerstein's musical *Carousel* to lift the powerful ballad 'You'll Never Walk Alone'. When released as a single, the song knew no boundaries. It soared to the top of the British chart during November 1963 for a four-week stay. It became the group's biggest-ever selling single, with sales in excess of 800,000 copies. And, more importantly, it represented Gerry and the Pacemakers' third consecutive chart-topper with their first three singles. This record stood until 1984 when fellow Liverpudlians Frankie Goes to Hollywood equalled it with 'Relax', 'Two Tribes' and 'The Power of Love'.

'You'll Never Walk Alone' grew legs. It was adopted by Liverpool Football Club as its anthem, indeed, Gerry Marsden has been requested to sing the song at countless football ceremonies. He has also, on the other hand, sung it on solemn occasions. For instance, in June 1985 he sang it at the memorial service for Bill Shankly, held at Liverpool Cathedral. Following the horrendous fire which killed spectators in the grounds of Bradford City Football Club, Marsden led a charity recording of 'You'll Never Walk Alone' credited to 'The Crowd'. The proceeds went to the fire victims' families. This version once more dominated the British chart during 1985, giving Marsden the distinction of being the first artist to enjoy a chart-topper with two versions of the same song.

Meantime, in 1964 and 1965, Gerry and the Pacemakers were rarely away from the British chart with singles that included Marsden's self-penned 'Don't Let the Sun Catch You Crying' and 'Ferry 'cross the Mersey'. The latter track was taken from the movie of the same name, written by Tony Warren, the creator of *Coronation Street*. The movie starred Gerry and the Pacemakers as themselves, along with Cilla Black and The Fourmost. The 'Ferry 'cross the Mersey' single raced to No. 8 in the British chart, and when the movie was released in America, gave the group a No. 6 hit there. It was their last Top Ten single in both countries.

Gerry and the Pacemakers toured America and Britain until December 1965 when they issued 'Walk Hand in Hand', a fifties ballad in the mould of 'You'll Never Walk Alone'. It faltered in the Top Thirty and was their last British hit.

After touring further for one year, Gerry and the Pacemakers disbanded, unable to keep abreast of the changing musical trends. However, Marsden recorded numerous solo singles, but all bombed. So he moved to the stage to perform in *Charlie Girl* in the West End of London for four years. He then became involved in children's television.

Midway through 1973, a new line-up of The Pacemakers backed Gerry Marsden at Madison Square Garden in New York. The event was *The British Re-Invasion Show*, starring a selection of other regrouped acts like Herman's Hermits and The Searchers.

Gerry and the Pacemakers have continued to work regularly on the cabaret circuit, particularly stints at Butlin's holiday camps, where capacity audiences relive the group's success story.

Also see: 'How Do You Do It?' April 1963; 'I Like It', July 1963

THE BEATLES

I Want to Hold your Hand

With a thriving fan club of at least 85,000 members, which The Beatles supported wholeheartedly with specially written newsletters, unique Christmas discs and *The Beatles Christmas Show*, the group's merchandising wheels were well and truly in motion. Although Brian Epstein, through his expanding NEMS enterprise, had eventually copyrighted 'The Beatles', hundreds of bootlegged items had already slipped through the net. All types of merchandise could be freely bought bearing the group's name; manufacturers were making a small fortune while The Beatles themselves earned nothing from these efforts. Even when the name was copyrighted, Epstein was powerless to take legal action against all the perpetrators. Yep, The Beatles signified big money.

Meantime, the drummer The Beatles left behind, or rather the drummer Brian Epstein sacked, was struggling to earn a living on the club circuit. The anger felt by Pete Best and his fans slowly simmered, but the fame and fortune of The Beatles was denied him. Eventually Best turned his back on music to become a civil servant. However, in 1995, those Beatles' wounds were reopened. A six-CD set, *The Beatles Anthology* and a six-part television series devoted to the group's career, and featuring the remaining Beatles, Paul McCartney, Ringo Starr and George Harrison, was screened by the ITV network. The early part of that story naturally included Pete Best, who was the group's drummer up until the time Ringo Starr joined for the 'Love Me Do' recording session. It took thirty years for Best to be acknowledged as the fourth Beatle, and his overdue public recognition reputedly turned him into a multi-millionaire without him lifting a finger.

'I Want to Hold your Hand' was rush-released in 1963. Like the singles before it, this was straightforward 'pop' with basic verses and repetitive chorus. With advance sales of one million, 'I Want to Hold your Hand' shot straight to the top of the British chart in December 1963, where it stayed for five weeks. The single became the fastest-selling title in British history, and when released in America notched up sales of 1.8 million copies, with eventual world sales in excess of fifteen million.

After many attempts by Brian Epstein, Capitol Records had agreed to release 'I Want to Hold your Hand' in America while claiming they expected it to bomb. The prediction was wildly off-base because buyers pushed it to the top of the chart where it stayed for a staggering seven weeks. In actual fact, Capitol Records was forced to issue the single prior to its scheduled release date in January 1964 when a radio DJ was given a copy of the British single. He played it non-stop; other stations subsequently wanted a copy, so Capitol upped the advance order and brought the release date forward to December 1963.

When 'I Want to Hold your Hand' started its American life, The Beatles were performing at the Olympia Theatre in Paris. They were notified of their pending success by cable. From Paris the group headed for Kennedy Airport in New York for their first American trip. They landed on 7 February 1964 and were met with advertising announcing 'The Beatles Are Coming' and a screaming mass of hysterical youngsters, way outshining any British welcome to date. Unknown to The Beatles, though, Capitol Records were so determined to cover their previous blunders that they decided to give The Fab Four a riotous welcome. To do this they recruited two New York radio stations to announce that anyone who met the group at the airport would receive a free T-shirt.

The Beatles had first been presented to the American viewing public in January 1964 when film clips of their performances were shown on the *Jack Paar Friday Night Show*. On this visit, seventy million viewers watched them on *The Ed Sullivan Show* performing five titles including 'She Loves You' and 'All my Loving'. Crime among the young dropped drastically that night. To ensure every angle was covered, The Beatles crammed in media interviews, photo sessions and the like, before debuting on the American stage with The Chiffons and Tommy Roe at the Washington Coliseum. This was a standing-room-only concert, likewise the following two at New York's Carnegie Hall.

The Beatles' fame imprisoned them in their hotel rooms. Visitors needed special concessions to pass through the security guards, and to avoid adolescent fans being caught in their bedrooms, Brian Epstein encouraged the group to spend time with prostitutes who themselves would undergo the same scrutiny. Epstein was terrified of The Beatles attracting bad press, particularly as their career was just beginning in America. Yet the stories flooded the media. For example, a woman claimed Paul McCartney was the father of her child. Certainly the group's press agent Brian Somerville worked overtime to ensure the group's squeaky clean image was maintained.

America had succumbed. She had acceded defeat, and was bowing down to Beatlemania. And all because of a little piece of vinyl bearing the label 'I Want to Hold your Hand'.

Also see: 'From Me to You', May/June 1963; 'She Loves You', October 1963; 'Can't Buy Me Love', April 1964; 'A Hard Day's Night', August 1964; 'I Feel Fine', January 1965; 'Ticket to Ride', May 1965; 'Help!', August 1965; 'We Can Work It Out'/'Day Tripper', January 1966; 'Paperback Writer', July 1966; 'Yellow Submarine'/'Eleanor Rigby', September 1966; 'All You Need Is Love', August 1967; 'Hello Goodbye', January 1968; 'Lady Madonna', April 1968; 'Get Back', May 1969; 'The Ballad of John and Yoko', July 1969

January 1964

THE SEARCHERS

Needles and Pins

In the midst of the Liverpool music explosion, The Searchers introduced a sweet, white sound on singles that were, by and large, swiped from American originals. This quartet was not managed by Brian Epstein, despite public belief, although most of its members were born in Liverpool and, indeed, their groundwork was done in that city.

In 1961 Mike Pender, born Michael Prendergast on 3 March 1942, and John McNally, born on 30 August 1941, both in Liverpool, called themselves The Searchers, and performed as a duo in local public houses. In time they met and teamed up with two more musicians, namely, drummer Norman McGarry and bass guitarist Tony Jackson, born on 16 July 1940 in Liverpool. The Searchers were hired to support Johnny Sandon, a local singer, until he joined The Remo Four, leaving them to fend for themselves once more.

As a quartet they secured dates at The Cavern Club, The Iron Door, and other notable Liverpool club haunts, attracting audiences with their tight group harmonies. However, a line-up change occurred during 1962 when Norman McGarry left to join Rory Storm and the Hurricanes as Ringo Starr's replacement. Chris Curtis, born Christopher Crummy, on 26 August 1941 in Lancashire, replaced McGarry.

111

Like most groups on the Liverpool circuit, The Searchers were shipped to perform at The Star Club in Hamburg, Germany. While there, one of their performances was taped by a representative from Phillips Records. However, that company didn't offer them a recording contract, though Pye Records did, through the intervention of its A. & R. manager, Tony Hatch.

During May 1963, The Searchers recorded 'Sweets for my Sweet', a version of The Drifters' hit, also recorded by The Sweet Inspirations, among other American acts. The song was released that August to race to the top of the British chart. Yet another group with Liverpudlian origins enjoyed a chart-topper with their debut single. No wonder record companies were falling over themselves to sign up any artist with a scouse accent.

After a series of prestigious television performances, the group embarked upon a lengthy British tour with headliner Roy Orbison, and support groups that included Brian Poole and the Tremeloes. 'Sweet Nothin's', taped from their live Hamburg performances, was released to reach the British Top Fifty, while their next single, 'Sugar and Spice', soared to No. 2 in October 1963. Established in the chart once more, The Searchers toured Britain again, this time supporting headliner Dusty Springfield.

The group's next release, 'Needles and Pins' (pronounced 'niddles and pinsa'), again had American origins; it was written by Jack Nitzsche and Sonny Bono and had already been a hit for Jackie De Shannon. The Searchers took their version to the top of the British chart in January 1964. It stayed there for three weeks, selling in excess of 80,000 copies. When issued in America, 'Needles and Pins' sold one million copies to reach the Top Twenty during April 1964. Following a further exhausting British tour, again with Dusty Springfield, The Searchers made a quick trip to America to appear on *The Ed Sullivan Show*.

The Shirelles' 'Don't Throw your Love Away' was covered by The Searchers, and when released it soared to the top in Britain during April 1964, the group's third chart-topper in two years. When issued in America it stalled in the Top Twenty. (Doubtless the Americans were tiring of the British stealing their classics.) In May The Searchers debuted on television's most popular show, *Sunday Night at the London Palladium*, before flying to America to perform at New York's World Fair.

The follow-up to 'Don't Throw your Love Away' was yet another cover version. Titled 'Someday We're Gonna Love Again', it was originally recorded by American singer Barbara Lewis. The group could only manage a Top Twenty hit in Britain during August 1964, at which point Tony Jackson left The Searchers to pursue a solo career. Frank Allen, born on 14 December 1943 in Middlesex, and swiped from Cliff Bennett's Rebel Rousers, replaced him.

A second Jackie De Shannon track, 'When You Walk in the Room', was The Searchers' next single during September 1964 and reached No. 3 in Britain. But before 1964 was over, the group drastically changed musical direction to record 'What Have They Done to the Rain?'. Penned by Malvina Reynolds, this anti-nuclear protest was reproduced as a folk song Searchers-style and reached No. 13 in the British chart, Top Thirty in America.

Through 1965 the group enjoyed four British hits. Only one, though, 'Goodbye my Love', reached the Top Ten because it had The Searchers' distinguished sound. 'He's Got No Love', written by Chris Curtis, peaked No. 12; 'When I Get Home' only made the Top Forty, and 'Take Me for What I'm Worth' scraped into the Top Twenty. In between tours of Britain, The Searchers appeared with Dusty Springfield in *The Bacharach Sound*, a television special dedicated to the music of Burt Bacharach and Hal David, whose American protégé Dionne Warwick also appeared.

For the first three months of 1966 The Searchers toured America and the Far East, then Britain. During the latter tour, drummer Chris Curtis retired from the group through ill health. John Blunt, born on 23 March 1947 in Surrey, replaced him. He could be heard on the two singles which charted during 1966, namely, 'Take It or Leave It' which stalled in the Top Thirty, and 'Have You Ever Loved Somebody' which struggled into the Top Forty, and became The Searchers' final British hit.

Two years later, Pye Records dropped The Searchers because they had by now lost their way, unable to decide whether to stick to their tried and tested musical formula or follow the folk-song path. In the midst of this dilemma they signed to Liberty Records, then RCA Records. Neither association produced hit singles.

Although British sales were nil, The Searchers continued to score in America. To capitalise on their success, in 1973 they toured there as part of *The British Re-Invasion Show* with other home acts, while further spasmodic touring schedules occupied them until 1985.

At the start of the nineties when the lucrative oldies-but-goldies package tours became popular, The Searchers joined several of their ilk to enjoy success once more, notably on the Solid Silver Sixties Show 30th Anniversary Tour in 1993.

113

Also a No. 1 single in January 1964: 'Glad All Over' by The Dave Clark Five

February 1964

BILLY J. KRAMER AND THE DAKOTAS

Little Children

Up to this point in his career, Billy J. Kramer had diligently followed Brian Epstein's advice and suggestions. However, when the time came to record the fourth single, singer and manager clashed.

Brian Epstein wanted the group to stay with Lennon/McCartney compositions because the formula worked. But Billy J. Kramer had heard the song he intended to record, written by Mort Shuman and John McFarland, two American composers. Kramer stood his ground, defied Epstein, and 'Little Children' became his biggest-selling single ever. Daily sales alone were in excess of 70,000 copies. So it was a 'natural' for the top spot in February 1964. It then went on to become an international million-seller.

'Little Children' also gave Billy J. Kramer and the Dakotas their first American hit, by reaching the Top Ten. 'Bad to Me' was on the flipside. The latter had bombed when it was originally released. Eventually, it attracted more attention than 'Little Children', and replaced it in the Top Ten.

For their next single Kramer and the Dakotas returned to Lennon/McCartney to release 'From a Window'. It stalled at No. 10 in the British chart during July 1964. This relatively poor showing worried Epstein, and with good reason. It was unheard of for a Beatles composition to falter in this way. It marked another disappointment. The year 1965 started off badly because it heralded Billy J. Kramer's first bomber, namely 'It's Gotta Last Forever'. Mind you, it fared marginally better Stateside by crawling into the Top Seventy.

The next single was all-important; it needed to return Kramer to a healthy British chart position. Penned by Burt Bacharach and Hal David, 'Trains and Boats and Planes' did just that, despite Bacharach releasing his own version at the same time. The battle was fought for chart status – Billy J. Kramer lost with a No. 12 position, while Bacharach soared to No. 4. The composer's version wasn't issued in

America, enabling Kramer to enjoy a Top Fifty hit. An album carrying the single's title quickly followed.

'Neon City', the final single of 1965, disappeared without trace largely due to the Merseybeat explosion coming to an end. Music was changing once more and acts like Billy J. Kramer and the Dakotas were unable to move with the tide. However, they could still perform. Most of 1966, therefore, was taken up on the cabaret circuit where, despite line-up changes in The Dakotas, audiences filled theatres.

At this point in his career, Kramer had hoped to turn to the big screen in much the same way as The Beatles had done. 'Acting is something I've never done so far, but it's a challenge I want to take . . . I could really run riot then.' Unfortunately, his ambition remained a pipe-dream.

During 1967, Billy J. Kramer recorded two solo outings. The first was 'Sorry' for EMI Records. When that bombed, the company dropped him. The other was for Reaction Records. Titled 'The Town of Tuxley Toy Maker', it was a version of The Bee Gees' original. That also flopped.

In mid-1968, The Dakotas disbanded, leaving Kramer little option but to continue as a solo act. He recorded '1941', a copy of Nilsson's original, and a version of Peter and Gordon's 'A World without Love', both for NEMS Records, followed by 'The Colour of my Love' for MGM Records. During 1971, he recorded another flop, 'And the Grass Won't Pay No Mind', under his real name.

From 1973 onwards, Billy J. Kramer and a re-formed Dakotas toured the oldies-but-goldies circuit, while solo Kramer recorded at least another dozen singles without success, before relocating to New York.

Kramer said in 1965, 'If you want to stay, you have to grow up in this business and I can see my styles changing in the future. I also hope to start recording a lot of top-class ballads, which is something I've longed to do.'

Unfortunately, the record-buying public didn't agree with him.

Also see: 'Bad to Me', September 1963

Also a No. 1 single in February 1964: 'Diane' by The Bachelors

CILLA BLACK

Anyone Who Had a Heart

'Somehow I have always had an image of being approachable, and people don't feel inhibited about coming up for a quick chat or to ask for an autograph . . . That is the image I am happiest with.' – Cilla Black

Born Priscilla White on 27 May 1943 in Liverpool, Black worked at the BICC Cable Company. Early in 1963 a part-time job as cloakroom attendant in The Cavern Club, the centre of Liverpool's young music, led to her being the occasional guest vocalist for groups like The Big Three and Kingsize Taylor and the Hurricanes.

Midway through 1963, Black auditioned for EMI Records and, with help from George Martin, signed a recording deal with EMI's subsidiary label, Parlophone. She went on to be the support act to The Beatles when they headlined a residency at Southport's Odeon Cinema, and became the first female artist to be signed by Brian Epstein to his NEMS Enterprise in August 1963. Following a printing error in a Liverpool newspaper, White became 'Black' and her first name was shortened to 'Cilla'.

Author Philip Norman noted in *Shout*, 'Cilla Black was to be, not a discovery like The Beatles and Gerry [and the Pacemakers] but a creation, wrought by Brian's own feminine taste. For weeks he lavished attention on Cilla; on her clothes, her hair, her makeup [while] . . . Tony Barrow . . . was producing the usual stylish NEMS press release, describing Cilla's recherché taste for wearing men's jeans, and relaying Cavern Club slang like "gear", "fab" and "endsville".'

Meanwhile, the music beckoned. Paul McCartney had penned and canned 'Love of the Loved'. When he discovered Cilla Black wanted material he offered it to her. She first sang the track on *Ready, Steady, Go!* in September 1963; a month later the ballsy single became her debut.

The exposure of the televised music show helped push 'Love of the Loved' into the British Top Forty. This minor success led to her joining The Beatles, among others, on their prestigious Christmas show staged at London's Finsbury Park Theatre.

The follow-up to 'Love of the Loved' displayed a total change of style and was a cover version of Dionne Warwick's wistful ballad 'Anyone Who Had a Heart', written by Burt Bacharach and Hal David. Black delivered the song like a snippet of drama, with her deep nasally voice straining at the notes. In fact, it was a difficult melody for her to master, but after several concentrated attempts she achieved what Bacharach had intended for the song. 'Anyone Who Had a Heart' sold in excess of 900,000 copies to top the British chart in March 1964, distinguishing Black as the first songstress since Helen Shapiro and 'Walkin' Back to Happiness' to enjoy one of Britain's top-selling singles. With the single dominating the chart for four weeks, Black wanted to celebrate her success by buying a Rolls-Royce. Brian Epstein thought otherwise and persuaded her to buy a Bentley instead, saying, 'A Princess of the Road for the Queen of Pop.'

While 'Anyone Who Had a Heart' was still selling, Black embarked upon a lengthy British tour with stable-mates Billy J. Kramer and the Dakotas, and Gene Pitney. Black wrote in her book *Step Inside*, 'Slowly I began to learn that I had a responsibility towards the audience. The paying public. Instead of taking it for granted that every house would be packed to the roof with cheering fans, I started to distinguish between one audience and another . . . Gradually I learned professional habits, like how to move on stage with presence and make a good entrance . . . In 1964 my world was turning very fast, it's hardly surprising I didn't learn everything overnight.'

In May 1964, Black recorded 'You're my World', an impassioned adaptation from the Italian original, titled 'Il Mondo'. The single raced to the top of the British chart, Black's second chart-topper in as many months, establishing her as an artist of value and one who was outselling her Mersey colleagues except, of course, The Beatles. She then turned to the stage at the London Palladium. 'I had a more regular life working on a traditional variety bill with Frankie Howerd and Tommy Cooper, plus The Foremost to add a little bit of Liverpool.'

For her next single, Black recorded another canned McCartney track titled 'It's for You'. The Beatle also played piano on the song which reached the British Top Ten during August 1964. The single also became her second American hit after 'You're my World', which soared into the Top Thirty. During November Black was invited to perform on the Royal Variety Show, and the following month she sang 'Is It Love' in the movie *Ferry 'cross the Mersey*, starring Gerry and the Pacemakers. Cilla Black's selling power proved beyond argument that she was the most successful songstress of 1964.

Another British tour started 1965, this time with Tommy Roe and P.J. Proby, among others. Black said, 'I learned a lot about travelling from one date to another. It was the age of the coach when everyone went by coach including the star. Later we had Americans coming over who refused to go on a coach and insisted on having their own limos . . . and as a result of that everyone wanted a limo.'

Once the lengthy trek was over, Black released a further cover version. She chose The Righteous Brothers' 'You've Lost that Lovin' Feelin'' but the plan backfired. She had competition this time from the American duo, and the outcome was: Cilla Black, No. 2; The Righteous Brothers, No. 1. Nonetheless, it was an achievement not to be knocked.

Following an Australian tour, Black flew to America to debut on *The Ed Sullivan Show*, where she followed performing chimpanzees in the programme's schedule. Unfortunately, not all the creatures left the stage on cue and as Black sang, one remained, clinging to her leg.

During May 1965 'I've Been Wrong Before', written by Randy Newman, was issued as Black's next single; a No. 17 British hit. Over the next three months, she performed again in America, co-starring with The Beatles on *The Ed Sullivan Show*, represented Britain in the 'Grand Gala Du Disques' held in Holland, and toured Britain for the last time with The Everly Brothers.

The first single of 1966 was 'Love's Just a Broken Heart', a No. 5 British hit. Two months on she recorded 'Alfie', the title song from the Michael Caine movie of the same name. Written by Bacharach and David, it reached the British Top Ten, but it was only No. 95 in America, where it failed to compete with Cher's version which soared into the Top Thirty. Two further British singles were issued during the year, namely 'Don't Answer Me', a Top Ten hit, and 'A Fool Am I', which reached the Top Twenty.

Early in 1967 and after performing with Frankie Howerd in *Way Out in Piccadilly*, a revue written by Eric Sykes, Ray Galton and Alan Simpson, Black made her film debut (her appearance in *Ferry 'cross the Mersey* was a cameo spot) in *Work . . . Is a Four-Letter Word* with Alfred Marks, among others. Meanwhile, singles had to be recorded and her first of the year was 'What Good Am I', a Top Thirty British hit during June 1967, while 'I Only Live to Love You' closed the year, peaking in the Top Thirty.

Like Dusty Springfield, Black hosted her own television series. It was titled *Step inside Love*, taken from a song specifically written by Paul McCartney for her shows (and which, when issued as a single, returning Black to the British Top Ten), and enabled the singer to flex her expanding showbiz muscles. 'Where Is Tomorrow' followed during June 1968 but, surprisingly, stalled in the British Top Forty. It was a minor setback, because when Bill Martin and Phil Coulter wrote 'Surround Yourself in Sorrow' for her, it re-established Black as a top-selling artist, reaching No. 3. In defiance of the sombre mood of the single, Black married her personal manager, Bobby Willis, a marriage that has lasted through the decades – unlike so many of the sixties'.

Following the last single of 1969, 'Conversations', Black notched up two further hits during the next two years, namely, 'If I Thought You'd Ever Change your Mind' and 'Something Tells Me (Something's Gonna Happen Tonight'), the title of her next television series. There then came a two-year gap before her next hit. Titled 'Baby We Can't Go Wrong', it was issued during February 1974, and was the theme from her third television series. It staggered into the British Top Forty and marked the end of her remarkable charting career.

From 1974, now no longer considered to be a 'pop' singer but rather a fledgling all-round entertainer, Cilla Black turned to the cabaret circuit where she built up a strong middle-of-the-road following. Through to the early eighties, she combined occasional live appearances with raising her family. Then in 1983 she returned to the public spotlight as a television personality, hosting two peak-viewing shows, *Blind Date* and *Surprise Surprise*. Both programmes ran into the nineties, with Black becoming one of the highest-paid entertainers on British television.

During 1993 she attempted to resurrect her recording career by releasing a comeback album, *Through the Years*. The duet with Dusty Springfield titled 'Heart and Soul' was lifted from that album to become a Top Eighty single.

Cilla Black: 'What happened in the early sixties in Liverpool was a rebellion. We did it through music, whereas today they use violence, but the causes weren't that different.'

THE BEATLES

Can't Buy Me Love

At this time in The Beatles' career, John Lennon and Paul McCartney wrote whenever they could, sometimes when they were travelling, or backstage waiting to perform, or any time when they could snatch a few minutes' free time. They worked together, and alone; often lyrics would be scribbled on cigarette packets or on numerous scraps of paper. A melody would usually be worked out on the guitar some time later. Only when Lennon and McCartney were actually in the recording studio did they know how a song would sound. With the group's immensely tight schedule, it really was a miracle they had the energy, let alone the inspiration, to compose.

The writing credit on record labels and such always read 'Lennon/McCartney' and when this was first discussed Paul McCartney felt it should read 'McCartney/Lennon' because he did the bulk of the work. This was rejected by the others, who felt 'Lennon/McCartney' looked better and rolled from the tongue that much more easily. However, on rare occasions, Paul McCartney did get his own way.

On 23 March 1964 The Beatles broke the record held by Elvis Presley with ten singles in the American Top One Hundred chart. Prior to the advent of the Fab Four, Presley had had nine singles in the chart. A month later, four further Beatles tracks charted, bringing the overall total to fourteen.

Prior to the release of 'Can't Buy Me Love', the group had started filming their first full-length movie *A Hard Day's Night*. Essential promotion time for the single, therefore, had to be squeezed in between shooting. Luckily, the first location shots were based in and around London, thus allowing the group easy access to the radio and television studios.

'Can't Buy Me Love' was simultaneously released in Britain and America. Advance British sales were a staggering one million plus, the largest ever in Britain, while in America double that figure sold within a week. It was a monumental achievement for an unheard record, but fans supported it because it was the official follow-up to 'I Want to

Hold your Hand' and was not included on any album to date. The single shot to the top of the American chart. The Beatles dominated the upper section with 'Please Please Me' at No. 5; 'I Want to Hold your Hand' at No. 4; 'She Loves You' at No. 3; and 'Twist and Shout', at No. 2. The group's *Second Album* was also issued Stateside in April. This predictably replaced *Meet The Beatles* at the top of the album chart. Spin-off albums like *The Beatles with Tony Sheridan and their Guests* likewise charted. Anyone connected with the name 'Beatles' was making money. The pity was Brian Epstein never thought to control this. Also a slew of singles were released in America only; a glut indeed.

While 'Can't Buy Me Love' was in its prime, The Beatles collected yet another award, this time for Showbusiness Personalities of 1963, presented by Harold Wilson at the twelfth annual Variety Club of Great Britain ceremony held at London's Dorchester Hotel. Madame Tussaud's paid tribute to The Beatles by installing their wax images in the Edgware Road exhibition.

John Lennon also published his first book, *In his Own Write*, with an initial print run of 50,000 copies. When published in America, the initial run was 100,000 copies. The book featured nothing more than Lennon's verses and cartoons which he had scribbled in his spare time. In April 1964 Lennon, wearing his author's hat, was guest of honour at Foyles's literary lunch at the Dorchester Hotel to celebrate William Shakespeare's four-hundredth birthday.

That June, The Fab Four embarked upon their first world tour. As Ringo Starr had been rushed to London's University College Hospital with pharyngitis and tonsillitis, Jimmy Nicol replaced him until Starr rejoined the group in Melbourne, where a quarter of a million fans watched them perform. When they returned to London, two more Lennon/McCartney compositions had been recorded by Brian Epstein's acts, namely, Cilla Black's 'It's for You' and Billy J. Kramer and the Dakotas' 'From a Window'.

Ella Fitzgerald, meanwhile, became the first artist to enjoy a British hit with a cover version of 'Can't Buy Me Love', which reached No. 34.

Also see: 'From Me to You', May/June 1963; 'She Loves You', October 1963; 'I Want to Hold your Hand', December 1963; 'A Hard Day's Night', August 1964; 'I Feel Fine', January 1965; 'Ticket to Ride', May 1965; 'Help!', August 1965; 'We Can Work It Out'/'Day Tripper', January 1966; 'Paperback Writer', July 1966; 'Yellow Submarine'/

'Eleanor Rigby', September 1966; 'All You Need Is Love', August 1967; 'Hello Goodbye', January 1968; 'Lady Madonna', April 1968; 'Get Back', May 1969; 'The Ballad of John and Yoko', July 1969

May 1964

PETER AND GORDON

A World without Love

Peter and Gordon were the acceptable face of British pop music: unassuming, but with a fashionable appearance. They were overnight sensations thanks to Paul McCartney, and were fortunate enough to be a big-selling act on both sides of the Atlantic.

Peter Asher was born on 22 June 1944 in London, while Gordon Waller was born on 4 June a year later in Scotland. They met at the prestigious Westminster boys' public school, both were doctors' sons and, as they had learned to play the guitar, decided to sing together, emulating their musical heroes The Everly Brothers.

In early 1964, Norman Newell, head of A. & R. at EMI Records, saw their act at the Pickwick Club in London. He invited them to audition for the record company where they sang the folk song '500 Miles' and 'If I Were You', one of their own compositions. Peter Asher told Joe Smith, 'Around the same time, Paul McCartney had met my sister Jane, and they started going out . . . At some point later he played me this song he'd never finished. It was "A World without Love".'

It appeared that McCartney had intended the song for Billy J. Kramer, but he had rejected it. Peter Asher believed in the song and asked McCartney to modify it for a duo.

'A World without Love' was rush-released by EMI Records and by May 1964 it had given an unknown duo a chart-topper with their debut release. It took all of two weeks and, of course, a helping hand from a Beatle. The single likewise stormed the American chart where it headed for the top spot. Within weeks, it had charted in most European countries as well.

To capitalise on their American success, Peter and Gordon performed at New York's World Fair during June 1964. According to Asher, 'It was fantastic. The whole thing was amazingly exciting. When we landed at the airport, there were crowds of screaming girls with signs, jumping all over us.' He also recalled that the World Fair's stage was separated from the audience by a body of water. Girls actually jumped or swam through this to get on stage with them. 'It was a terrific time to be in the music business and a terrific time to be an English rock 'n' roller.'

Paul McCartney also penned 'Nobody I Know', the follow-up single which, in June 1964, became a No. 10 British hit, No. 12 in America, and their third release, 'I Don't Want to See You Again', which, remarkably, bombed in Britain, yet reached the Top Twenty in America. Despite the hiccup with the singles chart, both their *Just for You* EP and their eponymous debut album became Top Twenty hits in their respective charts.

A change of composer occurred in February 1965, but that didn't work. During their Australian tour with Del Shannon, he gave them 'I Go to Pieces' to record. He had written it for The Searchers, who were also on the tour, but they turned it down. Once again, the duo had a flop on their hands in Britain, while American sales pushed the number into the Top Ten.

It was now obviously a crucial point in Peter and Gordon's career. Another British failure would signify the end. Happily, though, that didn't happen, as they turned to an established song, Buddy Holly's 'True Love Ways', which, in April 1965, reached No. 2. Across the Atlantic, the single struggled into the Top Twenty.

Another cover version followed, The Teddy Bears' 'To Know You Is to Love You', a Top Five British hit, No. 24 in America. Their career had been saved. As if to stabilise their position they recorded Van McCoy's 'Baby I'm Yours' (previously recorded by American soul singer Barbara Lewis) which became a Top Twenty British hit. This time, American sales were too low for it to chart, although its B-side, 'Don't Pity Me', scraped into the Top Ninety.

During March 1966, Peter and Gordon returned to Paul McCartney who gave them 'Woman'. Buyers were unaware of the Beatle connection because the composing credit on the record label read Bernard Webb. McCartney took this road because he was annoyed at suggestions that Peter and Gordon only reached hit status because of his name. To throw the Americans totally, McCartney added 'A. Smith' as the second composer's name! 'Woman' reached No. 28 in the British chart, No. 14 in America. An album titled after the single was released in America only, to reach the Top Sixty.

'Don't Pity Me', in June 1966, bombed, while their next, the tongue-in-cheek 'Lady Godiva' re-established them in the British Top Twenty that October. The fact that it was banned as 'indecent' in Coventry,

Lady Godiva's home town, might have had something to do with the high chart placing. When issued in America, it soared to No.6, with sales reaching in excess of one million copies.

During the following year, two singles were released, namely, 'Sunday for Tea' and 'The Jokers'. Both bombed in Britain, and charted poorly across the Atlantic. Hit singles generated money and sustained careers; without them acts, unless visually exciting on stage, couldn't survive. So it now seemed inevitable that Peter and Gordon would go their separate ways. According to Asher, '[We] broke up sort of gradually, as these things often do. Gordon wanted to do a solo record, and this friend of mine, Paul Jones [Manfred Mann's future lead singer] knew I was interested in production, and he asked me if I'd like to produce some records with him, which I did.'

When Gordon Waller released his solo single, 'Rosecrans Boulevard' early in 1968, Peter Asher, at Paul McCartney's invitation, joined The Beatles' Apple company as A. & R. manager, where his first production was James Taylor's eponymous album.

Waller pursued his solo career, albeit unsuccessfully, until May 1973, when he joined the London cast of *Joseph and his Amazing Technicolor Dreamcoat*. Peter Asher, meantime, left Apple when Allen Klein took over the running of the company, and climbed the ranks to become a highly respected and sought-after producer and manager. He is now based in Los Angeles, while Gordon Waller remained in Britain.

Also a No. 1 single in May 1964: 'Juliet' by The Four Pennies

June 1964

THE ANIMALS

House of the Rising Sun

'In the beginning, when people heard our name they used to come along expecting to see a scruffy, shaggy-haired group. They were amazed to see five tidy, ordinary young men.' – Eric Burdon

The Animals were born in Newcastle during 1962, and were so named because their stage act was on the wild side as they slammed home their own style of R. & B. Led by the rebellious Eric Burdon (born in Walker, Tyneside, on 11 May 1941), the band comprised Alan

Price on keyboards (born in Fairfield, County Durham, on 19 April 1941); John Steel, drums (born in Gateshead, County Durham, on 4 February 1941); Hilton Valentine, guitar (born in North Shields on 21 May 1943), and Chas Chandler, bass (born in Heaton, Tyneside, on 18 December 1938). Burdon had previously played trombone with John Steel on trumpet in various jazz outfits, while Hilton Valentine had been a member of The Gamblers.

After being the main attraction at Newcastle's Downbeat Club, The Animals changed their residency to the Club A Go-Go in 1963. According to Eric Burdon, 'We used to do late shows where we'd cater for all-male crowds. They'd bring in their own drink and we'd really have a ball. When we became better known, girls followed us around at dance halls. But the only image we ever tried to promote was that of a good musical act.' Soul singer Graham Bond was so enthusiastic about The Animals that he persuaded his manager, Ronan O'Rahilly, to represent them.

In answer to requests from their fans, The Animals recorded a tape of their material, which led to their first BBC radio spot on *Saturday Club*, hosted by Brian Matthews. So successful was this airing that the group moved to London to take the R. & B. club scene by storm. This excitement in a cult world was witnessed by countless record company personnel including producer Mickie Most (later head of RAK Records) who negotiated a recording deal with EMI Records' Columbia outlet.

In April 1964, The Animals' interpretation of the Bob Dylan track 'Baby Don't You Tear my Clothes' was released as their debut single under the title 'Baby Let Me Take You Home'. It broke into the British Top Twenty at No. 19.

Their second single was the immortal 'House of the Rising Sun', a folk song about a New Orleans brothel, written by Josh White, which Eric Burdon had first heard as a teenager. The group had been playing it on stage for some time, but until now no record company had shared the group's confidence in its hit potential. Following a tour with Chuck Berry, Mickie Most booked the group into a Kingsway recording studio at a cost of £8 an hour. The track was completed in fifteen minutes. It was then considered to be too long at 4½ minutes for radio play, and executives at Columbia went to great lengths to persuade the group to shorten the song. The group refused.

It took two weeks, during June 1964, for 'House of the Rising Sun' to reach the top of the British chart. It was a remarkable four-minutes-plus of British R. & B., with Burdon's soul-wrenching vocals and Alan

Price's extraordinary keyboard playing. According to Burdon, 'We worked five years to get where we are, and by our approach and the fact that we can support our discs on stage, have managed to make a spot for ourselves in the business.'

At this point in The Animals' career, they had no American outlet, despite Mickie Most's attempts to drum up interest. When he returned to London from one of his promotional trips, representatives from MGM Records were meeting EMI Records executives. When the Americans realised The Beatles were already signed to a Stateside deal, they agreed to sign The Animals instead. A shortened version of 'House of the Rising Sun' was subsequently issued in America; that too soared to No. 1, selling over one million copies to do so.

In October 1964, 'I'm Crying', an original composition from the group, was issued as follow-up to become a No. 6 hit in Britain; No. 19 in America. Because of the group's love of R. & B. it seemed logical they should pick the best material America had an offer. With this in mind – and, of course, their track record to date – it seemed ludicrous for Nina Simone to express her distaste when they covered her 'Don't Let Me Be Misunderstood' as their next single. She might have had a point; the group could well have prevented her from enjoying British success. It returned The Animals to the British Top Five, and reached the Top Fifteen in America during February 1965. Three months later, the group covered Sam Cooke's 'Bring It on Home to Me', another Top Five success, although it faltered in the American Top Thirty.

Barry Mann and Cynthia Weil wrote The Animals' next single, 'We Gotta Get out of This Place', and for the third time they enjoyed a Top Three hit, with a better showing in America this time at No. 13. Before 1965 closed, 'It's my Life' reached the Top Ten; Top Thirty in America.

Following the release of this single Alan Price quit the group. He had for some time been locked in argument with Burdon regarding the group's material, although Burdon later admitted it had more to do with him securing the publishing rights to 'House of the Rising Sun'. Whatever the reason, Price went on to become a successful artist in his own right, later forming the Alan Price Set. Dave Rowberry replaced him in The Animals.

However, the arguing continued. During January 1966, after a clash of musical opinion with EMI Records, The Animals signed a new recording deal with Decca Records, where they worked with Tom Wilson. A month later their debut single on the new label was released, namely, 'Inside Looking Out', a No. 7 British hit; No. 34 in America. All was still not well because the group suffered another upheaval when drummer John Steel left to be replaced by Barry Jenkins. By the end of the year the very existence of The Animals was in doubt. Dissent began when Eric Burdon's LSD habit grew alarmingly, and it led to him and newcomer Barry Jenkins forming another band, leaving the remainder to follow new ambitions.

'See See Rider' was the last single from the original Animals, and as if to prove how vital that line-up was, it became their best-selling American single, shooting to No. 10. It wasn't released in Britain but a solo Eric Burdon track (credited to The Animals) was, titled 'Help Me Girl'. It became a Top Twenty hit.

Eric Burdon retained the name 'The Animals' and relocated to California to start anew with the line-up Vic Briggs (from Steampacket), Danny McCullough, and John Weider (Family). Their first release, 'When I Was Young', issued in May 1967, was a combination of American psychedelia and Animals' R. & B. In time, Burdon cleaned up his act to enjoy hits with 'Help Me Girl' and 'San Franciscan Nights', and was an integral part of America's changing musical kaleidoscope. During 1969 he worked with the American group Nite Shift, later known as War. Together they recorded the *Eric Burdon Declares War* album from which 'Spill the Wine' was taken as a single. It shot to No. 3 in America. In retrospect, it was a disastrous combination. Burdon was intent on leading a musical revolution, while War was content to remain a funk outfit. During a British tour in the seventies, Burdon was once more caught up in hallucinatory drugs. He was unable to function, with the inevitable result: War dumped him.

From War, Burdon moved into films, but when his first project, conceived and presented through a drug haze, bombed, legal action ensued from companies who had invested in him. He lost his creative reputation, and in excess of $6 million which reputedly belonged to The Animals. By 1977, the legal wrangles had finished, and Eric Burdon was free to pursue a recording career.

Meanwhile, ex-Animal Chas Chandler had discovered the fiery Jimi Hendrix in Greenwich Village, and relocated him to London where the Jimi Hendrix Experience was formed. When Hendrix died in September 1970, Chandler went on to manage the British group Slade.

During October 1972, following the release of the compilation *Most of The Animals*, 'House of the Rising Sun' was lifted as a single. It became a Top Thirty hit. And again, in October 1982, the single was re-issued to soar to No. 11 in the British charts. A further re-issue is due . . .

ROY ORBISON

It's Over

Roy Orbison was one of the sixties' foremost singers who won his public support by crooning doom-laden songs. Not a sad character by nature, although rather shy and reserved, he excelled in tales that made people weep. His black hair, pasty white face half-hidden by sunglasses and black attire befitted a funeral parlour more than the top of the music charts. His falsetto voice soared from lips that barely parted and his static guitar playing on stage was in total opposition to the frenetic, sensual appearances of his idol (and one-time fellow artist at Sun Records), Elvis Presley.

Orbison was born on 23 April 1936 in Vernon, Texas. His father worked in the oil fields, and his mother was a nurse. They lived in Wink, Texas, where as a teenager Orbison sang with The Wink Westerners, a hillbilly band. He also joined Charline Arthur on a Sunday morning radio programme in Kermit. Later on, he studied at the West Texas State University to become a geologist. In 1955 those studies were pushed aside as he joined The Teen Kings instead to record 'Trying to Get to You' at Norman Petty's studios in Clovis, New Mexico. The single was later released on the Jewel Records label, and flopped. This just prompted Orbison to try again. 'I headed off to Sun Records because [Elvis] Presley and Carl Perkins did . . . We started recording everything we could get our hands on . . . it was all super-exciting. Little bitty studios, really small. But being there with everybody working actually made it seem like a workshop.' Orbison's debut there, 'Ooby Dooby', was rockabilly-influenced and entered the American chart to peak at No. 59 – his first taste of real success.

'Ooby Dooby' qualified Orbison to perform, and during 1956–57 he toured Pennsylvania with Gene Vincent, Eddie Cochran and others. Like Orbison, most of the acts only had one hit song to perform. 'I never wanted to be in the position where the only thing I could do was something I had already done. So I started writing songs,' he said. In 1958 he joined the music publishers Acuff-Rose Music in Nashville. 'Claudette', a song dedicated to his wife (whom he would divorce in 1964 following her adultery), was recorded by The Everly Brothers to become the flipside of their multi-million-seller 'All I Have to Do Is Dream'. Orbison told author Joe Smith, 'I didn't know if the songs were good, but the artists were good.'

A year later RCA Records signed the singer for one notable single, 'Almost 18'. From there he recorded 'Up Town' for Monument Records. This floated into the American chart to stall at No. 72. The dithering period was destined to end when during July 1960 Roy Orbison penned 'Only the Lonely' with Joe Melson. Elvis Presley was earmarked to record it, but Orbison opted to record it himself. A wise move, and a lucky break as the single raced to No. 2 on the charts in both America and Britain (where it was his debut), selling several million copies en route. 'Blue Angel' followed in November 1960, and like most clones it failed to repeat its predecessor's success but struggled to No. 11 in Britain and two notches higher in America.

It took almost a year for Roy Orbison to hit the big time again with the dramatic 'Running Scared', his second million-seller, which raced straight to the top of the American chart and peaked in the British Top Ten. Originally most of the high notes were sung falsetto but as this left the song gutless, Orbison alternated with full voice. 'I didn't know there was a difference between [them]. I could feel the difference but I didn't understand the technical differences. Then the power of the voice came.'

The third million-seller was the emotive 'Crying' (again penned by Orbison and Melson). It soared to No. 3 in America, yet surprisingly struggled into the British Top Thirty. It's fair to say that much of the singer's attraction was his voice and the vivid way he told his tale of emotional despair. It was a style peculiar to Orbison; he was the master, yet ironically, like his songs, his life was doomed to be scarred by tragedy.

A change of musical style marked the fourth million-seller. The mid-paced 'Dream Baby' peaked at No. 2 on both sides of the Atlantic, leaving its follow-up 'The Crowd' and 'Working for the Man' to break his chart run by stalling at No. 40 and No. 50 respectively in the British chart. Happily the lapse was short-lived because the first release of 1963 was the magnificent ballad 'In Dreams', one of the singer's most-loved songs. It shot into the British and American Top Ten. A month after the single had peaked, Orbison arrived in Britain for his first tour. Not only was the public to see the American perform on stage, but was to be introduced to a future trademark, albeit an unplanned one. According to Orbison, 'I was going to do a show with Patsy Cline and Bobby Vee [in Alabama] and I left my glasses on the plane. I only had the sunglasses and I was quite embarrassed to go on stage with them, but I did. Then I took the shades with me to England when I opened for The Beatles . . . I walked on stage with my sunglasses on, and all over Europe we were an instant success. Big time. I probably also wore something black that night, and that's how come the black outfits and dark sunglasses stuck.'

As 'In Dreams' descended, Orbison's next single, 'Falling', climbed into the British Top Ten. He also started another tour, this time with Freddie and the Dreamers, Brian Poole and the Tremeloes, among others. And before the end of 1963, 'Blue Bayou' became a No. 3 British hit.

In 1964, after 'Born on the Wind' hit the Top Fifteen, Orbison toured Britain once more, again with Freddie and the Dreamers. It was this that laid the foundation for his next British chart-topper, 'It's Over', in July 1964. It was a further slice of emotional drama, written by the singer and Bill Rees, and held the top spot for two weeks, while in America it surprisingly peaked at No. 9. Nonetheless, the high calibre of Orbison's music was unquestionable; each release held a magic of its own. But in spite of his preference for sad melodrama, his most enduring song was the uptempo and timeless 'Oh Pretty Woman', follow-up to 'It's Over'. With sales in excess of seven million the single topped the charts on both sides of the Atlantic, and even with the passing of time it refused to die. In 1990 the movie *Pretty Woman* starring Richard Gere and Julia Roberts gave it renewed life, earning Orbison a Grammy Award for the Best Pop Vocal Performance in 1991.

A regular British touring schedule during the sixties ensured Orbison's high public profile; in fact, he was said to have adopted Britain as his second home, even though that home would bring him suffering.

While touring with Lulu and The Walker Brothers during 1966, he fractured his foot in a motorcycle accident and appeared on stage on crutches. Behind the scenes and after a stormy relationship, Orbison and his wife Claudette remarried in 1966, only to be parted again. In June Claudette was killed in a road accident in Texas. Two years later, and as the singer was touring Britain, two of his three sons died in a blaze at his Nashville home.

Happily, time healed Roy Orbison's wounds as he eventually found a new life for himself by marrying Barbara Wellborn in 1969. They'd first met in Britain.

Professionally speaking, Orbison's career continued to be successful although the high chart placings evaded him. During 1980, though, after a thirteen-year absence, he returned to the American listing duetting with Emmylou Harris on 'That Lovin' You Feelin' Again', lifted from the *Roadie* movie soundtrack. The single went on to win a 1981 Grammy Award for the Best Country Performance by a Duo or Group with Vocal.

In fact, Orbison earned a lucrative living from the movie world. For instance, 'In Dreams' was featured in David Lynch's *Blue Velvet*, and in 1988 Orbison's duet with k.d. lang, 'Crying', was included in *Hiding Out*. However, he did return to the studios for the first time in four years to record his own work on the *Big O Country* album. This was followed a year later by 'Problem Child'. Various 'greatest hits' packages were regularly released and because of his enormous contribution to music, Orbison was honoured with handfuls of awards, as well as being inducted into the prestigious Rock 'n' Roll Hall of Fame during 1987.

Following his 52nd birthday in April 1988, Roy Orbison joined the all-star outfit The Traveling Wilburys. Alongside Tom Petty, George Harrison, Jeff Lynne and Bob Dylan he recorded the album *The Traveling Wilburys*. In November 'Handle with Care' was lifted from that album to reach the British Top Twenty. According to George Harrison, 'One of the things that really clinched the thing with The Wilburys with respect to me and Roy was when I found that Roy knew every word to every Monty Python song and the dialogue to all the movies and the TV series. I mean, he was a gentle person, but he had a good sense of humour . . . He was so pleased to be working and singing. To sit in a room and try to write tunes with him, it was a great thrill.' Orbison himself believed that 'The Wilburys was a wonderful experience . . . Most of the time we'd get together, have some laughs and play guitar. Then I'd realise they were superstar people.' (Quotes from 'The Roy Orbison Story' 1997 tour programme)

Yes, indeed, the singer threw himself into his new career, but, sadly, before he could reap the rewards of that success, he died on 6 December 1988 in the Henderson Hospital following a heart attack in his mother's bathroom.

A month after his death, a further track, 'You Got It', was issued and went to No. 3 in Britain, followed by 'She's a Mystery to Me', which reached the Top Thirty. A handful of Orbison singles and duets were subsequently re-issued; he was posthumously inducted into the Songwriters Hall of Fame; and in 1991 'Oh Pretty Woman' won another Grammy award for Best Pop Vocal Performance!

'I Drove All Night', released in 1993, was Roy Orbison's last British Top Fifty hit, while in tribute to his life and music Bill Kenwright devised the musical *The Roy Orbison Story*, based on the book written by Shirlie Roden and Jon Miller. The touring show featured Peter Howarth as Orbison, in a performance that spanned both the fame and the despair of the singer's life. It was a wonderful tribute to the legendary 'Big O'.

'Someone asked me, "How would you like to be remembered?", and I said, "I would just like to be remembered."' – Roy Orbison

August 1964

THE BEATLES

A Hard Day's Night

Prior to The Beatles' American success, Brian Epstein had negotiated a three-picture deal with United Artists. Due to his inexperience in this field, he accepted £25,000 for the group plus 7½ per cent of the movies' takings. It was a ludicrously low deal which United Artists representatives quickly closed in on. Another oversight was the discovery that The Beatles' recording contract with EMI Records excluded soundtrack albums. This meant United Artists had also purchased the music from the three movies.

A Hard Day's Night, The Beatles' first full-length film, started its life as *Beatlemania* but was changed at the last minute to the phrase Ringo Starr constantly used when a gruelling day's filming had finished. Conceived by Walter Shenson, written by fellow-Liverpudlian Alun Owen and directed by Richard Lester, the film was intended to portray The Beatles as themselves in a variety of situations which spanned two days of their working life. Two experienced actors, Norman Rossington and Wilfred Brambell, were the group's co-stars, and both slipped happily into the mayhem.

Filming started at London's Paddington Station, and later at Marylebone Station, where one hundred fans were paid to scream at the group as they ran for a train. The fact that they would have done this for nothing seemed to have slipped the director's mind. Patti Boyd was among the screaming crowd; she later married George Harrison, in January 1966. British Rail reputedly charged £600 a day for the five days' filming on the train and at the stations. The bulk of the movie was shot in London, at Gatwick Airport and Twickenham Film Studios. It took six weeks to complete with a budget of £200,000.

To date, most movies about music and artists had been pretty mundane affairs, but *A Hard Day's Night* broke the mould. With the experienced team behind them, The Beatles' zany personalities and many talents were highlighted, making the movie extremely entertaining. It was premiered in July 1964 at the London Pavilion in the West End before Princess Margaret and Lord Snowden. The second premiere was naturally held in Liverpool. The Beatles attended both, but in their home city they were welcomed by the Lord Mayor and over 200,000 Liverpudlians who lined the route from Speke to the city centre.

A month later *A Hard Day's Night* was released throughout the world, including America, where it opened in 500 cinemas, earning approximately $1.3 million during the first weeks. Predictably, the film caused outbreaks of screaming masses; at some cinemas the soundtrack was totally obliterated due to the noise from the audiences.

The 'A Hard Day's Night' single and album (the first to contain only Lennon/McCartney compositions) were released on the same August day, and both shot to No. 1 in their respective charts. Across the Atlantic this was repeated, with a specially compiled album, *Something New*, propping up the top spot at No. 2. With *A Hard Day's Night* in all three configurations in full swing, The Beatles left London for their second (and fully fledged) tour of America and Canada with co-stars Jackie De Shannon and The Righteous Brothers. Starting in San Francisco, they performed at venues in Philadelphia, Chicago, Detroit, Montreal, Cleveland and Dallas, among others. When they eventually returned to Britain and landed at London Airport on 21 September, fans were shoulder to shoulder. To cater for the unprecedented crowds at the airport, the roof of the Queen's Building was opened, while Beatles music was piped through the airport's PA system.

In October 1964, the group embarked on yet another British tour, the only one of the year, with Motown's first lady, Mary Wells, as support act. The Beatles had made no secret of the admiration they had for Motown, the Detroit-based record company headed by Berry Gordy Jr. Indeed they, like Dusty Springfield, had recorded a handful of Motown cover versions as album tracks.

A year after its original release date, Peter Sellers recorded his own unique version of 'A Hard Day's Night'. He recited the song as

Richard III impersonating Sir Laurence Olivier, no less. Released in December 1965, this unlikely combination of talent reached the Top Twenty in Britain.

Also see: 'From Me to You', May/June 1963; 'She Loves You', October 1963; 'I Want to Hold your Hand', December 1963; 'Can't Buy Me Love', April 1964; 'I Feel Fine', January 1965; 'Ticket to Ride', May 1965; 'Help!', August 1965; 'We Can Work It Out'/'Day Tripper', January 1966; 'Paperback Writer', July 1966; 'Yellow Submarine'/ 'Eleanor Rigby', September 1966; 'All You Need Is Love', August 1967; 'Hello Goodbye', January 1968; 'Lady Madonna', April 1968; 'Get Back', May 1969; 'The Ballad of John and Yoko', July 1969

September 1964

HONEYCOMBS

Have I the Right

Like most acts that are eventually signed by a record company, this group served its apprenticeship performing on the club circuit. But, as a rule, this learning experience doesn't necessarily lead to a No. 1 record with the first release. The Honeycombs were among the lucky few, when 'Have I the Right' hit the top of the British chart. Unfortunately, this success couldn't be sustained, and again, as for so many during this decade, their fall was as quick as their rise.

The nucleus of the band was formed by Martin Murray, rhythm guitarist, in 1963. Born on 7 October 1941 in London, he was actually a hairdresser by trade, but his ambition was to be a professional musician. He recruited Ann Lantree, born on 28 August 1943 in Hayes, Middlesex, as drummer, whose nickname was 'Honey' due to her hair colour. Her brother John, born 20 August 1940 in Berkshire, was hired as bass guitarist; Alan Ward, born 12 December 1945 in Nottingham, as lead guitarist, and vocalist Denis D'ell, born 10 October 1943.

As The Sherabons they played anywhere they could secure a booking on the North London circuit before composers Alan Blaikley and Ken Howard caught one of their performances. The couple took over the group's management and due to their music business contacts, quickly secured a recording deal with Pye Records. Producer Joe

Meek was assigned to them and the result was the Blaikley/Howard composition 'Have I the Right', a song that had previously been passed on by other companies. 'Have I the Right' might have turned gold for the group, but it marked the downward trail for Joe Meek. After a career that was studded with million-sellers, producing hit singles for the likes of John Leyton, Mike Berry and The Tornados, Meek's talent seemed to disintegrate, as his business concerns and personal life collapsed. Sadly, he never recovered and shot himself in February 1967.

With a debut single pending, The Sherabons desperately needed a new name. The Honeycombs was a combination of Ann Lantree's nickname and 'combs', a reminder of their past hairdressing days, although it was also reported that the name was swiped from a Jimmie Rogers song.

The jumpy, happy-go-lucky 'Have I the Right' rocketed to the top of the British chart past Jim Reeves's 'I Won't Forget You' and Manfred Mann's 'Do Wah Diddy Diddy'. Once publicity photographs had been circulated to the media it was obvious that Ann Lantree was the group's main attraction, and when television cameras zoomed home on the line-up, Ann at her drum kit was singled out for the close-ups. So with this female gimmick and a solid new sound the Honeycombs looked set for a healthy career. As 'Have I the Right' earned a gold disc, crashing into the American chart to peak in the Top Five, selling in excess of a million copies, the group could have been forgiven for resting on their laurels.

However, embarking on a lengthy Australian tour was not the wisest of moves when a No. 1 single was leaving the charts. By being out of Britain the Honeycombs lost the momentum; the public forgot. Even so, no one could have been prepared for what happened next. With Peter Pye replacing Martin Murray, the second single 'Is It Because' died when it stalled at No. 38. 'Eyes', which followed it, bombed totally. To the outsider, the Honeycombs had fallen into the dreaded one-hit wonder syndrome and before long would be stacked on the rejection pile. But their luck did change during 1965 when, following 'I Can't Stop', which was released in America only to reach the Top Fifty, The Kinks' Ray Davies gave them 'Something Better Beginning' which struggled into the British Top Forty. Not that healthy, but certainly better than nothing in this crucial stage of their tottering career.

Reassured of their selling power, Ann Lantree and Denis D'ell issued their duet 'That's the Way' in September 1965. It soared to No. 12, but had no follow-up.

The Honeycombs could do nothing else but keep their name alive through touring, as they knew their recording days were now numbered. In February 1966 'Who Is Sylvia?' bombed, and they continued to wander along the cabaret trail until that too petered out. Within two years the Honeycombs had disbanded.

Apart from the singles, the group issued two albums, *All Systems Go*, and *Here Are the Honeycombs,* released only in America.

During the seventies, Denis D'ell made an abortive attempt at a solo career, and seventeen years after 'Who Is Sylvia?' was released, a compilation, *Meek and Honey*, was available.

Also No. 1 in September 1964: 'You Really Got Me' by The Kinks; 'I'm into Something Good' by Herman's Hermits

October 1964

THE SUPREMES

Baby Love

Three skinny young kids from Detroit, Michigan, became the world's most successful, and most famous, female trio ever. Their recordings are immortal; their image has been imitated, but no one can equal the magic of The Supremes.

Two Detroit friends, Florence Ballard and Mary Wilson, sang in their local church and attended the same school. Wilson, one of three children, was born in Greenville, Mississippi, on 6 March 1944 to Sam and Johnnie Mae, and raised in Detroit by an aunt and uncle. Like other future members of The Supremes, Wilson moved to the Brewster Projects (where low-salary families lived in small but decent houses). Ballard, one of thirteen children, was born to Lurlee and Jessee on 30 June 1943. While a teenager at school she wanted to form her own group – Wilson was her first recruit and another school friend, Betty Travis, was the second.

As quartets were popular, the girls searched for a fourth member. A young singer, Paul Williams, lived in the same neighbourhood and, with his singing partner, Eddie Kendricks, suggested Diane Ross be the fourth member. Ross was one of seven children born to Ernestine and Fred on 26 March 1944. She became obsessed with music during her last two years at the Cass Technical High School where she graduated with fashion illustration and costume design awards. She jumped at the chance to complete the all-female quartet. Williams and Kendricks sang with their own group, The Primes (later to became The Temptations) so the four girls decided to become The Primettes, their sister group.

Ernestine Ross was not keen on her daughter wasting time singing and rehearsing, and insisted that Diane remain in high school. The mothers of Ballard and Travis were equally anxious about their daughters' education and both eventually pulled their offsprings from the group. Eventually, though, the mothers relented and the four Primettes rehearsed in earnest, working their way towards a recording deal. The girls (with Barbara Martin replacing Betty Travis) auditioned for Robert West, owner of the newly opened Lu-Pine label. He signed them to work with his in-house writers/producers, Richard Morris and Wilmar Davis. The result was two singles, 'Tears of Sorrow' and 'Pretty Baby'. Ross sang lead on the former; Wilson on the latter. Wilson said, 'We sold enough records locally to start getting a few little gigs.'

Some time later, Motown Records' scout, Robert Bateman, saw The Primettes perform at a talent show in Canada. He recommended them to Berry Gordy, owner of the record company, who auditioned them, but recommended they finish their schooling. Undeterred, the girls visited the company's offices every afternoon, watching, listening and hoping. In time, Gordy relented and allowed them into the recording studios to hand-clap for $2 a time and provide vocals for other signed artists.

However, it gradually became obvious to the producers that Wilson and Ballard had the best voices, while Ross had a strong personality and a young determination that attracted Berry Gordy. Robert Bateman and Brian Holland had recently written 'I Want a Guy' for The Marvelettes but when Ross heard it she wanted to record it. Gordy conceded and took The Primettes (now minus Barbara Martin, who left to get married) into the studio. The track became their first single when they signed a recording contract with Motown in January 1961. No one liked the name 'The Primettes' so Ballard was given a list of fifteen names; she chose 'The Supremes'. As the girls were still at school, future recording sessions were slotted in between lessons. They were all potential lead singers but at the instigation of Gordy, Ross was promoted to permanent lead vocalist and songs were written with her voice in mind. She also changed her name from Diane to Diana, maintaining there was an error on her birth certificate.

'I Want a Guy' was released on Tamla, Motown's subsidiary label, in March 1961, followed by 'Buttered Popcorn' in the July. Both were released in America only, and both bombed. For their third single (and flop), 'Your Heart Belongs to Me', in May 1962, The Supremes switched to the Motown label where they were to stay for the remainder of their career. Their seventh single, 'When the Lovelight Starts Shining thru his Eyes', released in October 1963, was their first to be issued in Britain, in January 1964. It flopped in both countries. However, the tide was to turn when The Supremes hitched up with Motown's in-house trio of composers/producers, Holland-Dozier-Holland. The combination was irresistible; they worked so well together that success was unavoidable. It started with 'Where Did our Love Go', originally written for Mary Wells. When it was released in America in June 1964 The Supremes were touring with Dick Clark's Cavalcade of Stars. When the track leapt up the chart to No. 1, selling one million copies on the way, the trio found themselves taking on a different role with their audiences. According to Ross, 'We started noticing that when we sang the single on stage during the remainder of the tour the kids started screaming and really responding. Previously they hadn't taken too much notice of us.'

'Where Did Our Love Go' also signified the start of the girls' British career, when following its release during August 1964 it soared to No. 3, their first Top Ten single. Its follow-up, 'Baby Love', became The Supremes' first (and only) British chart-topper, in October 1964, and became their second million-selling American No. 1. Being elevated to top recording artists, they found doors began opening for them, particularly those previously barred to black artists. According to Ross, 'We were amazed. We were working constantly and our dreams were coming true. We were so busy we didn't have time to think about the fact that we were becoming stars.'

Diana Ross put her costume design training to good use by making the group's clothes. They looked resplendent both in sleek gowns or simple cotton dresses and coiffured wigs (they had over three hundred between them). With soaring commitments, the girls spent little time in Detroit; it was usual for them to perform for seventy consecutive nights, or thirty-six cities for eleven months a year. The strain was unbearable, yet they maintained their touring schedules to cash in on their recorded success. A visitor to Ross's Detroit home remarked that the singer had never cooked at the stove, nor sat down in her kitchen.

In addition to single sales, The Supremes' albums were also huge money-spinners. *Meet The Supremes* was the first in 1964, followed by

Where Did Our Love Go, A Little Bit of Liverpool (retitled *With Love (from Us to You)* for the British market) and, in 1965, *Supremes Sing Country, Western and Pop, We Remember Sam Cooke* and *More Hits*.

The Supremes' first major trip to Europe was during 1964. According to Ross, 'It was something we had dreamed of since we were kids. We drove through England and saw all the things that we had read about in school but never imagined to be real.'

In January 1965 'Come See about Me', the follow-up to 'Baby Love', stalled in the British Top Thirty, while 'Stop! In the Name of Love' fared better at No. 7. The single introduced to the world the famous Supremes' pose of outstretched arms and hands. Two further singles were issued before the close of the year, namely 'Back in my Arms Again' and 'I Hear a Symphony', No. 40 and No. 50 hits respectively in Britain; all were American chart-toppers.

In between single releases, the first Motown Revue toured Britain in March 1965. Featuring acts like The Supremes, The Temptations, Little Stevie Wonder, Martha and the Vandellas, The Miracles and Earl Van Dyke and the Soul Brothers, it was a financial flop, but did much to promote Motown's music and artists. After working with Motown acts in America, Dusty Springfield persuaded Rediffusion Television to build a show around the artists touring Britain. On 28 April *The Sound of Motown* was not only the first programme of its kind to be screened on British television, but the only one devoted to a particular style of music or record company. With the demise of Rediffusion the show's tape was thought destroyed; however, when Dave Clark (from the Dave Clark Five) bought the rights to the *Ready, Steady, Go!* footage, he also secured the rights to *The Sound of Motown* which has since been released on commercial video.

During 1966, The Supremes enjoyed two British Top Ten hits with 'You Can't Hurry Love' and 'You Keep Me Hangin' on'. Their first release of 1967 was 'Love Is Here and Now You're Gone', which peaked in the British Top Twenty, followed by 'The Happening', a Top Ten hit. The single also signified a change in The Supremes' line-up when Florence Ballard was sacked during the August, following a performance at The Flamingo Hotel, Las Vegas. According to Ballard, 'Berry Gordy told me if I went on stage, he would throw me off. I didn't go on. I couldn't fight any more.' Upon leaving the group, Ballard admitted herself into Detroit's Henry Ford Hospital to recover from stress and exhaustion. Within a year, she was penniless. Ross: 'Flo would begin to get lazy, where she wouldn't show up for rehearsals or recording sessions which threw everybody off . . . It wasn't Flo's fault, she was just tired.' It transpired that Ballard was angry that the group she had formed had been overtaken by Diana Ross. This resentment had built up during the years and had led to drinking bouts, which in turn had resulted in her lackadaisical attitude towards her Supremes' commitments. Following an abortive attempt to embark upon a solo career, Ballard was found dead by her sister in February 1976. The police report stated, 'She ingested an unknown amount of pills and consumed alcohol.' The pills were for her weight problem and high blood pressure, taken to prepare herself for a pending offer of a new career.

An ex-member of Patti LaBelle's Bluebelles, Cindy Birdsong, born on 15 December 1943 in Mount Holly, New Jersey, replaced Florence Ballard. Her first single as a Supreme was 'Reflections' released during 1967, where the record label credit was Diana Ross and the Supremes.

To start 1968, the trio opened a season at London's prestigious nightclub, Talk of the Town, before becoming the first Motown act to appear in the Royal Command Performance, held in the November, attended by The Queen Mother, Princess Margaret, Prince Charles and Princess Anne. On the singles front, three releases were British hits, namely 'Forever Came Today', 'Some Things You Never Get Used to' and 'Love Child'.

Meanwhile, in America, following the Los Angeles stage success of Diana Ross and The Supremes and The Temptations, it was decided to record them together. The first hit single, 'I'm Gonna Make You Love Me' was released in January 1969, swiped from the album *Diana Ross and The Supremes Join The Temptations*. This success led to two joint American television specials and further albums and singles. But the magic that was associated with Motown's most famous trio was waning; the singles were less adventurous and the ladies were getting tired.

It came as no surprise when, following the release of 'Someday We'll Be Together' late in 1969, Diana Ross announced her intention to leave The Supremes to embark upon a solo career. As the single peaked in the British Top Twenty, and topped the American chart, her replacement, Jean Terrell, was introduced to the public at the trio's farewell concert, staged on 14 January 1970 at the Frontier Hotel, Las Vegas. The concert was released as a double album, *Farewell*, in August 1970. According to Terrell, 'I knew people would compare me with Diana but I felt I was enough of an individualist to break through. It was tough because I hadn't done much recording.'

Tough or not, The 'new' Supremes with Terrell as lead vocalist went on to enjoy renewed success with singles like 'Up the Ladder to the Roof' in 1970; 'Stoned Love' and 'Nathan Jones' a year on, followed by 'Automatically Sunshine' and 'Bad Weather' during 1972 and 1973 respectively. In between their group releases, they teamed up with fellow act, the Four Tops on record, and scored two British hits, namely 'River Deep Mountain High', a cover version of the Ike and Tina Turner classic, and 'You Gotta Have Love in your Heart'.

However, with line-up changes and inferior material, The Supremes had no choice but to disband in 1976, although their farewell tour spanned months, ending with their final British performance at London's Drury Lane Theatre in June 1977. According to Mary Wilson, 'I wanted to see The Supremes through to its natural conclusion.'

Meanwhile, Diana Ross was working towards becoming an international solo star, a position she holds today.

November 1964

SANDIE SHAW

(There's) Always Something There to Remind Me

Sandie Shaw became a star at the right time. She had the looks, the model figure; painfully thin with long arms and legs, and a face that appeared to be stretched over her high cheekbones. Shoulder-length, straight, dark brown hair, with, of course, the obligatory fringe, fell across both eyes. Indeed, such was the impact of the look, that Sandie Shaw clones could be seen on every street. At one point this was more popular than her records.

With her high-pitched voice that wasn't unattractive, Sandie Shaw forged her way to the top of her profession, despite solid competition from Lulu and Cilla Black, although all three stood in tne shadow of Dusty Springfield, who was in a league of her own.

Born Sandra Goodrich on 26 February 1947 in Dagenham, Essex, Sandie Shaw was the only child of Raymond and Rosina. Following an education at the Robert Clack Technical School, she easily found a position in the local Ford plant as an IBM machine operator. At this point in her life the teenager's exposure to music was listening to records and of course Radio Luxembourg, with singing confined to her spare time. Emulating her music icons James Brown, Dionne

Warwick and Dusty Springfield, Shaw gradually developed a nasal, untrained, yet controlled singing voice that gelled with mid-paced melodies rather than the ballad.

Given the lack of media exposure for pop stars during the early sixties, the surest method of gaining public exposure was to tour Britain and it was during 1964 when Adam Faith and The Roulettes, Eden Kane and Dave Berry hit Dagenham that Shaw talked her way backstage to give Adam Faith an impromptu version of 'Everybody Loves a Lover'. Eve Taylor, Faith's manager at the time, while being mildly amused by the teenager's antics, recognised a raw talent and agreed to represent her within a management deal. Sandra Goodrich became Sandie Shaw. Her ambitions were soon to be realised.

Management wheels were put in motion as Eve Taylor got to work. She enlisted the talent of another of her clients, Chris Andrews, former leader of Chris Ravel and the Ravers, who also wrote for Adam Faith. Taylor felt he would be the perfect match for the young Sandie. Andrews was reticent at first but after hearing certain demo records, he likewise recognised that same raw talent that had encouraged Taylor to take a chance. Together, Andrews and Shaw worked on his composition 'As Long as You're Happy' which became her debut single for Pye Records in July 1964.

Despite great hopes, the single bombed. Undeterred, the search for a follow-up began, but not before it was decided to hold a photo session in the recording studios. What emerged was more than the visual image, because the photographer chanced on one of the most memorable gimmicks of the decade. He noticed Sandie Shaw had kicked off her shoes because her feet were aching, and from this moment the singer's trademark was born. Doubtless bare feet became a liability because irrespective of where she was pictured, lounging at home, in the TV studios or walking along Piccadilly, she was shoeless. How many Sandie Shaw clones suffered injuries to their feet is not clear!

'(There's) Always Something There to Remind Me', written by the American partnership of Burt Bacharach and Hal David, was first recorded by Lou Johnson. The chirpy-style song was ideal for Shaw's voice and was released as her second single in 1964. Selling in excess of 25,000 copies daily, it replaced Roy Orbison's 'Oh Pretty Woman' at the top of the British chart where it stayed for three weeks, holding off fellow British acts The Searchers and Julie Rogers with 'When You Walk in the Room' and 'The Wedding' respectively. With this single, Sandie Shaw began a two-year run of hit singles.

Meanwhile, as Lou Johnson took his version of the song into the American Top Fifty, Shaw struck a deal with Reprise Records. Plans were put in hand for her to visit the States to promote her single as it dithered around the American listing. Unfortunately, her work permit was refused at the eleventh hour and the trip was cancelled. Not only did this deny the British singer an immediate Stateside hit, but lost her the chance to join the British invasion of artists who had taken an unexpected stranglehold on the music business there. It was America's loss because throughout the rest of the world, the story was much different – and happier.

A new barefooted star had been born.

Also see: 'Long Live Love', June 1965; 'Puppet on a String', May 1967

December 1964

THE ROLLING STONES

Little Red Rooster

The greatest rock 'n' roll band in the world.

Mick Jagger was born Michael Philip on 26 July 1943 to Basil Joseph and Eva. His brother Christopher was born in 1947. The family lived in Denver Road, Dartford, and Jagger attended Maypole Infants School, later Wentworth County Primary. After passing the eleven-plus examination he moved to Dartford Grammar School, where he passed seven GCE 'O' Levels enabling him to study Advanced English, French and History for two years. He passed 'A' Level History and English before enrolling at the London School of Economics.

Outside school hours Jagger's main interest was music – not rock 'n' roll that was introduced to Britain during the mid-fifties via Bill Haley, but American R. & B., from Little Richard and Chuck Berry. However, one white American artist did impress him – Buddy Holly – and when he saw him perform in Woolwich, he remembered one track in particular, 'Not Fade Away'.

Jagger's first attempt at singing the blues was as lead vocalist in a school friend's group, Little Boy Blue and The Blue Boys, although they never performed before an audience.

Keith Richards was born on 18 December 1943 to Doris and Bert, and the family lived in Chastillian Road, a few streets away from the Jaggers. As a child Richards's soprano voice took him to Westminster Abbey where he sang in the choir. He left when his voice broke. 'I think that was when I stopped being a good boy and started to be a yob,' he once said.

Like Jagger, Richards attended Wentworth County Primary School, but their friendship was short-lived because Richards moved to the Temple Hill Estate on the other side of Dartford. At school he refused to accept discipline, he played truant and his school work suffered. In the hope of changing their son's attitude, his parents enrolled him at the Dartford Technical College. His stay was short. In 1958 he was expelled, with the suggestion he attend Sidcup Art College, the last stop before finding employment. At Sidcup, Richards (having learned to play the guitar by ear) was introduced to American R. & B. and with a group of friends would listen to Little Walter, among others, while 'popping pills'.

Keith Richards and Mick Jagger re-established their friendship on a train journey from Dartford to Sidcup, discovering a mutual friend, Dick Taylor. Jagger invited Richards to play with Little Boy Blue and The Blue Boys. Hence, the two became soulmates.

Brian Lewis Hopkin Jones was born on 28 February 1942 in Cheltenham to Louisa and Lewis. They also had two daughters, but only one survived. Brian Jones, a sickly child, prone to chronic asthma and bronchitis, attended Dean Close School where he excelled at sport. At the age of six he learned to play the piano, later the clarinet and recorder. He passed the eleven-plus examination to attend Cheltenham Grammar School, where he joined the school orchestra as a clarinettist. As a teenager, Jones discovered Charlie Parker, the American saxophonist, and traded his clarinet for a second-hand alto saxophone. In time, he was proficient enough to join local Trad Jazz outfits who played in coffee bars and public houses.

With Advanced Level passes in Chemistry and Physics, plus nine GCE 'O' Levels, Jones was expelled from Cheltenham Grammar School when a fourteen-year-old student became pregnant by him. He worked at a variety of jobs, including shop assistant and bus driver. In his spare time, music consumed him, and he moved from Trad Jazz to join The Ramrods, a rock 'n' roll group. In 1961 and for the second time, Jones fathered a child. This time the mother was Pat Andrews, whom he promised to marry. However, Alexis Korner, from Blues Incorporated, and whom Jones had befriended following his performance in Cheltenham, asked him to move to London to join his outfit. Using the name Elmo Jones, Brian, playing a Gibson, made his debut guest appearance with Blues Incorporated at the Ealing Club. Mick Jagger, Keith Richards and Dick Taylor were in the audience.

In time they formed The Rollin' Stones, a name Jones swiped from a Muddy Waters track, with Mick Avory on drums, Ian Stewart on piano, Rick Taylor on bass, Elmo Lewis and Keith Richards on guitar, supporting Jagger on vocals. By 1962, The Rollin' Stones had regularly supported Alexis Korner's Blues Incorporated and had played at cult clubs like the Marquee. When drummer Mick Avory missed performances, Charlie Watts, part-time drummer with Blues Incorporated, stepped in.

Charlie Watts was born on 2 June 1941 in Islington, and like his parents, was a true Cockney. Throughout his teenage years, he was drawn to jazz and mastered the drums to emulate his heroes. When he left Harrow Art College, he worked for Charles Hobson and Gray, a Regent Street advertising agency, and it was a position he didn't want to jeopardise by playing drums at night. However, when The Rollin' Stones asked him to be their permanent drummer he succumbed to the pressure.

In 1962 bassist Dick Taylor left the group to attend the Royal College of Art. Bill Perks, later known as Bill Wyman, was suggested as his replacement. Born on 24 October 1936 to Kathleen and William Perks in Lewisham, London, Bill attended Beckenham Grammar School where he excelled in mathematics and art. His first job was with City Tote, bookmakers in London's West End, before he was drafted into the Royal Air Force for two years. While stationed in West Germany, he discovered rock 'n' roll, courtesy of the American Forces Network, bought his first guitar and adopted the surname Wyman from a fellow serviceman. When demobbed he worked as a storekeeper with a Streatham engineering company.

By late 1962, Wyman was playing bass guitar on a semi-professional basis, working for entrepreneur Larry Parnes. With this experience behind him, he auditioned for The Rollin' Stones, and debuted as a member in December 1962 at a youth club benefit held in Putney, London.

In January 1963 – with the line-up of Charlie Watts, Bill Wyman, Brian Jones, Ian Stewart, Keith Richards and Mick Jagger – the group performed at The Flamingo Club in London's Soho. This led to a Saturday residency at a Richmond hotel and a daytime spot at Studio 51 in London. However, it was their night-time gigs that attracted a large following. At one such performance Andrew Oldham and Eric

Easton from the Impact Sound Company offered to manage them. Oldham, disliking Ian Stewart's straight appearance, ousted him from the line-up into the role of studio musician and roadie. 'It wasn't done very nicely. I just turned up one day to find the others had stage suits and there was no suit for me,' Stewart told Philip Norman. Oldham also added a 'g' to The Rolling Stones while Keith Richards lost his 's'.

Signing a three-year recording contract with Impact Sound, which in turn leased material to Decca Records, The Rolling Stones recorded their debut single, 'Come On', a version of a lesser-known Chuck Berry track. The single was issued in June 1963 and after much television exposure (which included a spot on the music show *Thank your Lucky Stars* where the group wore matching Carnaby Street outfits) and live promotion it peaked at No. 21 in the British chart. Surprised that their first release had done so well, the group was in two minds how to follow it, although they felt 'Poison Ivy', previously recorded by The Coasters, was a good contender. However, while they were rehearsing in Studio 51, John Lennon and Paul McCartney stopped by and played them a partly finished track, 'I Wanna Be your Man', destined for The Beatles' second album. The song was finished before the two left, and The Rolling Stones recorded a new and previously unissued Beatles track.

Midway through their first British tour as support act to Bo Diddley and The Everly Brothers in November 1963, 'I Wanna Be your Man', with an R. & B. overcoat, was released to soar to No. 12 in the British chart. Early in 1964, the group embarked upon two British tours as headliners. Their first had support acts like The Swinging Blue Jeans and Phil Spector's The Ronettes, while the second included Mike Berry and Billie Davis, among others. During these tours The Rolling Stones destroyed their stage suits for street clothes and sported long hair. According to Jagger, 'The first time I remember talking about anything remotely connected with image was when I was wearing some kind of layered look . . . and either Brian or Keith said it was too effeminate. I didn't understand why I couldn't be effeminate, or be whatever I wanted.' In later years, Jagger believed 'the image stuff' contributed to Jones 'cracking up completely' and to Richard becoming a drug addict.

During March 1964 'Not Fade Away', which had so impressed Jagger during Buddy Holly's performance in Woolwich, was finally recorded during a drunken party that included Gene Pitney, The Hollies' Graham Nash and Alan Clarke, and Phil Spector on maracas. It was released as a single to soar to No. 3 in Britain, establishing The

Rolling Stones as consistent sellers. By now, they also attracted riotous scenes at concerts, the most notable being when they performed at the *Ready, Steady, Go!* Mad Mod Ball and at the *New Musical Express* Poll Winners' concert, both held at Wembley, Middlesex, during April 1964. Their performances also generated hate mail: unlike the clean-cut Beatles, parents believed The Rolling Stones were corrupting teenagers in Britain. Letters screamed of their 'dirty appearance', 'a disgrace to pop music' and 'the ugliest group in Britain'. Yet, the music rolled on.

The Rolling Stones' eponymous album, with advance orders in excess of 100,000 was released during the May. It replaced *With The Beatles* at the top of the British chart. The artwork of the album, similar to *With The Beatles* set a precedent, as The Rolling Stones' name was not featured anywhere on the front sleeve.

On the personal front, Mick Jagger was dating Chrissie Shrimpton, Brian Jones was involved with Linda Lawrence and Charlie Watts had married Shirley Ann Shepherd. (Bill Wyman was married when he joined the group.)

While touring Britain again in 1964, the group were refused admittance to a Bristol hotel for not wearing ties. This was the first in a succession of incidents which would splash the group's name across the tabloids' pages; a price they had to pay for rebelling against the Establishment.

Four months after The Beatles had taken America by storm, The Rolling Stones began their first promotional tour there. This included their television debut on *The Les Craine Show* (an off-peak viewing talk programme) and a verbal backlash from Dean Martin on the ABC TV networked show *The Hollywood Palace*. Sharing the bill with an elephant and acrobats, Martin said when introducing the trampolinist, 'That's the father of The Rolling Stones and he's been trying to kill himself ever since.'

Before returning to Britain, the group received news that they had toppled The Beatles as Top British Group in the *Record Mirror*'s annual readers' poll, and Mick Jagger had been voted Top British Group Member. The group's series of live dates ended in New York at a concert promoted by Murray The K at Carnegie Hall. It was a packed house: America had finally accepted The Rolling Stones. Promoted as 'England's Newest Hitmakers' they were following bands they most despised, like The Searchers and Billy J. Kramer and the Dakotas. Bill Wyman told Philip Norman, 'Everyone we really hated seemed to be doing far better in the States than we were. They'd had a No. 1 record, done a good tour, good TV. We'd got nothing like that to look forward to. No wonder we were depressed . . .'

However, while in America, the group recorded some material at the Chess Studios in Chicago (where they also met Muddy Waters and Chuck Berry) and the first single from these sessions was released in July 1964, with advance orders in excess of 150,000 copies. Titled 'It's All Over Now', it was a sharp-edged rock version of The Valentinos' original, and gave The Rolling Stones their first British chart-topper. As it dominated the chart, two policemen and several fans were hospitalised following their concert in Blackpool, and in the September they embarked upon a further lengthy British tour with The Mojos and Charlie and Inez Foxx, where mass hysteria from young fans equalled that experienced by The Beatles.

After refusing to perform in South Africa before segregated audiences, The Rolling Stones returned to America, where they debuted on *The Ed Sullivan Show*. The television audience caused such mayhem that Sullivan promised the group would never step foot on his stage again, saying, 'It took me seventeen years to build up my show and I'm not going to have it destroyed in a matter of weeks.' Undeterred, The Rolling Stones went on to record the *TAMI Show* in Santa Monica, alongside acts like Marvin Gaye, The Supremes and The Beach Boys; later this was released as the *Gather No Moss* movie in 1966.

Before their next single, 'Little Red Rooster', could be released, Jagger made a court appearance following driving offences in Lancashire and Staffordshire. His lawyer refuted remarks that long hair and criminals were synonymous in a speech that included the argument, 'The Duke of Marlborough had much longer hair than my client and he won some famous battles. He powdered his too, because of the fleas. My client has no fleas . . . Barristers, too, wear long hair in the shape of wigs with curled-up ends. They are not long-haired idiots, but highly intelligent university men.' Mick Jagger was still fined.

In December 1964, the group released its version of Willie Dixon's 'Little Red Rooster', originally recorded by Howlin' Wolf. Many believed The Rolling Stones had taken a chance recording such a blatant blues number, but with Jagger's interpretation of the lyrics and Jones's slide guitar swaying like a musical pendulum, it couldn't fail to reach the top of the British chart. Live performances of the song saw Jagger pouting suggestively, his stance befitting a posing lord-of-the-manor, while Richard, Wyman and Watts appeared totally uninterested, leaving Jones to hold the music together.

It would be a familiar scene.

Also see: 'The Last Time', April 1965; 'Get off my Cloud', November 1965; 'Honky Tonk Women', August 1969

January 1965

THE BEATLES

I Feel Fine

At the close of 1964, *Beatles for Sale*, the group's fourth album, containing eight new Lennon/McCartney tracks and eight cover versions, replaced *A Hard Day's Night* at the top of the album chart. Ringo Starr was rehospitalised to have his tonsils out, while John Lennon read poetry on the Peter Cook and Dudley Moore satirical television revue *Not Only . . . But Also*.

The follow-up to 'A Hard Day's Night' was 'I Feel Fine', which had advance orders in excess of 750,000 copies. It became The Beatles' sixth chart-topper in both Britain and America, and for the first time on disc it featured John Lennon's subtle musical experiments.

Three months prior to the release of 'I Feel Fine', The Beatles once more received a handful of important awards, including Ivor Novello Awards for the Most Outstanding Contribution to Music, Top Selling Single for 'She Loves You' and Second Best Selling Single for 'I Want to Hold your Hand', and lastly, Second Most Outstanding Song for 'All my Loving'.

By this time the group were regular performers on *Ready, Steady, Go!*, the most popular music programme of the decade, screened on Friday evenings. It was the programme to be seen on because, as its opening credits screamed, 'The weekend starts here!' It was a strictly 'live' show, hence the occasions when warts and all (like Dusty Springfield's hair being sellotaped to her cheek) were seen by millions of viewers. However, at the time of the release of 'I Feel Fine' The Beatles were touring Britain and were unable to perform in the studio on the particular Friday night. The show's producers were so keen to include it that they agreed the group could record their appearance for later transmission. It transpired that this was one of several tapings allowed to ensure the single had maximum television exposure.

Following the release of the single, Ringo Starr married Maureen

Cox, and plans were put in operation for the group to start filming their second full-length feature film, *Help!*.

The year 1965 was one of progression. The Beatles were becoming more experimental musically and their lifestyles had altered drastically. The price they paid was enormous, or was it? The total loss of privacy meant they were protected in the world of the privileged. They lacked nothing materially; money flowed like water, they had fabulously expensive clothes and cars, and drugs and sex were always on tap. John Lennon once said, 'We were like kings,' and that their tours 'were like *Satyricon*'.

Their fame and fortune were well established now on an international basis; they were the envy of their contemporaries because every note they recorded turned to gold. How long could this last? With the public's acceptance and encouragement, the quartet of long-haired Liverpudlians was slowly becoming part of the British Establishment. Or were they?

Within a short time, The Beatles would snub their British heritage, deliver a huge blow to their faithful public and eventually strike out in defiance.

Also see: 'From Me to You', May/June 1963; 'She Loves You', October 1963; 'I Want to Hold your Hand', December 1963; 'Can't Buy Me Love', April 1964; 'A Hard Day's Night', August 1964; 'Ticket to Ride', May 1965; 'Help!', August 1965; 'We Can Work It Out'/'Day Tripper', January 1966; 'Paperback Writer', July 1966; 'Yellow Submarine'/ 'Eleanor Rigby', September 1966; 'All You Need Is Love', August 1967; 'Hello Goodbye', January 1968; 'Lady Madonna', April 1968; 'Get Back', May 1969; 'The Ballad of John and Yoko', July 1969

Also No. 1 singles in January 1965: 'Yeh Yeh', Georgie Fame and The Blue Flames; 'Go Now', The Moody Blues

February 1965

THE RIGHTEOUS BROTHERS

You've Lost that Lovin' Feelin'

On first listening to 'You've Lost that Lovin' Feelin'', one could be forgiven for thinking it was recorded at the wrong speed. Nevertheless, the song was one of the few chart-toppers to enter the American Top Thirty on three separate occasions. Following The Righteous Brothers, Dionne Warwick enjoyed a No. 16 hit during 1969, and eleven years on Daryl Hall and John Oates took their version to No. 12.

Bill Medley was born on 19 September 1940 in Santa Ana, California, while Bobby Hatfield was born on 10 August 1940 in Beaver Dam, Wisconsin. Both grew up in Orange County, California, where their musical history started with two groups.

Medley was a member of The Paramours; Hatfield served his apprenticeship in The Variations. Both released singles – The Paramours 'There She Goes' and the solo Bobby Hatfield 'Hot Tamales' on the Moonglow label. Neither were happy with their group's progression so the two worked together as a duo. Bill Medley: 'In Orange County, no white kids sang R. & B., much less sounded black. We idolised Don and Dewey, who were real big in California. To us, they were like two Little Richards. So we ended up doing a lot of their songs and a lot of Ray Charles's songs.'

During a series of school concerts, black marines, who had attended a Santa Ana date, nicknamed the duo 'The Righteous Brothers' and the name stayed. During their act they included Medley's composition 'Little Latin Lupe Lu' which was later released as a single by Moonglow Records during June 1963. When a local record shop had sold its entire stock of two thousand, and when the radio station KRLA used it as a commercial, the single shot to No. 49 in the American chart. Due to this success, Moonglow signed The Righteous Brothers. Two more discs were issued – 'Koko Joe', written by Sonny Bono, and 'My Babe'. Both flopped.

At a concert in 1964 held at Cow Palace in San Francisco, co-starring The Ronettes, among others, Phil Spector conducted the back-up band throughout the entire show. The Righteous Brothers interested him sufficiently for him to buy them out of their Moonglow contract and sign them to his own Philles label. They were his first white artists. Spector then requested the husband and wife team Barry Mann and Cynthia Weil (who worked for Aldon Music) to write for his new signing. Bill Medley told author Joe Smith: 'We went to the Chateau Marmont in Hollywood, and there was a piano, and Barry Mann and Phil Spector sang "You've Lost that Lovin' Feelin'". They had these little high, thin voices. To me they sounded like The Everly Brothers . . . All we did was lower the tune to accommodate my baritone voice and it became like another song.'

151

'You've Lost that Lovin' Feelin'' was The Righteous Brothers' first single under the Philles label early in 1965. It had a big, boomy 'Wall of Sound' Spector production, almost like a controlled explosion, for the few minutes it ran, over which the duo's vocals were deep and thundery, especially Bill Medley's pure baritone/bass voice. 'My love for Little Richard, Chuck Berry and Ray Charles probably accounts for me singing the way I do,' he said. It was a monstrous slice of music that astounded listeners and pushed the single to No. 1 in America, and likewise to the top in Britain, preventing an inferior cover version from Cilla Black doing so. She stalled at No. 2, and rightly so. According to Medley, 'We always felt like we were the tool. "Lovin' Feelin'" was Barry Mann and Cynthia Weil's song, which Phil produced and we sang. We never felt like creative geniuses. We just felt like pretty good rock 'n' roll singers who could get a point across and have a good time.'

In January 1965, while the single was alive in America, the duo's previous record company, Moonglow, cashed in by issuing their early album, *Right Now*, from which 'Bring your Love to Me' was the lifted single; a Top Eighty hit. Moonglow Records continued to release early material which charted. However, they failed to detract attention from the new disc, issued in May 1965, 'Just Once in my Life', this time from the pen of Gerry Goffin and Carole King. Another timeless masterpiece that became a No. 9 American hit.

The Righteous Brothers' success was practically an overnight sensation, and quite frightening for them. They were young, white men who sounded black, from ordinary family backgrounds, and suddenly between two thousand and three thousand fans were flocking to see them perform. According to Medley, 'The good news was that it was happening so fast and we were so busy that we didn't have a clue as to what was going on . . . Our first indication of how big we were getting was when we actually got caught in traffic on the way to our own show!'

'Hung on You', again from the Goffin/King partnership, was next, but it was the B-side that attracted media attention, namely 'Unchained Melody'. The public supported it sufficiently to give The Righteous Brothers a No. 4 hit; No. 14 in the British chart.

'Unchained Melody' had previously been a hit song four times, starting with Jimmy Young, whose version was a British chart-topper; followed by American vocalist Al Hibbler who took it to No. 2: the Les Barter Orchestra and Chorus, who reached No. 10; and Liberace, with a No. 20 hit. All four were released in 1955. Following The Righteous

Brothers' version the most notable was Leo Sayer's 1986 rendition which reached the Top Sixty.

To start 1966, another established song, 'Ebb Tide', was issued. British support was poor, it stalled outside the Top Forty, while in America it shot into the Top Five. It became apparent at this stage in the duo's career that Phil Spector was losing interest in them, preferring to concentrate on new signing, Tina Turner. And when MGM Records offered him a reputed $1 million for The Righteous Brothers' contract, he sold them.

When the Mann/Weil team wrote 'You've Lost That Lovin' Feelin'', they also penned '(You're my) Soul and Inspiration' as its follow-up. When that was passed over, the song was canned, but not lost, because it was The Righteous Brothers' debut single for MGM Records' subsidiary label, Verve. '(You're my) Soul and Inspiration' raced to the top in America, with its sales certifying it gold status, while it had a disappointing British showing in the Top Fifteen.

Sporadic success followed Stateside, and the next time the Brothers charted in Britain was during November 1966 with another 'standard', 'White Cliffs of Dover', re-issued from their days with Phil Spector. British support ensured the duo enjoyed a No. 21 hit. But, once more, the struggle was on, because before 1966 ended, 'Island in the Sun' struggled into the Top Forty.

By 1968, as the hits slacked off, Medley and Hatfield went separate ways. Medley pursued a solo career with no success while Hatfield found a replacement for him and continued as The Righteous Brothers. However, legal problems prevented them from using the name for recording purposes. After seven years of independence, Medley and Hatfield re-formed The Righteous Brothers to release their tribute to a handful of late great artists with 'Rock 'n' Roll Heaven', a No. 3 American hit. Other Stateside hits followed, notably 'Give It to the People', but in 1981 the duo once more split up.

Bill Medley's professional career was the most successful. For instance he duetted with Jennifer Warnes on '(I've Had) The Time of my Life', a song lifted from the *Dirty Dancing* movie. It won the singers a Grammy Award for the Best Pop Performance by a Duo or Group in 1988. He sang 'He Ain't Heavy, He's my Brother' in *Rambo III* but lost out in Britain to The Hollies, who re-issued their original version to take it to No. 1. Finally, he was featured in *Ghost* with 'Unchained Melody'. As this movie reached the status of the biggest grosser during 1990, the single remained in the British top spot for four weeks. Hot on the heels of this unexpected success, the album *The Very Best of The Righteous Brothers* was issued late in the year. The song lifted from that compilation soared to No. 1 in Britain. What was it? 'You've Lost that Lovin' Feelin''.

Also a No. 1 single in February 1965: 'Tired of Waiting for You' by The Kinks

March 1965

THE SEEKERS

I'll Never Find Another You

This Australian quartet was, to all intents and purposes, an extension of The Springfields. When the trio disbanded, Tom Springfield needed a vocal vehicle for his compositions. The Seekers provided just that.

The Seekers, three male vocalists and musicians, were formed during 1963 in Melbourne, Australia, comprising guitarists Keith Potger, born in Colombo, Sri Lanka, on 2 March 1941, and Bruce Woodley, born in Melbourne on 25 July 1942; and Athol Guy, born in Victoria on 5 January 1940, on double bass. All attended the same school, but it wasn't until 1962 when they left school that they met up with Ken Ray to form The Seekers.

By day the group members worked nine-to-five jobs, but at night they played in bars and other venues where they could secure a booking. This lasted for one year, until Ken Ray left the line-up. The Seekers had been booked to perform on a Pacific cruise; not wanting to lose the job, the remaining trio fulfilled the booking. This culminated in them organising all the entertainment aboard the liner, and realising they desperately needed a female vocal attraction in the act.

Meanwhile, Judith Durham, born in Melbourne on 3 July 1943, was singing with jazz bands in her home state. During the day she was a secretary and, by chance, was hired by Athol Guy's company. Within a short time, he had persuaded her to abandon jazz and perform with The Seekers. By 1964, such was their popularity, they were turning down bookings. And it was at this juncture that the quartet decided to cross into the perilous world of professional artists.

It was this line-up that travelled to Britain by accident during 1964. They were booked to perform on a liner cruising between Europe and Australia, and upon arrival in Britain had a couple of weeks' sightseeing break before the return voyage. They failed to make the trip back. While still in Australia, they had sent a tape of their material to the Grade Organisation in London. This in turn prompted a company executive to hasten to Southampton to meet the docking liner. Three weeks later The Seekers had appeared on the popular variety television programme, *Sunday Night at the London Palladium*. The unknown group attracted considerable public acclaim, and before the end of 1964 had guested on over eighteen television shows and countless radio programmes, including *Easy Beat* and *Saturday Swings*.

Two weeks after their Sunday night television debut, The Seekers appeared on the same bill as Dusty Springfield. She encouraged them to remain in Britain and to this end, recruited the help of her brother Tom. For some time, he had searched for a vocal group as his mouthpiece, and asked if they wanted to record his material, including 'I'll Never Find Another You'.

A recording deal with the Columbia label (an EMI Records' offshoot) was negotiated, and 'I'll Never Find Another You' was released as their debut single. With The Seekers' appearances prior to this release building up public interest, the single (predictably) shot to the top of the British chart in March 1965. With no Springfields as competition, The Seekers' future was predicted as successful.

'I'll Never Find Another You' earned the group their first gold disc which was presented to them on BBC TV's music chart show *Top of the Pops* for sales in excess of one million copies. It was the first of two chart-toppers, immediately beating The Springfields who had failed to top the British chart. The single also became The Seekers' first American hit.

The British media quickly hailed the Australians as the most famous folk artists in music history (so far). But there was more to come . . .

Also see: 'The Carnival Is Over', December 1965

April 1965

THE ROLLING STONES

The Last Time

'Every band did outrageous stuff on the road, but we were always singled out. We did stupid things, but we also did do-goody things, like going to hospitals and visiting sick children . . . If you don't do charity work, then you're looked upon as some kind of weirdo.' – Mick Jagger

To start 1965 The Stones toured Australia and the Far East with Dionne Warwick and Roy Orbison. The group was met at Sydney Airport by 3,000 fans who tore down a chain-wire perimeter fence and wrenched up rails from their steel bolts. The media condemned the group out of hand, while audiences crammed into theatres to watch their performances. By the time The Stones left Australia for the Far East, they had four singles in their Top Ten, including their version of The Drifters' 'Under the Boardwalk'. While they were out of Britain their second album *Volume 2* had replaced *Beatles for Sale* at the top of the album chart.

For some time now, Andrew Oldham had wanted Jagger and Richard to compose material for the group in much the same way as Lennon and McCartney did for The Beatles. To date, nothing had been suitable. Then Mick and Keith wrote 'The Last Time' which they recorded at RCA's studios in Hollywood with Phil Spector and Jack Nitzsche as producers. The single was issued in Britain during April 1965 and within eight days it soared to the top of the chart. The Stones also dominated the album chart, while their EP *Five by Five* was the best-selling multi-tracked disc. 'The Last Time' also became an American Top Ten hit.

To capitalise on this across-the-board success, The Stones toured Britain once more, doing seventy sell-out shows. The group also hit the headlines, not with reviews of their performance but rather an incident that concerned Charles Keeley, manager of a service station in Stratford. Keeley testified at West Ham magistrates' court that late at night on 18 March a chauffeur-driven Daimler pulled into his garage forecourt. Bill Wyman (whom he described as a 'shaggy monster') asked to use the toilet. Keeley replied it was 'out of order' and refused to allow him to use the staff one. At this juncture, Mick Jagger and Brian Jones, accompanied by eight youngsters, alighted from the car, pushed Keeley aside, saying, 'We piss anywhere, man.' Jones, Wyman and Jagger then stood in a line and urinated against the forecourt wall. The court convicted the three of 'insulting behaviour' and fined them £3 each, plus costs. The case had been brought to court privately by Charles Keeley and a garage customer Eric Lavender.

The group faced persecution wherever they travelled, particularly from restaurants and hotels, apart from those venues who catered for music business personnel. The Stones had little option but to eat in motorway cafés and the like. The general public too were quick to insult them, claiming both their appearance and manners were crude, while the police harassed them with spot checks and traffic offences.

Following a short stint at the Olympia Theatre in Paris during April 1965, The Stones embarked upon a tour of North America. There they experienced first-hand the power of a (possibly) misguided police force. In Ottawa, a police cordon stood on stage with them, blotting them from audience view, and in Ontario, the chief-of-police unplugged the microphones and amplifiers to stop their performance. Jagger: 'We felt sorry for the fans, not getting a proper show, so we did sort of gang up on the police.' The newspaper headlines the following day were predictable.

Part-way through the tour Keith Richard wrote the riff to a song which he called 'I Can't Get No Satisfaction', although he said it could easily have been called 'Auntie Millie's Caught her Left Tit in the Mangle'. Jagger and Richard subsequently worked on the idea until it was formulated into '(I Can't Get No) Satisfaction', which they recorded at RCA's studios in Hollywood. It became an A-side despite Richard arguing that the public would realise his riff had been swiped from Martha and the Vandellas' 'Dancing in the Street', itself an international chart-topper.

Before they left America, and despite his remark that The Stones would never again appear on his programme, the group performed on *The Ed Sullivan Show* with Dusty Springfield and Tom Jones. They actually appeared twice, once to sing 'The Last Time', and again for a four-song encore that included 'Little Red Rooster' and 'Everybody Needs Somebody'. As The Stones left America, '(I Can't Get No) Satisfaction' topped America's chart for four weeks.

During August The Stones re-signed to Decca Records and Allen Klein became their co-manager with Andrew Oldham. Times were achanging. 'We started out simply to be a good R. & B. band. A few years later, things got a little twisted. The road to success is a very slippery one.' – Mick Jagger

Also see: 'Little Red Rooster', December 1964; 'Get off my Cloud', November 1965; 'Honky Tonk Women', August 1969

Also a No. 1 single in April 1965: 'Concrete and Clay' by Unit Four Plus Two

THE BEATLES

Ticket to Ride

The year of 1965 signified the start of The Beatles' rebellion when their private lives crossed over into the public domain, when the media began splashing headlines about them that were far from welcome.

It was also the year of three chart-toppers. The first was 'I Feel Fine', followed by 'Ticket to Ride', issued during the filming of the group's second movie, *Help!*. John Lennon composed the track prior to leaving for the Bahamas where production of the film was due to start. Before their departure, in April, when 'Ticket to Ride' was issued, The Beatles appeared at the annual *New Musical Express* Poll Winners' concert, held at the Empire Pool, London. They then devoted the bulk of their time to filming and recording.

Within a month of the single's release, news broke that the members of The Beatles were to receive the MBE upon the recommendation of Prime Minister Harold Wilson. The reaction from some past recipients was not favourable, to say the least. In fact, such was the extent of the outrage that several were returned. Among those people to take this course were several Army officers, which angered John Lennon sufficiently for him to tell the media that they received their medals for killing people, while The Beatles entertained them, and deserved them more. It was arguable because the group had generated money for Britain, being one of the country's biggest and most lucrative exports. Others claimed Prime Minister Wilson had bowed down to public pressure, while believing that such a move would increase his popularity among the young.

Whatever the motive and despite the outrage, The Beatles received their MBEs on 26 October 1965 at an Investiture held at Buckingham Palace. The group members, relaxed from smoking marijuana secreted into the Palace in John Lennon's boots, were among approximately 180 people due to be decorated by the Queen. Outside the Palace, hundreds of fans thronged against the gates singing 'God Save The Beatles'. John, George, Paul and Ringo were to be members of the Most Excellent Order of the British Empire, although many believed the MBE stood for Mr Brian Epstein, the man who wasn't honoured but who had only discovered them. In typical showbusiness fashion, after posing with their medals for the ever-hungry photographers, The Beatles held a press reception at the Saville Theatre, which Epstein owned, in London.

Prior to this event. *The Beatles (Invite You to Take a Ticket to Ride)* was the last of BBC Radio's Bank Holiday specials broadcast in June 1965. Since 1963, the group had recorded these programmes, titled *From Us to You*, but for this finale they insisted on a title change to reflect their current image. At the end of June, John Lennon's second book, *A Spaniard in the Works*, was published, while midway through July, Paul McCartney attended the Ivor Novello Awards ceremony in London to collect more awards including Highest Certified British Sales and Most Performed Work of 1964 for 'Can't Buy Me Love'.

The British public may now have been split in its opinion of The Beatles, but the fans stayed loyal. In time that loyalty would also be tested. Yet, for the time being, The Beatles had no equal.

Also see: 'From Me to You', May/June 1963; 'She Loves You', October 1963; 'I Want to Hold your Hand', December 1963; 'Can't Buy Me Love', April 1964; 'A Hard Day's Night', August 1964; 'I Feel Fine', January 1965; 'Help!', August 1965; 'We Can Work It Out'/'Day Tripper', January 1966; 'Paperback Writer', July 1966; 'Yellow Submarine'/'Eleanor Rigby', September 1966; 'All You Need Is Love', August 1967; 'Hello Goodbye', January 1968; 'Lady Madonna', April 1968; 'Get Back', May 1969; 'The Ballad of John and Yoko', July 1969

Also No. 1 singles in May 1965: 'King of the Road' by Roger Miller; 'Where Are You Now (My Love)' by Jackie Trent

June 1965

SANDIE SHAW

Long Live Love

Sandie Shaw's biggest rivals, Cilla Black, Dusty Springfield and Lulu, all failed to achieve a chart-topper in 1965. Instead it was left to newcomer Jackie Trent with 'Where Are You Now (My Love)' and the established barefooted singer with the acceptable face of sixties pop music.

Early in 1965, Sandie Shaw released the follow-up to her British chart-topper '(There's) Always Something There to Remind Me'. Titled 'I'd Be Far Better off without You', it was penned by Chris Andrews, who, like Shaw and Adam Faith, was managed by Eve Taylor. But it was the single's flipside, 'Girl Don't Come', that attracted media attention; therefore the disc was flipped and Shaw enjoyed a British No. 3 hit. 'Girl Don't Come' also charted at No. 42 in America. Once again the singer was refused a work permit by the American Immigration authorities on the grounds that too many bigger-selling British acts were already performing in America. She visited Canada instead.

During February 1965, Shaw debuted in concert as support act to Adam Faith at the De Montfort Hall, Leicester. A month later, her fourth single, 'I'll Stop at Nothing', was released. Chris Andrews had originally written this track for Adam Faith, but changed his mind after hearing Shaw's version. The single was tailor-made for her, as proven when it soared to No. 4 in the British chart. While this single peaked, her debut album *Sandie* became a No. 3 seller; her first and only charting album.

'Long Live Love', another Chris Andrews song, became Shaw's second chart-topper. It stayed at the top for three weeks. The singer had, in actual fact, been offered 'It's Not Unusual' for her next single. When she rejected it, Tom Jones took it to the top of the British chart in March 1965.

'Long Live Love' also cracked the American Top One Hundred, and after two attempts, Shaw finally worked in America, promoting the single on television. It was her final American hit. A misjustice, because if she had been able to promote her work earlier, she could easily have joined her fellow artists in the big-selling league. With America now out of reach, Shaw concentrated on Europe and Australia, where she toured in August 1965. Two months later 'Message Understood' was issued to reach No. 6 in the British chart, with her last single of the year, 'How Can You Tell', faltering in the Top Thirty.

When Burt Bacharach and Hal David wrote 'Alfie', the title track from the movie of the same name starring Michael Caine, Sandie Shaw had the first refusal. She did, leaving her rival Cilla Black to take her version to No. 9 in the British chart, and Cher to enjoy an American hit with her interpretation. Instead, Shaw released 'Tomorrow', her first of 1966 and a Top Ten entrant.

Europe beckoned, and once more she embarked upon a lengthy tour, strengthening her popularity. When this ended, she recorded

'Nothing Comes Easy' as her next release, during June, which stalled in the Top Twenty, while 'Run' and its follow-up, 'Think Sometimes about Me', fared worse by struggling into the Top Forty.

With Shaw being a big-named artist in Europe, and with the Eurovision Song Contest pending, she was the obvious choice to represent Britain. All that was needed was the right song.

Also see: '(There's) Always Something There to Remind Me', November 1964; 'Puppet on a String', May 1967

Also a No. 1 single in June 1965: 'I'm Alive' by The Hollies

July 1965

ELVIS PRESLEY

Crying in the Chapel

In March 1965 Elvis Presley and Colonel Tom Parker celebrated the tenth anniversary of their partnership. Parker revealed that Presley had sold in excess of 100 million records earning an estimated $150 million worldwide. He also confirmed that Presley's 17 movies to date had grossed a further $130 million. Yet, by the start of the seventies, Presley was forced to return to live appearances because the bulk of his earnings had been spent.

As impressive as these dollar signs are, it must be remembered that one half of Presley's income went to Colonel Parker and an estimated 40 per cent in American taxes. Also by the mid-sixties Presley supported a considerable entourage that included members of his family; his employees (who included servants, bodyguards, nursing staff, gardeners, etc.); his drug habit and the medical costs attributed to that (doctors' bills, emergency hospital treatment), his fleet of jet planes, his various properties including the expensive upkeep of Graceland. His generosity, on occasion, knew no bounds.

To the public, Presley was still the King and following a two-year absence, he dominated the British chart once more with the sentimental ballad 'Crying in the Chapel', a song left over from the 1961 recording session for the *His Hand in Mine* album which went on to win him his first Grammy Award for Best Sacred Performance of 1967. The song had previously been recorded by The Orioles, but

Presley's version peaked at No. 3 in the American chart, selling one million copies on the way.

As the single flourished Presley's latest movie, *Tickle Me*, opened in London, while across the Atlantic the singer worked on another, titled *Paradise Hawaiian Style*. In November, *Harum Scarum* opened in America, and for later British release it was retitled *Harem Holiday*. Another was in the pipeline, namely *Frankie and Johnny*. When that opened in London during April 1966, Presley had started another, *Spinout*, which for British release was renamed *California Holiday*.

The movie conveyor belt finally ground to a halt in 1969, leaving Presley no choice but to retire from the big screen. He had starred in 31 films, earning an estimated $400 million (in 1969) without the bonus of associated merchandising and soundtracks. By nineties' standards, Presley's career as an actor had reached blockbusting proportions but as good scripts became scarce and producers dwindled, his usefulness to Hollywood was over.

On the personal front, however, the singer finally married Priscilla Beaulieu on 1 May 1967. The eight-minute ceremony before 100 guests was held at The Aladdin Hotel in Las Vegas; the couple honeymooned in Palm Springs. Their daughter, Lisa Marie, was born on 1 February 1968, and four years later her parents separated.

Elvis Presley would rise again but the price he eventually paid was fatal.

Also see: 'It's Now or Never', November/December 1960; 'Are You Lonesome Tonight', February 1961; 'Wooden Heart', April 1961; 'Surrender', June 1961; 'Rock a Hula Baby'/'Can't Help Falling in Love', March 1962; 'Good Luck Charm', June 1962; 'She's Not You', September 1962; '(You're the) Devil in Disguise', August 1963

Also a No. 1 single in July 1965: 'Mr Tambourine Man' by The Byrds

August 1965

THE BEATLES

Help!

The Beatles' second film, *Help!*, was originally titled *Eight Arms to Hold You*, an apt title because an eight-armed God Kali was a prominent feature in the plot which spun around Ringo Starr's ring and a mad scientist whose aim in life was to remove it from his finger. The movie began with a group of Eastern religious fanatics planning to sacrifice a beautiful girl to their god. The ceremony was due to commence when the high priest discovered the sacrificial ring was missing. Meantime, on the other side of the world, The Beatles were performing, and on the third finger of Ringo's right hand sat that very same ring. The high priest and priestess together with a band of followers travelled to Britain to retrieve it. The movie then concentrated on the chase, the near misses and such like. Unlikely? Totally true. For anyone else, the whole idea would have appeared preposterous. But for The Beatles it was just right.

Help!, produced by Walter Shenson and directed by Richard Lester, was written by Charles Wood and Marc Behm, among others. The Beatles' co-stars this time were Roy Kinnear, Victor Spinetti and Eleanor Bron, and like Wilfred Brambell and Norman Rossington before them (in *A Hard Day's Night*) they threw themselves into the crazy world of make-believe. From the moment when each Beatle entered his own front door in a terraced row, only to walk into a huge communal room stretching behind the four house fronts, fantasy time began. This section was actually filmed in a nearby street to the Twickenham Film Studios where, once again, the bulk of the movie was shot. However, shooting also took place in more exotic locations like the Bahamas, Austria, and at the other extreme, on Salisbury Plain in Wiltshire where the group had a recording session. The entire film was zany and humorous, and like *A Hard Day's Night* was made commercially available on video during the nineties.

'Help!' the single, reported to be John Lennon's plea for help during his depressed and overweight period, was issued worldwide to top the British and American charts during August 1965. The movie and soundtrack quickly followed; the latter, as was expected, immediately peaked at the top of the album charts on both sides of the Atlantic.

The film was premiered in Piccadilly Circus, London, during August, again with Princess Margaret attending. Approximately 10,000 fans crushed into the immediate area to see their four idols while police attempted, in vain, to control them. Ambulances ferried the fainting few to a nearby hospital. By now, of course, these scenes were second nature to The Beatles, but probably not Princess Margaret.

Also during August the Fab Four toured America once again. The opening night at Shea Stadium in New York attracted 55,000 people and broke the record for ticket sales at $300,000 gross. NEMS Enterprises and Ed Sullivan filmed the concert for future transmission, while Capitol Records taped a further performance at the Hollywood Bowl in Los Angeles for future release. It was during this tour that the group met Elvis Presley at his Bel Air Mansion; an occasion that both thrilled and disappointed them. And in San Francisco they met up with Bob Dylan who introduced them to marijuana. The group's LSD intake also escalated to such a pitch that John Lennon admitted he had dropped the drug at least one thousand times. A dentist had first introduced George Harrison and John Lennon to LSD at a dinner party. Harrison: 'It was as if I'd never tasted, talked, seen, thought or heard properly before.'

On a more solid level, in September, Ringo and Maureen Starr's first child Zak was born in Queen Charlotte's Hospital in London, and The Beatles debuted as cartoon characters in an American television series. To close 1965, the group toured Britain for the last time, and a television tribute, *The Music of Lennon/McCartney* was screened. It featured artists like Billy J. Kramer, Cilla Black and Peter Sellers, while The Beatles themselves previewed 'We Can Work It Out' with Lennon playing the harmonium used by Ena Sharples in *Coronation Street*.

Also see: 'From Me to You', May/June 1963; 'She Loves You', October 1963; 'I Want to Hold your Hand', December 1963; 'Can't Buy Me Love', April 1964; 'A Hard Day's Night', August 1964; 'I Feel Fine', January 1965; 'Ticket to Ride', May 1965; 'We Can Work It Out'/'Day Tripper', January 1966; 'Paperback Writer', July 1966; 'Yellow Submarine'/'Eleanor Rigby', September 1966; 'All You Need Is Love', August 1967; 'Hello Goodbye', January 1968; 'Lady Madonna', April 1968; 'Get Back', May 1969; 'The Ballad of John and Yoko', July 1969

September 1965

SONNY AND CHER

I Got You Babe

When the British public first saw the singers responsible for the cute, romantic folk/rock song 'I Got You Babe', everyone probably laughed in disbelief. On the one hand there was a tall, lanky girl with chest-length dark hair, looking every inch the Cherokee Indian, and on the other, a small, funny-looking guy with a silly haircut and big nose. When performing they appeared awkward in their American hippy/mod style of the day – striped flared trousers, leopard-skin waistcoats, shapeless blouses, moccasins and the obligatory sixties blank looks.

Yet despite all this, Sonny and Cher were immediately adopted, with almost a million British people buying 'I Got You Babe', a trend that was to be reflected across Europe.

Sonny wrote the song about two young lovers rich only in love, after a flash of inspiration, and due to its simplicity knew he had a hit on his hands. As Ahmet Ertegun at Atlantic Records in New York had shown an interest in signing the duo, Sonny sent him the song, with another of his compositions. In time, Ertegun contacted Sonny, enthusing over their new single titled 'It's Gonna Rain' with 'I Got You Babe' on the B-side. No amount of begging from Sonny would change Ertegun's mind, leaving Sonny with no option but to play dirty. He took 'I Got You Babe' to KHT, Hollywood's most influential radio station, where programme director Ron Jacob agreed to play it hourly if he could do so exclusively. Sonny agreed and within days Atlantic Records bowed down to public demand. 'I Got You Babe' was the official topside and soared straight to the top of the American chart during August 1965.

Sonny, real name Salvatore Phillip Bono, was born on 16 February 1935 in Detroit, Michigan. During his teenage years, his family moved to Inglewood, California. Music was his first love; his first song was actually inspired by a brand of biscuits, 'Koko Jo'. During 1957 he got the chance to work for Speciality Records, where he wrote and produced for in-house acts. Probably the most notable were 'Needles and Pins' which he co-wrote with Jack Nitzsche for soloist Jackie De Shannon (it was also a 1964 hit for The Searchers), and 'She Said Yeah', originally recorded by Larry Williams and later covered by The Rolling Stones.

Cher was born Cherilyn Sarkasian LaPier in El Centro, California, on 20 May 1946. Her mother, Georgia Holt, a single parent, desperate to become known as an actress, struggled to keep them both. (In fact, in 1946 when John Huston was casting for *The Asphalt Jungle* he hired Georgia for a bit part. At the eleventh hour he changed his mind to cast Marilyn Monroe instead.) Due to her mother's career, Cher was invariably fostered out to friends and family. Reputedly Georgia had four husbands and Cher's sister Georgeanne was born with number three, while Cher herself adopted the surname LaPier from the fourth.

Life for the youngster was obviously unpredictable, exciting and tiresome, but this was to change when she met Sonny Bono in late 1962 in a Hollywood Boulevard coffee house. She was sixteen, he was twenty-seven. Two years after this meeting they married in Tijuana. Sonny had what Cher craved, an inroad into the music business. At this time, Sonny was gofer for producer/composer Phil Spector, and his job included booking singers and musicians for studio work. Through him, young Cher worked as back-up vocalist for a pair of Spector's top female groups, The Ronettes and The Crystals, and also with a duo that was heading for the big time, The Righteous Brothers.

Sonny was keen for Spector to rub some of his musical genius on to Cher but he refused, except for one song, a Beatlemania cash-in, 'Ringo I Love You', issued under the name Bonnie Jo Mason on Annette Records, one of Spector's subsidary labels. If Spector wouldn't help further, Sonny had no choice but to produce Cher himself. He borrowed $135 and booked a session at RCA's Hollywood studios. The result was a duet not by intention but because Cher was too nervous to sing alone. Titled 'Baby Don't Go', it was released as the follow-up to 'I Got You Babe' in September 1965. While working with Sonny, Cher had also secured a solo deal with Imperial Records, where her debut was the Spector-cloned 'Dream Baby' credited this time to Cherilyn, her real name.

But it was to be at Atlantic Records, or rather one of its offshoots, Atco Records, that they would enjoy their first taste of success. Signing as a duo, their recording debut was to have been 'Sing C'est La Vie' but that was replaced by 'Just You'. 'I Got You Babe' followed. The couple's recording career and Cher's solo recordings ran simultaneously now for some time. For instance, when 'I Got You Babe' dominated the American charts, her solo 'All I Really Want to Do' reached No. 15. It peaked at No. 9 in Britain. It was her next single, titled 'Bang, Bang (My Baby Shot Me Down)', produced by Sonny, which became her first solo million-seller in 1966. A cover of Cilla Black's 'Alfie', from the movie of the same name starring Michael Caine, reached the American Top Thirty, but wasn't issued in Britain where Black cleaned up. However, when the movie was issued in the States, Cher's version replaced Black's on the film credits. 'I Feel Something in the Air' replaced 'Alfie' in Britain, followed by Bobby Hebb's 'Sunny'. Both were Top Fifty hits.

By this time Sonny and Cher, as a duo, had enjoyed four consecutive British hits following 'Baby Don't Go', namely 'But You're Mine',

'What Now my Love', 'Have I Stayed Too Long' and 'Little Man'. By 1972, with three further hits – 'Living for You', 'The Beat Goes On' and 'All I Ever Need Is You' – the carnival was over. So was their marriage, prompting Cher to record and release 'Living in a House Divided' – solo.

The next few years for Cher were topsy-turvy. She wandered through a succession of record deals, enjoying success and suffering failures. Her personal life hit highs and lows, all liberally reported in the tabloid press. But her star was rising in the movie world where she eventually shone. Following stints on Broadway, the singer was nominated for an Oscar in 1984 for Best Supporting Actress to Meryl Streep in *Silkwood*. A year later, her leading role in *Mask* delighted cinema-goers, while her best was yet to come, co-starring with Jack Nicholson in the celebrated *The Witches of Eastwick*. Yet it was for her role in *Moonstruck* that she finally won the Oscar for Best Actress. The date was 12 April 1988, the day before her ex-husband Sonny was elected mayor of Palm Springs.

When her acting career allowed, Cher returned to the recording studios, and 1987 saw her return after a fourteen-year chart absence as a singer of considerable note and interest. Not only was her material a blend of rock/soul, almost an emulation of Tina Turner, but her appearance had been transformed by plastic surgery. She was as stunning in appearance as she was raunchy in her music, and totally at ease with herself. The public fell at her feet, as her recording career entered a new and astoundingly successful phase, thanks to hits like 'I Found Someone', 'If I Could Turn Back Time' and, of course, 1991's 'The Shoop Shoop Song (It's in his Kiss)', taken from her movie *Mermaids*, which co-starred Bob Hoskins. It was an infuriating version of the Betty Everett original that the world loved.

'I Got You Babe' was probably the finest-produced single of its age that offered no complications, just the basic theme of life in the sixties. But Cher doesn't usually include it in her stage shows any more.

October 1965

KEN DODD

Tears

With his spiky hair, protruding teeth, a cheeky tickling stick and a gang of oversized Diddymen, Ken Dodd is still considered to be one of Britain's premiere stand-up comedians. He also has a more serious side – that of a straight singer. Indeed, when he cares to sing, his voice equals that of most contemporary male balladeers.

Born on 8 November 1927 in Liverpool, where he grew up, Ken Dodd was a regular vocal contributor to his church choir. In time he turned to comedy and devised an act that included his alter-egos Professor Yaffle Chuckabutty, Sausage Knotter and Operatic Tenor. He used these characters to sing cover versions of songs popular at the time.

In 1954 Dodd became a professional stand-up comic, performing on the theatre circuit and at summer seasons, notably in Blackpool. His growing popularity on stage led to support appearances at the prestigious London Palladium, before he hosted his own television series.

He signed a recording contract with Decca Records during 1960, and his first singles, 'Love Is Like a Violin', a ballad from the twenties, bolted into the Top Ten. 'Once in Every Lifetime' followed in 1961, a No. 28 hit, then 'Pianissimo' a year later, a Top Thirty entrant. When Dodd's deal with Decca expired, he joined the Columbia label, a subsidiary of EMI Records. Geoff Love, his musical director, steered him to a No. 35 hit with 'Still' during 1963, 'Eight By Ten', No. 22, and the immortal 'Happiness' during 1964 which, surprisingly, faltered at No. 31.

But it was the ballad 'Tears', produced by Norman Newell, that was the best of the bunch. Ken Dodd was in his publisher's office and came across the song's sheet music, claiming, 'I tried it on the piano and liked it.' He then sang it on his radio programme and letters poured in asking him to record it. At this point there were no less than eighteen other versions of the song, from its first recording by Rudy Vallee in 1929 to artists like Layton and Johnstone, Jack Payne, and Bob and Alf Pearson. The sad song captured the public's imagination and it sold in excess of two million copies to reach the top of the British chart in October 1965, where it stayed for five weeks. As 'Tears' peaked, the singer was appearing in *Doddy's Here* at the London Palladium. 'It's a bit different doing a show down south. Up north the more gags you tell, and the faster you tell them, the better the audiences like it. Down south, the audiences are a little slower but they laugh just as loudly. I've never enjoyed a season as much as this one.'

The follow-up to 'Tears' was taken from the Italian original 'The River (Le Colline Sono In Fioro)' which soared to No. 3, and during

1966 Dodd enjoyed a further three hit singles: 'Promises', 'More Than Love' and 'It's Love'. Early in 1967 'Let Me Cry on your Shoulder' re-established him in the Top Twenty but was his last hit until his Top Thirty single 'Tears Won't Wash Away These Heartaches' during July 1969.

The seventies were somewhat kinder to the comic. Over the span of five years he enjoyed four notable hits, although one, 'Brokenhearted' (his second Italian cover version) charted twice, the first time in December 1970 when it peaked at No. 15, and again during February 1971, when it was a Top Forty hit. Dodd's third Italian interpretation, 'When Love Comes Round Again (L'Arca Di Noè)' re-established him in the Top Twenty in July 1971, while 'Just out of Reach (of my Two Empty Arms)' and '(Think of Me) Wherever You Are' both faltered outside the Top Twenty in 1972 and 1975 respectively. The last time Ken Dodd's name appeared in the British Top Fifty was with 'Hold my Hand' in 1981.

With his recording career behind him Dodd continued to make audiences laugh, although his public life took on a sombre note in 1990 when he hit the headlines in a clash with the Inland Revenue. He was accused of tax evasion and to prove his innocence took the Inland Revenue to the High Court. Needless to say, once the trauma of the action was over, the incident was portrayed humorously in his stage act.

November 1965

THE ROLLING STONES

Get off my Cloud

From 1965 through to 1967, Mick Jagger, Keith Richard and Brian Jones would be hounded by the police, who were intent on busting them on drug charges wherever and whenever they could. Such was the extent of this harassment that many felt it contributed to Brian Jones's early death in 1969, while the group itself found working difficult for fear of possible imprisonment. Indeed, one would be forgiven for thinking it was open season on The Rolling Stones.

The British police did not always confine their campaign against the group to drug-related matters. For example, during a tour of 1965, The Stones' concert in Southend was cancelled because the police chief declared their officers would be controlling crowds who flooded to see its illuminations. None would be available for a concert.

However, there was another pressure to be controlled. As Richard said, 'Each single you made . . . had to be better and do better. If the next one didn't do as well as the last one, everyone told you you were sliding. Every eight weeks, you had to come up with a red-hot song that said it all in two minutes, thirty seconds.'

The fast-paced 'Get off my Cloud', hinting at the effects of drug use, was The Stones' next single to race to the top of the British chart, during November 1965. True, the lyrics were subtle, yet to the connoisseur they extolled the delight of being stoned. The single likewise topped the American chart while the group was touring there. It was a depressing trek; they were transferred from one hotel to another, while the media attempted to discredit them. But, more importantly, the public loved them. Their last performance at the Sports Arena, Los Angeles, before an estimated audience of 14,000 people could have seen only four Stones on stage. Keith Richard had been electrocuted the previous evening when his guitar had touched a live microphone. He was, thankfully, only unconscious for a few minutes.

In February 1966, their aptly-titled '19th Nervous Breakdown' stalled at No. 2 in the British chart, ending a run of five consecutive singles chart-toppers. Following its release, The Stones toured Europe before returning to America. By this time, Brian Jones had met Anita Pallenberg. She has said, 'I fell in love with Brian, in love all the way. [Mick] was the one most against my seeing Brian and being around The Stones. He told Chrissie Shrimpton she wasn't to have anything to do with me.'

'The Rolling Stones Tour '66' hit Britain in September with Ike and Tina Turner in support, plus a handful of British acts. The opening night at London's Royal Albert Hall was the scene of massive mayhem where fans stormed the stage, threatening the abandonment of the evening's entertainment. Once again the group was blamed – and they weren't even on stage!

With publicity stills showing the group members dressed in drag, 'Have You Seen your Mother Baby, Standing in the Shadow' was also issued in September. It stalled at No. 5 in the British chart; No. 9 in America. When they appeared on *The Ed Sullivan Show* to promote their next single, 'Let's Spend the Night Together', the lyrics were hastily altered to 'let's spend some time together'. Yes, The Stones continued to rebel.

Following in the British musical tradition, The Stones appeared for the first and only time on the television special *Sunday Night at the London Palladium*. One of the show's highlights was the revolving stage at the close of the programme where all artists stood and waved to the audience. The Stones refused to do this; the media jumped on them with blaring headlines.

As 'Let's Spend the Night Together' sat in the British Top Three, one of the most bizarre drug busts occurred, and one that was remembered through the years for varying reasons. Mick Jagger had ended his relationship with Chrissie Shrimpton to start dating Marianne Faithfull. She was a successful singer in her own right with hit singles that included, 'As Tears Go By', 'Come and Stay with Me', 'This Little Bird' and 'Yesterday'. She had also married John Dunbar in May 1965 when she discovered she was pregnant by him. When she left her husband, she had a son, Nicholas, and a drug habit. Before long, Jagger and Faithfull were seen publicly as a couple and she would also accompany him on tour.

However, probably the most memorable incident in their relationship was the drugs bust at Keith Richard's home in West Wittering, Sussex, during 1967. Richard had invited several friends, including Jagger and Faithfull, to stay for the evening, during which they drank wine, smoked joints and took LSD. Eighteen policemen burst into the house. Faithfull, wrapped in a large rug, who had reputedly been sharing the delights of a Mars bar with Jagger, was whisked into a bedroom and told to let the rug drop, while other guests were frisked by police officers. An amount of drugs was confiscated; Richard was later charged with knowingly letting his house be used for drugs consumption, while the others were charged with possessing unlawful substances. It later transpired that the group had been set up by the same person who had alerted the Sunday scandal sheet the *News of the World* that they would be in residence in Sussex. In turn, the newspaper alerted the Sussex police. While Jagger and Richard made an appearance in court at a committal, Brian Jones was arrested in his London flat on drugs charges.

Musically speaking, one of the most significant projects to be released during 1968 following a series of battles with the Establishment, was The Stones' *Beggars' Banquet* album. Midway through the year, it was delivered to their record company Decca. The company refused to release it, objecting to the artwork showing a toilet covered in graffiti. The group vented its anger by finally releasing *Beggars' Banquet* in a white sleeve, in the form of an invitation. Decca went on to hold a press banquet in London to launch it, but it ended in a custard-pie-throwing circus.

Another era was due to start. This time without Decca and Brain Jones.

Also see: 'Little Red Rooster', December 1964; 'The Last Time', April 1965; 'Honky Tonk Women', August 1969

December 1965

THE SEEKERS

The Carnival Is Over

With The Springfields disbanded, Tom Springfield used his composing talent to recreate their vocal image with The Seekers. This Australian quartet proved to be more successful than the original Springfield trio, until their lead singer embarked upon a solo career. Unfortunately, Judith Durham failed to repeat Dusty Springfield's lead in the chart, although The Seekers' name lived on under another guise.

'A World of our Own' was the follow-up to The Seekers' first chart-topper, 'I'll Never Find Another You'. Although it failed to reach the top, it peaked at No. 3 during April 1965. This was, of course, the year when The Beatles began their career, but The Seekers held on, and against great odds, enjoyed their second No. 1 single with Tom Springfield's composition, 'The Carnival Is Over', during December 1965.

'The Carnival Is Over' sold in excess of one million copies and became the top-selling British single of the year, with Ken Dodd's 'Tears' as runner-up. Horst Jankowski's 'A Walk in the Black Forest' was third, with The Seekers' 'A World of our Own' at No. 4.

Their next single, released in March 1966, was Paul Simon's 'Someday One Day', which reached No. 11 in the British listing, while the second of the year, 'Walk with Me', rose one rung higher, leaving the last of 1966, Malvina Reynolds' 'Morningtown Ride', to re-establish them at No. 2. Prior to the release of this single, and foregoing a sunny Christmas in Australia, the group performed in pantomime in Bristol, opening on Boxing Day. According to Judith Durham, 'We think there's nothing nicer than performing before an audience consisting mainly of children. And there's no greater Christmas present for us than the sound of children enjoying themselves at a pantomime.'

No one could have foreseen the demise of The Seekers at this juncture, but nonetheless, the struggle was to begin. Their final British Top Ten single was the cheery Tom Springfield/Jim Dale composition 'Georgy Girl', taken from the movie of the same name. However, the single fared much better Stateside where it sold in excess of one million copies. A further two singles charted during 1967, namely Kenny Young's 'When Will the Good Apples Fall', a Top Twenty hit in September, and their final British hit, 'Emerald City', which struggled to No. 50 in December.

It seemed inexplicable that after such a strong impact on British music, The Seekers were powerless to sustain their success. But fail they did, and with no hits they disbanded in 1969.

It was inevitable that Judith Durham would embark upon a solo career. She enjoyed limited success, though, with 'Olive Tree' during 1967 her only hit.

Keith Potger, on the other hand, was reluctant to let The Seekers' name die altogether, and encouraged the formation of The New Seekers. Their first hit was Melanie's 'What Have They Done to my Song, Ma' in October 1970, while their most popular, 'I'd Like to Teach the World to Sing', written by Roger Greenaway and Roger Cook, became a No. 1 single during 1971. (The song was later adopted by the Coca-Cola drinks company to promote Coke.) After an extremely successful career, The New Seekers likewise disbanded during 1974. Both the female singers, Lyn Paul and Eve Graham, became soloists, without any great success.

The Seekers re-formed during 1975, when Judith Durham was replaced by Louisa Wisseling, a young Dutch songstress. They were signed to Columbia Records and enjoyed two minor hits during 1977 and 1978, namely, 'I Wanna Go Back' and 'Anthem (One Day in Every Week)'.

Following a handful of compilations celebrating The Seekers' work released between 1974 and 1988, the original Seekers re-formed for a sell-out tour of Britain. This was followed by the Top Ten compilation *Carnival of Hits*, issued by EMI Records.

Judith Durham then continued as a soloist, and as recently as 1995 toured Britain, and during April 1996 returned to promote her album *Mona Lisas*, issued by EMI Records' Premier label.

All it took was one man's inspiration. Tom Springfield masterminded his own trio, The Springfields; later The Seekers, who through Keith Potger gave birth to The New Seekers. All three groups spawned solo female singers.

Also see: 'I'll Never Find Another You', March 1965

January 1966

THE BEATLES

We Can Work It Out/Day Tripper

Following the success of The Beatles' second movie, *Help!*, and bearing in mind that Brian Epstein had signed a three-film deal with United Artists, Richard Lester had begun looking for a suitable third vehicle for the group. He was interested in *The Three Musketeers* featuring Brigitte Bardot as co-star; *A Talent for Loving*, based on Richard London's book, and the rights to which Brian Epstein had already purchased; and Joe Orton's script *Up Against It*, in which a female prime minister was assassinated. Brian Epstein rejected the script because, in his opinion, the idea of Britain having a female prime minister was ludicrous. None of the movies featured The Beatles.

Meantime, the music continued. Both 'We Can Work It Out' and 'Day Tripper' were written by Lennon/McCartney in November 1965, and as a top title couldn't be agreed upon, EMI Records decided to release the titles as a double A-sided single. Promotional films for both songs had already been screened on BBC TV's music show *Top of the Pops* during December 1965, ensuring that public demand would guarantee high chart placings.

Both titles became American hits although 'We Can Work It Out' went on to become The Beatles' eleventh American chart-topper. 'The Sound of Silence' by Simon and Garfunkel knocked the disc from the top, only for it to climb back up again.

When the single was issued in Britain in January 1966, it became the group's ninth No. 1, and the first to have both titles at the top. As the single dominated the chart, George Harrison married Patti Boyd, whom he had first met on the set of *A Hard Day's Night*.

The Beatles' album *Rubber Soul* was issued and, like its precedessors, dominated the album chart in Britain. Before the year was out, the group acknowledged the importance of pirate radio when they recorded a special Christmas greeting for Radio Caroline which was followed by a pre-recorded interview with Paul McCartney. During the broadcast, McCartney was actually staying with his father in Cheshire. His short holiday was marred when he had an accident on his moped; his mouth needed stitching, leaving a five-inch scar.

While McCartney was licking his wounds, John Lennon had some opened for him when his father recorded 'That's my Life (My Love and my Home)' for Pye Records.

Also see: 'From Me to You', May/June 1963; 'She Loves You', October 1963; 'I Want to Hold your Hand', December 1963; 'Can't Buy Me Love', April 1964; 'A Hard Day's Night', August 1964; 'I Feel Fine', January 1965; 'Ticket to Ride', May 1965; Help!', August 1965; 'Paperback Writer', July 1966; 'Yellow Submarine'/'Eleanor Rigby', September 1966; 'All You Need Is Love', August 1967; 'Hello Goodbye', January 1968; 'Lady Madonna', April 1968; 'Get Back', May 1969; 'The Ballad of John and Yoko', July 1969

Also no. 1 singles in January 1966: 'Keep on Running' by The Spencer Davis Group; 'Michelle' by The Overlanders

February 1966

NANCY SINATRA

These Boots Are Made for Walkin'

When your father is Frank Sinatra, choosing a career in music is an easy option. But when Nancy Sinatra decided entertaining was for her, the last thing she wanted was her father's help. She succeeded. Many felt 'These Boots Are Made for Walkin'' was an irritating slice of nothing, held together by an infuriating bass line. When it sold one million copies, they conceded defeat.

Born on 8 June 1940 in Jersey City, New York, Nancy Sinatra was the oldest of three children born to Frank and Nancy Sinatra. While she was still a child, the family moved to Southern California where she attended high school in Los Angeles, before moving on to the University of Southern California where she majored in economics. Naturally, entertainment was in her blood, but she was determined not to rely on her father's fame and influence, so learning to play the piano, taking vocal and dance lessons ran parallel with her studies.

In 1961 she recorded her first single, 'Cufflinks and a Tie Clip', on her father's Reprise label. In fact, she was one of the first artists to be signed to the roster. The media made much of the fact that Frank Sinatra's daughter was following in his footsteps; automatic success was predicted. Unfortunately, the furore was premature, although she subsequently issued a handful of singles including a version of 'True Love', written by Cole Porter. She enjoyed success in Japan but remained an also-ran in her home country. That was until 'So Long Babe' in 1965 which peaked in the American chart at No. 86.

Personal problems clashed with her budding professional life. In a blaze of publicity, she married and subsequently divorced Tommy Sands in 1966, then met Lee Hazlewood. He wrote 'These Boots Are Made For Walkin'' for her because he believed she had experienced enough of life's emotional upheavals to recognise the meaning of the lyrics.

The single was one of 1966's most imposing of songs due to the descending bass at its start. It raced to No. 1 in America, and within weeks was an international hit, including in Britain, where Nancy Sinatra became the first American female singer since Connie Francis with 'Stupid Cupid' in 1958 to reach No. 1. Sinatra had finally found her own niche without her father's help. 'Almost all my life I was Frank Sinatra's daughter. Now I am somebody on my own!' she said. Although the single told the tale of a determined, strong woman in the throes of a love affair, Sinatra was quick to point out the song didn't reflect her because 'I'm as soft as they come'.

More importantly, the single afforded her the opportunity to star in countless American television programmes before she hosted her own *Movin' with Nancy* special.

The follow-up, 'How Does that Grab You Darlin'', soared into the American charts, reaching No. 7; No. 19 in Britain in April 1966. 'Sugar Town' early in 1967 did even better, peaking at No. 5 and No. 8 in America and Britain respectively.

It was at this time that Nancy Sinatra persuaded her father to duet with her on record. The track was 'Somethin' Stupid', the first daughter/father single to top both the American and British charts, during March 1967. It was Frank Sinatra's second British chart-topper in as many years because in 1966 his 'Strangers in the Night' dominated the British listing.

Lee Hazlewood was Nancy Sinatra's second duettist on 'Jackson', the flipside to her solo 'You Only Live Twice', the theme from the

James Bond movie of the same name. This single became a No. 11 British hit.

'Lady Bird' was next, with a poor showing in the Top Fifty, followed by 'Did You Ever', in August 1971, a much stronger track, which took the combined talent of Sinatra/Hazlewood to No. 2 in Britain.

As well as recording, Nancy Sinatra pursued a lucrative acting career. In the mid-sixties she appeared in movies like *For Those Who Think Young*, *Get Yourself a College Girl* and *The Oscar*, in which she played herself. She'll probably be best remembered for her co-starring role with Elvis Presley (with whom she first performed as a five-year-old on a national television programme) in *Speedway* during 1967.

Following her last British hit in August 1971, Nancy Sinatra replaced her 'pop' success with middle-of-the-road releases including 'How Are Things in California'. She then went on to pen a biography about her father.

March 1966

DUSTY SPRINGFIELD

You Don't Have to Say You Love Me

'I was a convent girl and I knew from the age of eight or nine that I had this strange voice. Eventually I got the chance to act out my dream.' Dusty Springfield is considered by many to be the living legend of British pop music. The goddess of the swingin' sixties, the reluctant recluse of the seventies and the enigmatic icon of the eighties and nineties. She broke the mould of the accepted female singer. She wasn't a sex symbol, yet she attracted a passionate attention that is as powerful today as it was three decades ago.

Born Mary O'Brien on 16 April 1939 in Hampstead, London, she was educated in convent schools in High Wycombe and Ealing, West London. She had one older brother, Dion, later to be known as Tom. Their father was an income tax consultant, their mother a vivacious Irish woman. As a red-headed, bespectacled teenager, Dusty Springfield astonished her teachers by declaring her ambition to be a blues singer – even though she didn't know what it meant. She has said, 'I wasn't very good at anything at school . . . My brother passed fourteen subjects with honours. I left at fifteen, the moment I could. I just wasn't that kind of bright.'

Springfield's love of music was shared by Tom and was her means of escaping her strict Catholic upbringing in a middle-class family. However, the youngster had no idea how to pursue her musical ambitions, so worked in a variety of jobs until she was able to steal the limelight from her brother when he sang in local clubs.

During 1958, Dusty Springfield joined the female trio The Lana Sisters, staying for two years. It was an unspectacular yet educational period for her and prepared her to embark upon a second career with her brother and friend Tim Feild as The Springfields. At this point came the name change – Dusty (a nickname from one of her jobs selling dustbins) and Springfield because the trio was rehearsing in a field on a spring day. (Dusty has stuck to this explanation throughout her career, so who's to argue?)

The trio performed as a folk act in London clubs, until Philips Records signed them during 1961. Their debut single, 'Dear John', released that May, bombed, and a month later Tim Feild left to be replaced by Mike Pickworth, later known as Mike Hurst. The Springfields built up a solid reputation with a string of hit singles that included 'Island of Dreams', 'Say I Won't Be There' and 'Come On Home'. But it was the female vocalist with her strange, haunting voice, tightly-bodiced, stiff-petticoated dresses, and blonde bouffants who attracted the attention.

On the strength of their debut album, *Kinda Folksy*, The Springfields were voted by *New Musical Express* readers as the Best British Vocal Group, and when 'Silver Threads and Golden Needles' became their first American hit, they promoted the single there. Springfield fell in love with the country and its black and soul music. However, this love soon turned to frustration; she could not emulate her musical heroes within the confines of The Springfields. It was possibly this attitude that contributed to the trio playing its farewell concert at the London Palladium in 1963, leaving her free to pursue her solo ambitions; her brother Tom to become a full-time composer for other artists, notably 'The Carnival Is Over' for The Seekers, while Mike Hurst turned to record production before managing singer Cat Stevens.

In January 1964, following her debut solo appearance entertaining British troops in West Germany, and her British tour co-starring with Dave Berry and The Searchers, Dusty Springfield issued her first solo single, 'I Only Want to Be with You'. This Phil Spector-inspired song was written by The Springfields' writer/producer, Ivor Raymonde, and Helen Shapiro's lyricist, Mike Hawker. It immediately soared to No. 4 in the British chart, the first record by a British female vocalist to break into the Top Twenty since Vera Lynn in 1952. The single was also the first to be played on BBC TV's new music chart show *Top of the Pops*, although the presence of the St Bernard at her side was questionable. The song was later re-recorded by countless artists including The Tourists, The Bay City Rollers and Samantha Fox. 'I Only Want to Be with You' was also Dusty's first solo hit in America, peaking at No. 12, making her the second British artist after The Beatles to break into the American chart. Incidentally, the Americans refused to believe she was white and British because her vocals were so 'black'. Altogether 'I Only Want to Be with You' charted in nineteen countries.

As she completed a further British tour, this time with Bobby Vee and The Swinging Blue Jeans, Springfield released the clone of 'I Only Want to Be with You', titled 'Stay Awhile'. It was a stop-gap release, and faltered at No. 13 in the British chart during March 1965. A month later, she toured Australia with Gerry and the Pacemakers before undertaking an American promotional tour.

In July 1964, Springfield excelled herself on the Burt Bacharach and Hal David composition 'I Just Don't Know What to Do with Myself'. It was a ballsy monster of a ballad which narrowly missed the British top spot, peaking at No. 3. Meanwhile, a track from her debut album *A Girl Called Dusty* was lifted for American release. Titled 'Wishin' and Hopin'', it became a Top Ten single there, leaving The Merseybeats to enjoy a British No. 13 hit with it.

A further trip to America to record a handful of tracks including the American hit 'All Cried Out', led to a lengthy British tour late in 1964. This stint with Herman's Hermits and Brian Poole and the Tremeloes coincided with the release of 'Losing You', written by brother Tom and Clive Westlake. It became a British Top Ten hit.

In December, Springfield embarked upon a tour of South Africa on the proviso that her performances would be for non-segregated audiences only. A clause to this effect was written into her contract. Yet, when the singer was due to appear in Cape Town, she discovered the audience was segregated and refused to perform. Springfield was placed under house arrest before being deported. She had inadvertently walked into a political storm and it was open season on her when she returned to Britain. According to Springfield, 'My conscience wouldn't let me do it. When I got home I was slagged off. People like Max Bygraves publicly criticised me as a trouble-maker for making it difficult for them to go there to work . . . But what meant something to me was the airline workers, the black guys, lifted their hats when I got on the plane. I thought, "Ah, you did notice, even though I fucked it up.'"

Early in 1965 'You're Hurtin' Kind of Love' was issued. It signified a change in style inasmuch as it was a hard-edged sound where Springfield tore the notes from her throat. Surprisingly, it stalled at No. 37 during February. A month later she was touring Britain once more with The Searchers, among others.

A further change of style occurred during July 1965 with the dance-orientated 'In the Middle of Nowhere'. Its driving, thumping beat returned Springfield to the British Top Ten. The gentler 'Some of Your Loving' followed. Written by Gerry Goffin and Carole King and using back-up vocalists Doris Troy and Madeline Bell, it likewise raced into the British Top Ten. Before the close of 1965, the album *Everything's Coming up Dusty* was issued, packaged in a gatefold sleeve and containing more cover versions of her American peers' numbers than original material.

'Little by Little' was the first single of 1966. Similar in style to 'In the Middle of Nowhere', it failed to emulate its predecessor's success by faltering at No. 17.

If ever there was a 'best' single in Springfield's career, the next was certainly a contender, simply because it gave her a British chart-topper. 'You Don't Have to Say You Love Me', originally 'Io Che Non Vivo (Senzate)', was Italy's entry into the San Remo Song Festival. Springfield claimed, 'I adore Italian songs. They have so much emotion. I think the original was far superior to mine.' Vicki Wickham discovered the song, and asked Simon Napier-Bell to rewrite the lyrics before Springfield recorded it. The result was an intensely emotional song that had involved over forty takes before the singer was satisfied with the results. It sold one million copies to dominate the British chart in March 1966; across the Atlantic it peaked in the Top Five. The song subsequently won chart success for two further artists, Elvis Presley in 1971, when his version peaked at No. 9 in the British chart, and for Guys and Dolls in 1976 when it soared to No. 5.

'Goin' Back' was the follow-up single. Written by Goffin and King, it's considered to be the finest-ever vocal interpretation of one of their compositions. It raced to No. 10 in the British chart during July 1966. A month later, Springfield hosted the first of three television series, titled *Dusty*. The last was screened in 1968 as *It Must Be Dusty*. Meanwhile, 'All I See Is You' was issued before the end of 1966, a No. 9 British hit. She made her debut nightclub appearance at New York's Basin Street East, and returned to Britain for a less glamorous role in a pantomime, *Merry King Cole*, in Liverpool.

Springfield's songs always hinted at unspoken truths of personal emotions which had no gender. She presented her soul for public dissection against a backdrop of plush orchestration and wistful lyrics. However, she was torn between her passion to imitate the sound of black America and the commercial demands of British pop music. Her love of soul music was easily detectable in her early recordings when she slavishly copied songs by The Supremes, Ray Charles, and The Shirelles, among others. In fact, Cliff Richard affectionately nicknamed her 'the white negress', a soubriquet resented by certain black artists like Nina Simone who, on one occasion, threw whisky in Springfield's face, and Dionne Warwick, who accused her of stealing her songs.

At the peak of her success Springfield was also a fashion icon, with heavily lacquered bouffant hairstyles, long slinky gowns, and Panda-black eye make-up. According to her, 'The eyelids were jet black. I never took the stuff off for a week at a time because it took about six days to get a good build-up by using talcum powder and more eye-black. When I finally took it off, I needed an ice-pick!' The singer's clones religiously attended her concerts and at the London television studios of *Ready, Steady, Go!* on which she appeared regularly as singer and MC. Through her involvement with this programme she hosted the historical television special, *The Sound of Motown*. In America she performed with Motown artists at the Brooklyn Theater and while there discovered drugs and alcohol for the first time. Before long that interest became an addiction.

At the end of the sixties, Springfield's consuming ambition to be 'black' reached fruition when she was invited to record at the Atlantic Records studios in Memphis, using Aretha Franklin's musicians and session singers. The emotionally draining album, *Dusty in Memphis*, resulted, to be promoted as the finest soul record ever recorded by a white singer. Ironically, it was her first album not to chart in Britain. 'Son of a Preacher Man' (originally written for Aretha Franklin, who rejected it) was lifted from the album to become a Top Ten hit in both Britain and America during December 1968.

Springfield continued to enjoy minor hits through to the seventies. Then she charted for the last time in Britain in 1970 with a cover version of the Young Rascals' 'How Can I Be Sure?' which stalled in the Top Forty. Across the Atlantic, 'Silly Silly Fool' crawled into the American chart, her last hit. Springfield said, 'I did feel like knocking my head against a wall. You start telling yourself these dark thoughts that seem very real, that maybe your time has passed. Then the panic comes on another level and you start saying to yourself, "If you don't do this, what do you do?"'

In 1972, after refusing to follow her female contemporaries on to the British club circuit, and to escape escalating press attention in the wake of her flagging career, Springfield moved to California, where she disappeared into a haze of drugs and alcohol.

After a three-year hiatus, Springfield signed a recording contract with United Artists in America (Mercury Records in Britain) and released her 'comeback' album in 1978, aptly titled *It Begins Again*. Produced by Roy Thomas-Baker, known for his work with Queen, the album reached the British Top Forty. This success gave her the confidence to tour Britain once again.

From United Artists, the singer moved to 20th Century Records in 1980 to release two significant singles, 'It Goes Like It Goes', the bitter-sweet Oscar-winning track from the movie *Norma Rae*, and the dance-slanted 'Your Love Still Brings Me to my Knees'. Three years later, she moved to Casablanca Records to release the album *White Heat* which did little to rejuvenate her career as it wasn't available in Britain. A year on, she took the unusual step of duetting on disc with Spencer Davis. The track was a cover version of the Judy Clay/William Bell classic 'Private Number', but it failed to repeat the success of the original.

From America, Springfield turned to Britain when nightclub owner Peter Stringfellow persuaded her to record for his newly formed Hippodrome label, so named after his gay nighterie. It was a stormy relationship from the outset; only one single, 'Sometimes Like Butterflies', was issued, against the singer's wishes, in August 1985. When that bombed, Springfield returned to America.

Once more, her life was to change but not at her own hand. During 1987, after a seventeen-year absence, her name was once again listed in the American chart. Richard Carpenter had approached her to record the ballad 'Something in your Eyes', while in Britain pop music's computer wizards, The Pet Shop Boys, persuaded her to collaborate on their single, 'What Have I Done to Deserve This', released by the duo's record label, Parlophone. The single soared to No. 2 in both the British and American charts, and its home success culminated in Springfield performing with The Pet Shop Boys at the British Phonographic Institute's Awards Ceremony, held in London.

A year later, Springfield moved from America to Amsterdam, on her way back to Britain. The move to Holland was to avoid the lengthy quarantine period for her cats required by British law. This time, she did not avoid the media, but lost weight, shed her long, tightly-fitting gowns of the sixties for designer trouser suits, grabbed success with both hands, and ultimately adopted the role of the glamorous diva to reclaim her throne, as dictated by The Pet Shop Boys' music.

The follow-up to 'What Have I Done to Deserve This?' was her solo single 'Nothing Has Been Proved', written and produced by the duo and released during March 1989. The track was featured in the movie *Scandal*, the story of the Profumo affair which overturned the British Government in 1963. The single reached No. 16 in the British chart. 'In Private' followed late in 1989 and also became a Top Twenty hit.

Springfield's former record company, Phonogram, detected her growing popularity and capitalised on her new success by releasing 'The Silver Collection', a compilation featuring her biggest-selling singles. It sold in excess of half a million copies, and earned a gold disc, proving the singer's past was as popular as her present. Meanwhile, executives of the Parlophone label, one of EMI Records' subsidiaries, were suitably impressed with Springfield's pulling power that she was signed to record a solo album, *Reputation*. The title track was lifted as a single during May 1990; it stalled in the Top Forty. The album qualified for a silver disc in November 1990, and another single, 'Arrested by You', was issued, but by this time Springfield appeared to have lost interest in the project. Early in 1991 her deal with Parlophone ended. At the end of the year, though, Springfield once again hit the headlines when impressionist Bobby Davro portrayed her as performing drunk on one of his television shows. Springfield sued the television company and won £75,000 in damages.

Then followed a further hiatus until the singer returned to Nashville, Tennessee, to record the album *A Very Fine Love* released on Sony Records' Columbia label during 1995. During the recording sessions she was diagnosed with breast cancer and following months of gruelling treatment returned to the public spotlight. The first single from the Nashville album was 'Wherever Would I Be', a duet with Daryl Hall. With the record company's reputed lack of interest, the single bombed.

Having won the battle to wean herself off drugs and alcohol, and more recently to fight and win the battle against cancer, the Dusty Springfield of the nineties still commands loyal fan worship. The voice that launched a string of million-selling singles has mellowed, but the irrepressible magic that enthralled three generations remains the same.

THE WALKER BROTHERS

The Sun Ain't Gonna Shine Anymore

They stood on stage like three Hollywood actors – tall, lean and handsome. It was difficult to tell whether the screaming audiences came to look or listen. Walkermania was everywhere.

Scott Engel, born 9 January 1943 in Hamilton, Ohio, mastered the double bass in high school before majoring in music. As a teenager he recorded for a handful of Californian record labels before joining The Routers as their electric bassist. The group recorded 'Let's Go' during 1963, and its follow-up, 'Make It Snappy'.

Gary Leeds, born on 3 September 1944 in Glendale, Los Angeles, learned to play the drums as a teenager and attended New York's Aerospace Technology School. In 1963 he formed The Standells, but following the release of a few singles left to work with Johnny Rivers, later P.J. Proby, with whom he visited Britain.

John Maus, born on 12 November 1943 in New York, was a child actor in the American television series starring Betty Hutton, titled *Hello Mum*. Using the name John Stewart, he moved to the West Coast and met Scott Engel on a television show. The two joined forces during 1964 in Los Angeles, and before the year was out had signed to the Smash label, one of Mercury Records' offshoots, and recorded four tracks with Nik Venet and Jack Nitzsche, including Eugene Church's 'Pretty Girls Everywhere'. It was a moderate Los Angeles hit which led to their cameo appearance in the movie *Beach Ball* with The Supremes. British television producer, Jack Good, then booked them to appear on his show, *Shindig*.

Fresh from his recent British tour with P.J. Proby, Gary Leeds met Engel and Maus and enthused about the exciting new music across the Atlantic. As Maus and Engel were due to be drafted into the American Services, they decided to join Leeds when he returned to Britain.

Early in 1965, The Walker Brothers relocated to London, and were signed to a management deal with Maurice King and Barry Clayman. They, in turn, contacted Mercury's British company, Philips Records, where their head of A. & R., Johnny Franz, agreed to work with them.

'Pretty Girls Everywhere', with John Maus on lead, was their debut single, issued in March 1965. Despite a spot on the popular music programme *Ready, Steady, Go!* and other television appearances, the single bombed. Two months later they debuted on the British stage in Leeds.

For their next single, The Walker Brothers turned to an Everly Brothers flipside, recording 'Love Her', written by Barry Mann and Cynthia Weil, and produced by Nitzsche and Venet in Los Angeles. According to Scott Walker, 'What [they] were tryin' to do was achieve something similar to The Righteous Brothers, only a little more refined, because [they] felt they were gettin' to be a bit of a drag.' 'Love Her' introduced the public to Scott's magnificent, rich voice set against the backdrop of deep, roomy orchestration, almost on a par with Phil Spector's 'Wall of Sound'. The single peaked in the British Top Twenty in June 1965, which in turn led to their first concerts with the newly-formed Quotations as their back-up group.

The Walker Brothers next recorded Burt Bacharach and Hal David's 'Make It Easy on Yourself', previously recorded by Jerry Butler, among others. It was another powerhouse production and their first number recorded in London with Johnny Franz. The single soared to the top of the British chart in September 1965, leaving another version by Bern Elliot at the starting block. A month later it peaked in the American Top Twenty. It was another Phil Spector-influenced track. Scott told authors like Watkinson and Pete Anderson, 'The only way I could get that mammoth sound was to pre-plan everything before goin' into the studio. [At the time the Musicians Union had banned overdubbing, which was how Spector achieved his booming sound.] I did it by usin' large forces in the studio that "leaked" – at that time a very inferior studio which nobody was usin'. So all this leakage of sound – plus the fact I was usin', say, five percussionists, two basses, three pianos – was responsible. It was outrageous. In the studio everyone was on top of each other, but that's how it was done.'

Before their work permits expired the trio performed at the Finsbury Park Astoria, London, where the initial signs of Walkermania were present. Female fans were hysterical, much to the astonishment of the trio. This behaviour would, of course, become the norm as time went by, but to Scott these scenes were his personal nightmare. He cited the trio's arrival at the ABC studios in Birmingham, where they took little notice of a group of girls standing near the building. 'Suddenly they hit us and damn near tore us apart. I got inside and I was bleeding and shocked. I looked at John, and John looked at Gary. "Jesus Christ," was all I could say.' Performing on stage also petrified him and to blot out the audience, he would shut his eyes tightly, or wear sunglasses, while his hands shook uncontrollably. It was probably this nervous disposition that contributed to his heavy drinking sessions – twice he was thrown in jail for being drunk and disorderly, and twice it went unreported by the media.

The first single of 1966 was another cover version, this time Jimmy Radcliffe's 'My Ship Is Coming In', which raced to No. 4 in Britain and stalled in the Top Seventy in America. Meanwhile, their first album, *Take It Easy with The Walker Brothers*, stormed to No. 4.

Due to contractual reasons, Gary Leeds was unable to sing or play with Scott and John on record, although he could perform with them. Instead, he signed a solo contract with CBS Records' subsidiary Columbia, where his first single was titled 'You Don't Love Me'. It reached the British Top Thirty.

In March 1966, The Walker Brothers turned to a 1965 track recorded by Frankie Valli (lead singer of The Four Seasons) titled 'The Sun Ain't Gonna Shine Anymore'. The single raced to the top of the British chart that April where it stayed for four weeks. More powerful and demanding than its predecessors, this was a monstrously beautiful sound, enhanced by Scott's pure, rich vocals. The single also peaked in the American Top Twenty in May and represented the trio's last hit. While 'The Sun Ain't Gonna Shine Anymore' dominated the British chart, Gary Leeds was kidnapped by students from Harrow Technical College to raise funds for their Rag Week. The singer was taken to a London underground station and remained there until collected. The exercise cost Leeds £50.

As Leeds released his second solo outing, 'Twinkie Lee', The Walker Brothers issued '(Baby) You Don't Have to Tell Me' in August 1966, which reached No. 3 in Britain. Their cover version of the Gene McDaniels' classic, 'Another Tear Falls', hotly followed to soar to No. 12 that October. During the single's life, the trio embarked upon a major British tour with The Troggs, among others. The final single of the year was 'Deadlier than the Male' from the movie of the same name. Surprisingly, it stalled at No. 34 in the British chart.

The Walker Brothers' image was beginning to crack. Alongside the declining record sales, internal politics were causing grief between Scott and John, and this was starting to infiltrate their live performances. It had already affected their recorded output when an EP, *Solo Scott – Solo John* was issued late in 1966.

Early the following year, the trio toured Australia, with The

Yardbirds and Roy Orbison sharing the bill. On the flight from Britain, the plane developed engine problems, plummeting Scott into panic, whereupon he was sedated for the remainder of the flight. This in turn, marred the tour from the outset. In February 1971, 'Stay with Me Baby', a cover of the heart-wrenching Lorraine Ellison original, was issued. It faltered at No. 26 in the British chart.

Despite falling sales, The Walker Brothers continued to perform to sell-out, hysterical audiences, and that reaction looked likely to endure. However, in March they toured Britain for the last time with co-stars Jimi Hendrix and Cat Stevens. At the last performance they announced to a shocked audience their intention to break up.

John: 'I've known Scott for four years and now I can't even talk to him.'

Scott: 'Thank God it's over.'

A cover of The Ronettes' 'Walking in the Rain' was issued as The Walker Brothers' final single in June 1967, to become a Top Thirty hit in Britain.

John Maus was the first to be reviewed performing as a soloist in Paris. Gary Leeds followed by participating in the recording of The Beatles' 'All You Need Is Love' for the BBC TV *Our World* spectacular. Meanwhile, Scott Engel was rushed to a London hospital following a fall in Regent's Park.

The first solo Walker Brothers' release was 'Annabella' by John Maus in August 1967: a Top Thirty hit. The first of the trio to make a guest appearance on television was Scott Engel on *Down at the Old Bull and Bush*, and it was, surprisingly, Engel who would seriously pursue a solo recording career.

Using the name Scott Walker, he released the Jacques Brel composition 'Jacky' early in 1968, a stunning single which Radio One confined to late-night airing because of its lyrics pertaining to a man's bizarre reflection on his childhood. According to Scott, 'I felt it was so refined and beautiful even if it stands a good chance of being banned and crushed.' This limited exposure confined it to a Top Thirty hit. 'Joanna' followed that June to become his biggest-selling single to date, soaring to No. 7 in the British chart. Despite his loathing of live performances, Scott joined The Paper Dolls and others on a lengthy British tour at the end of the year. 'I'm prepared to over-prostitute myself to get money to live on,' he said.

Then Scott was offered the chance to host his own weekly television series. Eventually it ran for two months. The spin-off album, *Scott Walker Sings Songs from his TV Series*, was released during July 1969, the same month as his last hit, 'Lights of Cincinnati' was released.

Following a quiet spell and against all odds, The Walker Brothers re-united during 1975 to sign a recording deal with GTO Records. A year later they issued 'No Regrets', a cover version of the Tom Rush hit. Performed as only the three Walkers could do it, the track soared to No. 7 in the British chart in January 1976. An album bearing the single's title followed to become a Top Fifty hit. The trio subsequently stayed together for two further albums, *Lines* and *Nite Flights*, their last in July 1987.

After signing a recording contract with Virgin Records, Scott Walker issued the album *Climate of Hunter* during 1984. A year on, he switched to Fontana Records but no project was released. He was then persuaded to join other sixties' artists like Dusty Springfield, Sandie Shaw and Dave Dee, in an extra-special television advertisement for the soft drink Britvic. It was shot in black and white and was claimed by music fans to be the most outstanding advertisement of 1987.

With the advent of the nineties, Fontana Records issued a solo Scott Walker album, *Boy Child – The Best of 1967–1970*, and The Walker Brothers' compilation, *After the Lights Go Out – The Best of 1965–1967*. A further compilation was then issued in 1991 titled *No Regrets – The Best of The Walker Brothers 1965–1976*.

John Maus: 'Scott and I both have strong personalities and Gary used to be in the middle. We split because Scott and I disagreed on what we should do . . . who knows what we could have achieved if we had stuck it out together.' – *Sunday People*, 1992

Also a No. 1 single in April 1966: 'Somebody Help Me' by The Spencer Davis Group

May 1966

MANFRED MANN

Pretty Flamingo

'We had the reputation of being a rather stand-offish and unfriendly lot. This only came about through our reluctance to conform with the social side of showbusiness' – Manfred Mann, the keyboardist with the group of the same name. He also disputed that the group was R. & B.-based, yet a significant number of their singles were swiped from

American R. & B. artists. All's fair in love and music, someone should have said.

Manfred Mann originated in 1962 from the Mann-Hugg Blues Brothers, named after its two founder members, Manfred Mann and Mike Hugg. Mann, born Michael Lubowitz in Johannesburg, South Africa, on 21 October 1940, and Hugg, born in Andover, Hants, on 11 August 1942, first teamed up at a Butlin's holiday camp. Paul Jones, born Paul Pond in Portsmouth, Hants, on 24 February 1942, was introduced to the pair at London's Marquee Club. Jones was a former member of The Roosters with future Rolling Stones guitarist Brian Jones and Eric Clapton, among others. Manfred Mann's membership was completed by Tom McGuiness, born in London on 2 December 1941, and Mike Vickers, born in Southampton, Hants, on 18 April 1941.

In 1963, the group performed in a handful of 'in' London clubs including the Crawdaddy, and, of course, the Marquee. By May, after negative responses from countless record companies, they signed to EMI Records' HMV label, and were known as Manfred Mann, a name that annoyed them. According to Mann, 'It wasn't one we wanted. The record company chose it for us as we couldn't think of a better one. But right from the start it caused confusion because people only wanted to talk to me and not the rest of the group.'

'Why Should We Not?' was their debut single in July 1963. It was an instrumental, unlike its follow-up, 'Cock-a-Hoop'. Both bombed. Early in 1964, the producers of the Friday night television music programme *Ready, Steady, Go!* asked Manfred Mann to compose a new theme to replace their outdated 'Wipe Out' by The Surfaris. In February, with weekly television exposure, '5-4-3-2-1' was issued as a single to storm the British chart into the Top Five. 'Hubble Bubble Toil and Trouble' was next; a No. 11 hit.

Manfred Mann's style had been developed: it was British R. & B. (a phrase they loathed) with the lavish use of Paul Jones's harmonica and Mann's keyboard expertise. Mann believes, 'The style of our music was the result of huge failures. We started out as a jazz group and were a miserable flop. We changed to a kind of R. & B. outfit before leaning towards pop. More than anything else, we don't want to be tagged as a group who can only play one type of thing.'

Despite their reluctance to be known as an R. & B. band, Manfred Mann's third release was a cover version of the American soul group, The Exciters' 'Do Wah Diddy Diddy', written by Jeff Barry and Ellie Greenwich. It held the top of the British chart for two weeks in July

189

1964, and repeated that success in America during October. Their first album, *The Five Faces of Manfred Mann*, was also crammed with R. & B. cover versions. Before 1964 was out, they covered a further American soul group classic – The Shirelles' 'Sha La La', which reached No. 3 in Britain, and was a Top Twenty American entrant.

A lesser-paced 'Come Tomorrow' followed in February 1965. As Mann says, 'This surprised a lot of people as it was a beat ballad and a complete breakaway for us. You'd be amazed the difference it made in pulling in the crowds. We have been told we are one of the biggest ballroom draws in the country.' 'Come Tomorrow' raced to No. 4. For its follow-up, Manfred Mann once again turned to America to record the Maxine Brown classic 'Oh No Not my Baby', which faltered outside the British Top Ten.

The title track from the EP *The One in the Middle* pushed the four-tracker into the singles chart to peak at No. 6 in July 1965. Two months on, lead singer Paul Jones gave notice to leave the group, but agreed he would stay until a suitable replacement was found. In October, 'If You Gotta Go, Go Now' was issued to soar to No. 2 and as 1965 closed, Mike Vickers left the line-up to concentrate on record production. His replacements were Jack Bruce and a pair of brass players.

With Manfred Mann now settled for a time, 'Pretty Flamingo' was released to race to the top of the British chart during May 1966. Written by Mark Barkan, it dominated the chart for three weeks. Across the Atlantic, it became a Top Thirty hit.

When 'You Gave Me Somebody to Love' stalled in the British Top Forty, a worrying chart position for a recent chart-topping act, Paul Jones left the group. Jack Bruce followed to form the supergroup Cream with Ginger Baker and Eric Clapton. Both Long John Baldry and Rod Stewart were considered to replace Jones, but eventually Mike D'Abo, born 1 March 1944, from A Band of Angels, was chosen, leaving Jack Bruce's spot to be filled by Klaus Voorman, born in West Berlin, Germany. Further upheaval occurred when the group switched from the HMV label to Fontana Records, where, in September 1966, they chose Bob Dylan's 'Just Like a Woman' as their debut release with Mike D'Abo as lead singer. It reached the British Top Ten. 'Semi-Detached Surburban Mr James' quickly followed, the group's last hit of 1966.

For the next two years Manfred Mann was a charting name – 'Ha! Ha! Said the Clown' and 'The Mighty Quinn (Quinn the Eskimo)', among others – while ex-member Paul Jones enjoyed solo status with

'I've Been a Bad Bad Boy' and 'Thinkin' Ain't for Me'. He also co-starred with Jean Shrimpton in the movie *Privilege*.

During 1969 both Paul Jones's and Manfred Mann's chart runs came to an abrupt end. Jones's last was 'Aquarius' that February, while Manfred Mann's 'Ragamuffin Man' reached the Top Ten three months later. The group subsequently disbanded.

Initially, Manfred Mann formed a jazz outfit, before working with Mike Hugg under the title Manfred Mann Chapter Three. In turn, this became Manfred Mann's Earth Band in the summer of 1971. A year later, they signed a recording deal with Polydor Records, and eventually scored a Top Ten single with 'Joybringer'. Although the Earth Band was primarily a touring unit both in Britain and America, they did issue the occasional album from which singles were lifted. In 1976, with a change of record company to Bronze, the band enjoyed further success with 'Blinded by the Light', and 'Davy's on the Road Again' in 1978.

Right up to 1993 Manfred Mann (whose catchphrase must be 'never say die') has progressed with the Earth Band in spite of various line-up changes, and has recorded new material alongside the flow of re-issues from the sixties and seventies.

June 1966

FRANK SINATRA

Strangers in the Night

Frank Sinatra developed a style, born from swing bands, that encompassed all types of music from the mellowest of ballads to the flimsiest of 'pop' songs. Through his apprenticeship with the best band leaders America had on offer, Sinatra's reputation grew to unrivalled heights in the entertainment business. Even the dubiousness of his private life that included links with the Mafia did nothing to tarnish his international status. 'Ol' Blue Eyes' is part of the American institution, for better or worse.

Born Francis Albert Sinatra on 12 December 1915 in Hoboken, New Jersey, he started singing while at the Demarest High School. He left to work as a sports writer on *The Jersey Journal* but continued to sing locally in his spare time, later forming his first group, The

Hoboken Four, who went on to win first prize on *Major Bowes' Amateur Radio Hour* in 1935.

Sinatra moved on to become the vocalist with Harry Arden's Band and enjoyed regular radio spots on WNEW's *Dance Band Parade*. During 1939, orchestra leader Harry James chanced to hear the broadcast and was interested in the male vocalist, who wasn't identified on air. He went to the radio station and offered Sinatra a job as his vocalist. While with James, he recorded two tracks, 'Melancholy Mood' and 'From the Bottom of My Heart', Sinatra's debut single.

From Harry James's orchestra, Sinatra joined Tommy Dorsey's during December 1939, where he was featured vocalist on approximately ninety songs. He also appeared in the movie *Las Vegas Nights* with Dorsey's band, singing 'I'll Never Smile Again'. This song, incidentally, became the first chart-topper on *Billboard*'s singles listing, published in 1942.

Midway through 1943, Sinatra left Tommy Dorsey to concentrate upon a solo career, initially as a contributor to the radio programme *Your Hit Parade*, while Columbia Records re-issued 'From the Bottom of my Heart', this time credited to Sinatra. The resulting sales were sufficient for the record company to sign him as a soloist. A year on, the singer turned to the big screen where his first major role was in the movie *Higher and Higher*, followed by a spot in the musical *Anchors Aweigh*.

Using the Bobby Tucker Singers as support vocalists, Sinatra released a series of show tunes until he hitched up with arranger Axel Stordahl, to record approximately 200 songs like 'Nancy (with the Laughing Face)' and 'Full Moon and Empty Arms' during his ten-year stay with Columbia Records.

There followed a sluggish period at Columbia from 1950 to 1953 which prompted the singer to move to Capitol Records. As he was rebuilding his recording career, Sinatra was offered a role in the movie *From Here to Eternity*. He went on to win a Oscar in 1954 for Best Supporting Actor. As a Capitol artist Sinatra worked with Nelson Riddle and together they produced the big-selling 'Young at Heart' in 1954 which became his first British Top Twenty single in July 1954, followed by his first chart-topper, 'Three Coins in the Fountain', two weeks later. From the series of albums he recorded, including *Songs for Young Lovers*, Sinatra enjoyed several British hits in 1955, like 'You My Love', 'Learning the Blues' and 'Not as a Stranger'.

Working with material penned by Sammy Cahn and Cole Porter, among others, Sinatra's appearance in the British chart was practically monthly with songs like 'Love and Marriage' and '(Love Is) The Tender Trap' (a television and movie theme respectively), while 'All the Way', a Top Thirty British hit in December 1957, won him a Grammy. 'Witchcraft', his first single of 1958, reached No. 12, while his second of the year, namely, 'Mr Success' entered the British chart three times, finally peaking in the Top Thirty. Three singles charted during 1959: 'French Foreign Legion', 'Come Dance with Me' and 'High Hopes', which entered the chart twice, until it peaked at No. 6 during September.

Sinatra continued to record a slew of albums, usually with producer Dave Cavanagh, including *Only the Lonely* in 1958 and *Nice 'n' Easy* during 1960, when the album's title track reached No. 15 in the British chart in September, followed two months later by 'Ol' MacDonald', a Top Ten hit.

Early in 1961, Sinatra took the unusual step of forming his own record label, Reprise. His first release was the album *Sinatra Swings*, while his first British hit on the new outlet was 'Granada' in September 1961, a Top Thirty British hit. Other Reprise acts included Dean Martin and Sammy Davis Jr, but when, in 1963, Warner Brothers purchased the label, Sinatra was its only signing.

By this time, the singer had enjoyed a lucrative acting career. He had co-starred with Gene Kelly in *On the Town*, played opposite Doris Day in *Young at Heart*, and made starring appearances in *Guys and Dolls* and *High Society*. He was as much in demand as an actor as a singer.

Recording-wise, Sinatra worked through the sixties with Billy May, Duke Ellington, Count Basie and Ella Fitzgerald, and continued to enjoy single chart status with tracks like 'Me and my Shadow', and 'Hello Dolly'. Behind the scenes, however, Jimmy Bowen, A. & R. manager for the Reprise label, was given a handful of instrumentals composed by Bert Kaempfert which were destined for the movie soundtrack of *A Man Could Get Killed*. Among the tracks was a melody that Bowen felt would suit Sinatra. Charles Singleton and Eddie Snyder were asked to write English lyrics for this piece of music and by the time the song was finished, both Jack Jones and Bobby Darin were intent on recording it.

In a race against time, Sinatra recorded his version of 'Strangers in the Night' within hours of reading the sheet music. The single was shipped to American radio stations within a day, leaving the competition at the starting block. 'Strangers in the Night' took off at an alarming speed and became a British chart-topper in June 1966 where it stayed for three weeks; a month later it dominated the

American chart and went on to repeat the success in twelve countries.

Within a year Sinatra dominated both the British and American charts once again, this time as duettist with his daughter Nancy on the lightweight 'Somethin' Stupid', which earned them the distinction of being the only daughter/father duet to reach No. 1. On the film front, Sinatra appeared in his third non-singing role playing the main character in *The Detective* (following *The Manchurian Candidate* and *Tony Rome* in 1962 and 1967 respectively).

To date, Sinatra has not repeated his chart-topping success, but for an artist of his calibre does it matter? Nonetheless, 'My Way', adapted from the French song 'Comme d'Habitude' by Paul Anka (who doubtless wished he had recorded it before Sinatra), first issued during 1969, became a powerful contender; in fact, it entered the British chart eight times following its original release. The song has remained synonymous with Sinatra during the years, as has 'Theme from *New York New York*', which was issued twice. It was sung by Liza Minelli in the movie *New York New York* and later adopted as Manhattan's anthem. Sinatra's version peaked at No. 4 in the British chart during 1986.

A spate of recordings followed, but this side of Sinatra's career was second to his live performances in America, and occasionally Britain, where he would command extortionate ticket prices. However, in 1993 he took the unprecedented step of recording with artists like Barbra Streisand, Luther Vandross and Tony Bennett. The first album, *Duets*, was so successful that its sequel, *Duets II*, was issued the following year. Despite being classed as duet recordings, the truth was very few of the chosen artists actually stood at the same microphone as Sinatra. The joys of modern technology!

Frank Sinatra is at the time of writing in his eighties, and while the pace of his life is that much slower, he still holds that magic which the public flock to see during his rare performances. Without doubt he remains one of the finest vocal interpreters known to contemporary music.

THE BEATLES

Paperback Writer

During 1966 The Beatles no longer enjoyed public acclaim for everything they did. Musically they still had no equal, but in other areas the British were quick to condemn. This was a vogue that continued until the group disbanded.

In May 1966, The Beatles performed for the last time at the *New Musical Express* Poll Winners' concert. As in previous years, the 1966 concert was televised because it was such a prestigious music event, and it commanded a multi-million viewing figure. This year, though, The Beatles' performance wasn't televised, not at the group's instigation but because NEMS Enterprises and the television company had failed to reach financial agreement. This disagreement prevented millions from seeing one of the last performances by The Beatles on British soil.

A month after the concert, the Fab Four were escorted through the streets of Hamburg, Germany. The motorcade and police escort celebrated their first visit to the city since 1963. The group performed at Ernst Merck Halle, attracting a sell-out audience in excess of 7,000 people. This trip was followed by three concerts in Tokyo, Japan.

Although the record label credit of 'Paperback Writer' read Lennon/McCartney, it was Paul who actually wrote it, leaving Lennon to compose the B-side, 'Rain', at his Kenwood home studio. By accident the tape of this track was played backwards, and Lennon liked it so much that he added it to the song's ending.

BBC TV's music show *Top of the Pops* was the first programme to screen promotional films for both titles, whereupon The Beatles agreed to perform them 'live' on a later programme. 'Paperback Writer' soared to the top of the British chart during July 1966, but the publicity that surrounded it was hardly expected.

The outcry concerned a photograph used to promote 'Paperback Writer' in a trade magazine advertisement. It showed the group dressed in white overalls holding dismembered dolls and slices of raw red meat, a bloody and sickening mess that bore no relation to the music it was advertising. Across the Atlantic, the same photograph was used on the *Yesterday and Today* album compilation. Like the British before them, the Americans were disgusted with the pose, forcing Capitol Records to stick an innocuous picture of The Beatles on top of the offending sleeves. Further pressings were packaged in new sleeves, making the first run an extremely collectable item.

Also during July 1966, The Beatles flew to Manila for two shows before an audience estimated to be 80,000 strong. While there the group received a party invitation from Imelda Marcos, wife of the country's dictator. Brian Epstein turned down the invitation, claiming the group needed to rest. The British consulate impressed upon him that this was an unwise move but Epstein stuck to his decision. His refusal was televised, with the slant that by snubbing Imelda Marcos's invitation The Beatles had disappointed 300 disabled and orphaned children whom she had also invited to her party. The following day, The Beatles left Manila, fighting off an angry mob waiting for them at the airport. During the scuffle both Ringo Starr and Brian Epstein were injured.

Upon their return to the relative safety of Britain, the partnership of Lennon/McCartney won further Ivor Novello awards at the annual ceremony held in London. 'We Can Work It Out' collected the Highest Certified British Sales of 1965 award and 'Yesterday', the Outstanding Song of 1965 award.

'Yesterday', a soothing ballad of considerable note, written by McCartney, was hidden away on the *Help!* movie soundtrack album. It had been ignored by the media while some radio stations believed it to be a novelty track. Years later, of course, 'Yesterday' was hailed as McCartney's most significant composition and considered a classic by his peers and fans alike.

Also see: 'From Me to You', May/June 1963; 'She Loves You', October 1963; 'I Want to Hold your Hand', December 1963; 'Can't Buy Me Love', April 1964; 'A Hard Day's Night', August 1964; 'I Feel Fine', January 1965; 'Ticket to Ride', May 1965; 'Help!', August 1965; 'We Can Work It Out'/'Day Tripper', January 1966; 'Yellow Submarine'/ 'Eleanor Rigby', September 1966; 'All You Need Is Love', August 1967; 'Hello Goodbye', January 1968; 'Lady Madonna', April 1968; 'Get Back', May 1969; 'The Ballad of John and Yoko', July 1969

Also No. 1 singles in July 1966: 'Sunny Afternoon' by The Kinks; 'Get Away' by Georgie Fame and the Blue Flames; 'Out of Time' by Chris Farlowe and the Thunderbirds

THE TROGGS

With a Girl Like You

This group portrayed an image of being hard rockers to the public but behind scenes they were quietly unassuming. The media poked fun at them, not taking their music seriously. Yet the outfit held prolific songwriters whose work went on to be recorded by other artists. This was typified years after the group disbanded when Wet Wet Wet enjoyed their biggest-selling single of all time with Reg Presley's composition 'Love Is All Around'. Wet Wet Wet recorded it for the movie *Four Weddings and a Funeral* during 1995, earning over £1 million in royalties for the composer.

The Troglodytes were first formed in 1964, with the line-up of Ronnie Bond, born in Andover on 4 May 1943, on drums; Reginald Ball, born on 12 June 1943 (also in Andover), on guitar; supporting vocalist Tony Mansfield, and Dave Wright, second guitarist. They performed in the Andover area of Hampshire. Within a year, Pete Staples, born on 3 May 1944 in Andover, and Chris Britton, born in Watford, Herts, on 21 June 1945, had replaced Mansfield and Wright, leaving Ball to reluctantly take over as vocalist.

During their act, The Troglodytes played material first recorded by The Kinks, and when that group's manager, Larry Page, saw one of their performances, he decided to work with them also. Now known as The Troggs, they recorded and issued their debut single early in 1966. Titled 'Lost Girl', it was written by Reg Ball and issued by CBS Records. It bombed.

Two months on from its release, in April, Larry Page was given the sheet music of 'Did You Ever Have to Make Up your Mind', written by John Sebastian, and a Chip Taylor composition, 'Wild Thing'. The latter song had already been recorded by the American outfit, The Wild Ones, but that had flopped. After dispelling The Troggs' fears that the single's lyrics were pure rubbish, Larry Page whisked them into the recording studios to produce a hard-hitting and raw rock song, as Reg Ball growled his way through the inane lyrics.

'Wild Thing' was issued this time by the Fontana label, following an exclusive arrangement with Page One, Larry Page's own production company. The single soared to No. 2 in the British chart during May 1966, proving that the lyric content wasn't that important after all. In July 'Wild Thing' topped the American chart for two weeks, selling in excess of one million copies. As the American rights for the single had not been sorted out, it was released by two record labels – Atco and Fontana. It really couldn't fail – double promotion! Subsequently, 'Wild Thing' earned the distinction of being the first American chart-topper to be simultaneously released by two separate record labels.

With success came a name change. Following a suggestion from a music journalist, Reg Ball became Reg Presley, the surname borrowed from his idol Elvis. The Troggs, with their incredibly basic and rock-hard music, had by now secured a niche for themselves with the record-buying public. And it was a style that would stand them in good stead for a while yet.

'With a Girl Like You' was next. Written by Reg Presley, it was a diluted version of 'Wild Thing' and raced to the top of the British chart for a two-week stay during July 1966. In America, sales were slow because it had already been the flipside to the Atco release of 'Wild Thing'. Nonetheless, the group went on to enjoy a Top Thirty hit. *From Nowhere – The Troggs*, their first album, was released at this time to reach the British Top Ten, while The Troggs themselves embarked upon their first serious British tour with The Walker Brothers, among others.

At the end of 1966, the next single, 'I Can't Control Myself', again penned by Presley, was issued on the Page One label. It peaked at No. 2 in the British chart, but, surprisingly, stalled at No. 43 across the Atlantic.

To start 1967, the group turned again to Chip Taylor and his composition 'Any Way that You Want Me'; another Top Ten British hit. Following a further tour, the Troggs reverted to Presley for their next single, 'Give It to Me', which reached No. 12 in Britain. In June a change of style appeared with 'Night of the Long Grass'; the buying public lapped up this also to push it into the Top Twenty, yet when The Troggs released a version of Geno Washington's stomper, 'Hi Hi Hazel', it stalled in the Top Fifty. The decline of the group had started, but Reg Presley managed to temporarily halt the descent with 'Love Is All Around', a ballad of considerable note. It raced into the British Top Five; reaching No. 7 in America.

By 1968 their hit run had finished. 'Little Girl', a Top Forty hit, signified their last chart placing. Almost overnight the career of The Troggs was turned upside down, and this dilemma wasn't helped when, following a disagreement with Larry Page which led to a High Court hearing, the manager and group split up. The Troggs had little choice but to turn to the club circuit again, where for a time they earned a lucrative living. But that soon ended, and in 1969 The Troggs disbanded, leaving Ronnie Bond and Reg Presley to pursue solo careers with no success.

The mystique of The Troggs ensured a loyal American cult following, particularly when a bootleg tape of a recording session was made available to fans. Titled *Troggs Tapes* it comprised filthy language, West Country style, alongside unissued material. It was this interest that encouraged Presley and Bond to re-form The Troggs, with Tony Murray and Richard Moore, during 1972.

In time, the 'new' Troggs were reunited with Larry Page to record a version of The Beach Boys' 'Good Vibrations'. It bombed in 1975. This was followed by '(I Can't Get No) Satisfaction', previously recorded by The Rolling Stones and Otis Redding, which likewise bombed.

With American interest still aroused, The Troggs toured there during 1976 as part of a revival package, and when *Vintage Years*, a compilation of their sixties hits was also issued, additional interest was generated across Britain and Europe. But it was the American support that sustained the group, now a quintet with the addition of guitarist Colin Fletcher. Not only were they regular touring attractions there, but in 1980, recorded an album, *Live at Max's Kansas City*, for Basement Records.

Ten years on, in 1990, 'Wild Thing' received a new lease of life. First it was used on the Lion Bar television advertisement, encouraging viewers to eat a nutty chocolate bar, and then it was used on ITV's Saturday night *Gladiators* spectacular, where bulging-muscled bodies underwent the most incredible of athletic manoeuvres.

As recently as 1996, The Troggs were featured in a British touring sixties package promoted by the Flying Music Group.

September 1966

THE BEATLES

Yellow Submarine/Eleanor Rigby

At the time of this single's release, John Lennon believed The Beatles were destined to break up. The individual members had varying ideas about the direction they should follow which naturally led to dissatisfaction and frustration. Yet remarkably, those feelings were not reflected in their musical output; the fact that they worked so closely together was a miracle in itself. The Beatles as a whole, they felt, was far more important than any individual, and it was, they believed, unthinkable that the group should continue without its original membership. Happily, the dilemma was put on the back burner for at least three years.

The combination of the two songs, 'Yellow Submarine' and 'Eleanor Rigby', was strange to say the least. The first title featured Ringo Starr on lead, making people feel it was a song geared for children. To date, Starr's vocal contributions had been confined to album tracks and were, to all intents and purposes, simple, memorable tunes. However, this time the Ringo Starr track was significant. *Yellow Submarine* was the title of a cartoon film, written by Erich Segal and featuring The Beatles' music. It was also the last in the trio of movies that Brian Epstein owed United Artists.

The group distanced themselves from the movie as much as possible, although they did throw together a handful of songs and allowed impressionists to mimic their voices on screen. The animated film was premiered at the Pavilion Cinema, London, leaving Epstein free to negotiate film rights for The Beatles.

'Eleanor Rigby', on the other hand, was as complex as 'Yellow Submarine' was simple. Paul McCartney wrote the song in tribute to Eleanor Bron who co-starred with the group in *Help!*, and 'Rigby' he swiped from a shop front in Bristol. Despite the odd combination, the titles shot to the top of the British chart during September 1966; the second Beatles' single to bear two titles and became a chart-topper. The single went on to win the 1966 Grammy Award in the Best Contemporary (Rock 'n' Roll) Solo Vocal Performance category.

However, this success paled by comparison to yet another public outcry prompted by an interview John Lennon gave to *The Evening Standard*. He told journalist Maureen Cleave that 'Christianity will go. It will vanish and shrink. I needn't argue about that. I'm right and I will be proved right. We're more popular than Jesus now. Jesus was all right but his disciples were thick and ordinary.' The British public took little or no notice of Lennon's remarks but the Americans turned nasty, particularly those living in the southern Bible Belt. To prove their disgust, record stores refused to stock the group's records, radio stations banned their music and Beatle records were burned in the streets.

OCTOBER 1966

As The Beatles' final American tour was imminent and as Brian Epstein was loath to cancel it because of the millions of dollars involved, he demanded that Lennon apologise to the American nation. Major television networks screened Lennon's press conference, and the tour started.

Their final concert was held at Candlestick Park in San Francisco, before an estimated 25,000 people. The show was filmed and Lennon took photographs. America would never see The Beatles perform 'live' again.

Also see: 'From Me to You', May/June 1963; 'She Loves You', October 1963; 'I Want to Hold your Hand', December 1963; 'Can't Buy Me Love', April 1964; 'A Hard Day's Night', August 1964; 'I Feel Fine', January 1965; 'Ticket to Ride', May 1965; 'Help!', August 1965; 'We Can Work It Out'/'Day Tripper', January 1966; 'Paperback Writer', July 1966; 'All You Need Is Love', August 1967; 'Hello Goodbye', January 1968; 'Lady Madonna', April 1968; 'Get Back', May 1969; 'The Ballad of John and Yoko', July 1969

Also a No. 1 single in September 1966: 'All or Nothing' by The Small Faces

October 1966

JIM REEVES

Distant Drums

He was known as 'Gentleman Jim'. While the public screamed hysterically at pop groups, he wiped the floor with them with his smooth, stylish ballads. Jim Reeves loved country and western music, and songs that were passed down through generations from many origins, claiming, 'Don't get the idea these songs are faded and museum pieces. They're nothing of the kind. They are living, vital music.'

Born in Galloway, Texas, on 20 August 1923, Jim Reeves was raised on his family's farm. At nine years old he made his debut on the local radio station, but his main ambition in life was to be a professional baseball player. That was until a knee injury put paid to any sporting activities. As a youngster Reeves had a stammer, but after taking courses in public speaking, he spoke as easily as he later sang.

201

During 1947, he was a DJ in his home state before recording for the Macy label two years later. He moved to Abbot Records during 1952 to release a pair of country and western hits, 'Mexican Joe', his first million-seller, and 'Bimbo'. Reeves claims, 'I always loved music from the heart, music that spoke people's feelings, simply and directly, which is why country and western songs meant so much more to me, starting from my childhood days.'

In 1955, Reeves joined RCA Records, where he abandoned his country roots to concentrate on contemporary music, although his singles charted in both listings. This was typified by his first RCA hit, 'Four Walls', in 1957, which set the mould for his debut British hit, 'He'll Have to Go' written by Joe and Audrey Allison. Reeves's warm, soft voice boosted the single to No. 36 in March 1960, and No. 12 a month later upon re-entry. 'Country music is a main part of folk music, and it's spreading all the time,' he said. 'I'm really thrilled about the way it's been catching on outside the States. We all seem to be drawing closer and closer together. And that's good.'

During 1961, the velvet-voiced singer enjoyed two further British hits, 'Whispering Hope' in March, a Top Fifty hit, and 'You're the Only Good Thing' during November, which fared much better, peaking in the Top Twenty. With 'Adios Amigo' and 'I'm Gonna Change Everything' notching up further hits during 1962, the best was yet to come.

'Welcome to my World', a beautiful, smooth ballad, as soft as lambswool, soared to No. 6 in the British chart during 1963. Also during that year, Jim Reeves starred in *Kimberley Jim*, a movie shot in South Africa, a country he loved. He had previously toured there with Floyd Cramer and commanded a strong following.

Another classic in Reeves's unique style was issued the following year, namely 'I Love You Because'. Written by Leon Payne and previously recorded by Al Martino, it raced to the Top Five in the British chart, hotly followed by 'I Won't Forget You', which reached No. 3.

It was an immensely fulfilling career by any standards, but tragically Jim Reeves was destined not to enjoy it further. On 31 July 1964 he died when his private plane crashed in Nashville, Tennessee. His music, though, lived on; his record sales increased dramatically, proving death is a powerful selling point. For example, during 1965 he had six posthumous British hits, including 'It Hurts So Much', 'Not until the Next Time' and 'Is It Really Over', while the next year, he reached the top of the British chart in October with 'Distant Drums'. A haunting few minutes of Jim Reeves's magic, a song that has grown old gracefully to become a classic of the decade.

All in all, his singles were best-sellers for three decades, either Top Twenty or Thirty hits – 'When Two Worlds Collide', 'But You Love Me Daddy' and 'Angels Don't Lie' are fine examples – until his last chart entry during February 1972 with 'You're Free to Go', which stalled in the Top Fifty.

Gentleman Jim once summed up the origins of the music he treasured. He explained it had reached America from various parts of the world, and when the pioneers moved westward, they lived dangerously, worked hard and sang of their new lives in the open country. 'Frontiersmen and women wanted words and melodies with a breath of fresh air, and a proud, free spirit. The fiddle was their favourite instrument. It used to be said that the fiddle, the rifle, the axe and the Bible were the trusty friends and faithful allies of the pioneers.'

It was this music that Jim Reeves brought alive.

November 1966

FOUR TOPS

Reach Out, I'll Be There

While American record-buyers were fighting to buy Beatles' records in 1964, Motown Records issued a single that marked the beginning of an extraordinary career for a new group. That single was 'Baby I Need your Loving' from the Four Tops.

The male quartet – with its lead singer Levi Stubbs Jr, born 6 June 1936, and back-up vocalists Abdul 'Duke' Fakir, born 26 December 1935, Lawrence Payton, born in 1938, and Renaldo 'Obie' Benson, born in 1937 – were previously known as The Four Aims. All hailed from the North End of Detroit, Michigan, grew up together and attended the same schools. All were members of different groups until the decision was made to join forces to become The Four Aims. They performed at high school graduation parties, one-night stands and weekend gigs during 1954 before recording their first single, 'Could It Be You', on Chess Records. As there was already a group called The Ames Brothers, the Four Tops were born.

Under this name they toured extensively with middle-of-the-road crooner Billy Eckstine and under his guidance learned the tricks of the trade. Their talent was soon snapped up by Columbia Records where they recorded 'Ain't That Love'. Like their debut release, the single bombed.

Meanwhile, Berry Gordy had opened his record company, Tamla Motown, in Detroit. He'd known the Four Tops for some time and approached them to record for him. Gordy first signed them to his Riverside label, an outlet catering for jazz releases, where they joined fellow acts like Johnny Griffin and Pepper Adams. *Breaking Through*, their debut album, was quietly issued in 1964, followed by *Hello Broadway*, which like its predecessor contained 'standards' aimed at the older record-buyers.

After a rethink Berry Gordy decided to place his young quartet in the hands of his in-house writer/producers Holland, Dozier and Holland, and move the releases to his Motown label. The combination was a perfect musical liaison, as a string of stimulating singles was released one after the other, beginning with the passive 'Baby I Need your Loving' which soared to the top of the American chart. A strong follow-up was needed, so 'Without the One You Love (Life's Not Worthwhile)' was hastily written and released in November 1964.

However, it took another year for the Four Tops to enjoy British success with another American chart-topper, 'I Can't Help Myself', typical of Motown's storming sound, which reached No. 23 in 1965. This single was to be the first of nineteen hits before the Four Tops left Motown in 1972. The quartet could do no wrong as 'It's the Same Old Song', 'Something about You', 'Shake Me Wake Me (When It's Over)' and 'Loving You Is Sweeter Than Ever' paved the way for the cream of the crop in 1966.

Originally the Four Tops were reluctant to record 'Reach Out, I'll Be There' because it was so different to their previous releases, and they were, naturally enough, wary about a change in musical style at this point in their career. According to Levi Stubbs, 'When I first heard it, it was a little foreign from what I thought my bag was as lead singer. I suggested that maybe one of the other fellows could sing it, but they wouldn't go for it. So I gave it the best I had and it turned out to be a monster.' 'Reach Out, I'll Be There' became the group's biggest-ever seller, racing to the top of the world's charts including Britain where it stayed for three weeks. Nobody could escape the haunting, hypnotic sound, with its suffusion of oboes and flutes, or Levi's straining vocals as he tore his throat to reach the unreachable notes.

As the single began its chart descent, The Beatles' manager, Brian Epstein, booked the group for a promotional stint before a second tour was arranged for the following year. Four Tops hysteria gripped Britain. Fourteen thousand fans flocked to see them perform in London alone, where the Royal Albert Hall heaved with the sound of Motown. And it was this that sealed the group's future with British fans.

More million-sellers followed, as gold turned to platinum, with 'Standing in the Shadows of Love,' 'Bernadette', 'Seven Rooms of Gloom' and 'You Keep Running Away'. All carried the hallmark of the distinctive Four Tops' sound, so ingeniously created by Motown's in-house trio.

Then within a year, in 1968, the Four Tops' style drastically changed. Holland, Dozier and Holland were in a contractual dispute with Motown and were on the verge of leaving the company. This move not only affected the Four Tops but fellow artists like The Supremes, Marvin Gaye, and Martha and the Vandellas because they relied too heavily on the trio's material for hits. But like the Four Tops they had no choice, they had to change direction, to move on. An easy version of Left Banke's 'Walk Away Renee' and a relaxed Tim Hardin's 'If I Were a Carpenter' were the next from the quartet – and both were British charters. The Americans, on the other hand, seemed less enthusiastic about the new, softer sound, preferring the frenetic releases that were the past. When the Four Tops issued their most sophisticated album to date, *Yesterday's Dreams,* in 1968, it heralded the more mellow approach while tracks like a previously recorded Holland, Dozier and Holland track, 'I'm in a Different World', were treated as a trip down memory lane.

Now recognised as Motown's ambassadors, the Four Tops embarked upon another promotional visit to London during which Levi Stubbs was arrested on drug and possession of ammunition charges. He was fined, although why he was singled out in the first place remained a mystery. In June 1970 'It's All in the Game', lifted from the immortal *Still Waters Run Deep* album, produced by Frank Wilson, took their new mature sound one step further. The single peaked at No. 5, while the album reached the Top Twenty. Another change of direction also took place during 1970 when the Four Tops teamed up with The Supremes (Mary Wilson, Cindy Birdsong, Jean Terrell) on record. Their joint album was aptly named *The Magnificent Seven* from which their reworking of Ike and Tina Turner's 'River Deep Mountain High' was lifted as the first hit single. A second album, *The Return of the*

Magnificent Seven, and a pot-pourri of musical ideas in *Dynamite* rounded off their joint careers.

In 1971, the Four Tops once again moved on to release Jimmy Webb's 'MacArthur Park', and further still to record 'A Simple Game', produced by The Moody Blues' Tony Clarke. The song was one of two (the other being 'So Deep within You') recorded in Britain, marking the first time a Motown act had recorded outside America. 'A Simple Game', strong and dramatic, became the group's biggest hit at No. 3 since 'Walk Away Renee' in 1968, yet it, like their others, struggled into the American Top Ninety.

When Berry Gordy moved Motown from Detroit to Los Angeles, the Four Tops refused to move, and it was probably this that instigated their signing with Dunhill Records in 1972 to release 'Keeper of the Castle', both as single and album, and the single 'Ain't No Woman'. But despite an excellent start with their new Dunhill career, the Four Tops lost their Midas touch as 1974 turned out to be relatively quiet. By 1981, they had switched labels again, this time to the dance-orientated Casablanca with 'When She Was my Girl', which reinstated them in the chart at No. 3. It seemed the group drifted through record companies (including Motown) and different music styles, trying to find a niche, but nothing worked. Thankfully, Arista Records offered them a deal and heavily promoted their album, *Indestructible*, during 1988. It was bursting with commercial tracks, and the Four Tops were once again chartbound with the lightweight 'Going Loco in Acapulco', taken from the movie *Buster*.

Established as performers and singers for at least three decades, the Four Tops are now a way of life. Their line-up never changed until, tragically, Lawrence Payton died in June 1997 after losing his fight against cancer, and, unlike some, they've survived against the most remarkable odds as musical trends changed during the years. Although they are primarily a touring act, they returned home to Motown in 1995 with plans to record an album a year.

Also a No. 1 single in November 1996: 'Good Vibrations' by The Beach Boys

TOM JONES

Green Green Grass of Home

'The problem with Wales was that there were no record companies . . . People would say to me, "Jesus Christ, you're a great singer, you've got to make it."' – Tom Jones

Born Thomas Jones Woodward in Pontypridd, Wales, on 7 June 1940, Jones wasted no time in pursuing his singing ambitions. The Treforest Working Men's Club in Glamorgan was the venue for his professional debut during 1957, while his first television appearance was on *Donald Peers Presents*. He then went on to form his first group, Tommy Scott and the Senators, to record for EMI Records in 1963. It was an uneventful liaison. While performing in Pontypridd, the singer attracted the attention of Gordon Mills who worked for Leeds Music, and who offered him a management contract. The first move, however, was to change his name to Tom Jones, swiped from the movie of the same name; the second was to secure him a record deal.

Decca Records took up the challenge, and Tom Jones's first single was 'Chills and Fever', a cover version of Ronnie Love's sixties' hit, while behind the scenes Jones made demo recordings for other artists.

In March 1965, 'It's Not Unusual' was released. It soared to the top of the British chart. The song, in actual fact, was written by Gordon Mills and Les Reed for Sandie Shaw. While she pondered, Jones recorded it. When the single was issued in America, it became a Top Ten hit, and because the Americans believed Jones was black, it also charted in the R. & B. listing. Most certainly, his voice contained an emotive edge that was both powerful and soulful.

With a chart-topper to his credit, Jones needed to meet his audiences. For this purpose, he hired the backing group The Squires, and together they debuted at the annual *New Musical Express* Poll Winners' concert staged in London during the April. That same month, Jones appeared for the first time on television's top variety show, *Sunday Night at the London Palladium*.

In May 1965, 'Once upon a Time' was released as the follow-up to 'It's Not Unusual', a poor-selling single which staggered into the British Top Forty. Despite this, Jones embarked upon his first major

British tour that included theatres in Bristol, Nottingham and Cardiff. Due to his American success and following two appearances on *The Ed Sullivan Show*, Jones performed at the Paramount Theater in New York, followed by a spot at the Brooklyn Fox Theater as part of Murray The K's prestigious spectacular, alongside American artists like Ben E. King.

Tom Jones's third Decca single was a cover version of Billy Eckstine's hit, 'With These Hands', released during 1965. It sold better than its predecessor, reaching No. 13 in the British chart; and the Top Thirty in America. For his next release, the singer turned to a song he had recorded earlier with Burt Bacharach. Titled 'What's New Pussycat' it was the theme song from the movie of the same name, and peaked at No. 11 in Britain during August 1965; and at No. 3 in America. Once again, to capitalise on his American success, Jones undertook a lengthy tour there. Before the close of 1965, Jones had recorded a further movie theme, 'Promise Her Anything', again penned by Burt Bacharach, and had hosted his first British television show, *Call in on Tom*.

To start 1966, another movie theme gave the Welshman a Top Forty British hit, a low placing considering it was the title track from the fourth James Bond Film, *Thunderball*. Once more, American success was greater at No. 25. Jones's contribution to music (so far) was honoured during March 1966 when he won a Grammy Award for Best New Artist of 1965.

'Not Responsible' and 'This and That' both charted between June and August 1966, but it was during December that he was re-established as Britain's top-selling artist. Covering Jerry Lee Lewis's 'Green Green Grass of Home', Jones dominated the British chart just before Christmas and stayed there for a staggering seven weeks. Dripping with emotion, the single went on to sell in excess of one million copies – Decca Records' first and Jones's biggest-selling single ever. In America, though, it faltered at No. 11. The *Green Green Grass of Home* album subsequently soared to No. 3 in Britain, but stalled outside the American Top Sixty.

Following a short tour of South America, the singer released 'Detroit City' as the chart-topper's follow-up single. It was another cover version, this time from Bobby Bare, and reached the Top Ten in Britain in February 1967; Top Thirty in America. During this year, the singer fulfilled countless American commitments but was able to allocate time for a short season at London's top nightclub, Talk of the Town. That August, 'I'll Never Fall in Love Again' became a No. 2

British hit. It was, in actual fact, a Lonnie Donegan composition which, when recorded by him, bombed without trace. The last single of the year, 'I'm Coming Home' likewise hit the No. 2 spot in Britain.

By now, Tom Jones had found a niche for himself in the British market. The stronger his vocal delivery, the more records he sold. And none was more powerful than 'Delilah', released in March 1968. It became his third consecutive No. 2 hit in Britain, while in America it peaked at No. 15, following Las Vegas performances and the promise of further dates during the year. 'Help Yourself' and 'A Minute of your Time' completed his 1968 single releases. The former reached No. 5, while the latter faltered at No. 14 in Britain. Their American success was negligible.

After the success of the show *Spotlight* which was recorded in London and televised in America via the CBS TV network, Jones hosted a further variety show, *This Is Tom Jones*. The weekly programme for ABC TV was screened in America on Friday nights, and within two weeks, he commanded peak viewing figures as he fell into the role of entertainer rather than pop singer. Meanwhile in Britain, 'Love Me Tonight' reached the Top Ten in May 1969.

To start 1970, a cover version of Clyde McPhatter's original 'Without Love (There Is Nothing)' was issued to become a Top Ten British single; No. 5 in America. In May, the explosive 'Daughter of Darkness' soared to No. 5 in Britain; two rungs lower in America. The final single of the year was the much-recorded 'I (Who Have Nothing)' which stalled in the British and American Top Twenty. Jones spent the bulk of the year in America where, in particular, he appeared at New York's Madison Square Garden to break the box-office record by selling tickets worth $350,000. This was repeated at a later date in New Jersey.

Three singles during 1971 maintained Jones's profile in the British chart, namely 'She's a Lady', 'Puppet Man' and 'Till'. A further trio the next year also charted: 'The Young New Mexican Puppeteer', 'Letter to Lucille' and 'Something 'bout You Baby I Like'. By now, Tom Jones was the highest-paid singer in the world, and as the bulk of his wealth was in dollars, he took up residence in California in 1975.

With the singer now concentrating on his American career, British fans were left to muddle through in his absence, with recordings few and far between, his selling power diminished. During the eighties, he experimented with country and western music under a new recording deal with Mercury Records. In April 1987, he sang the lead role on the album of the musical *Matador*, based on a Spanish rags to bullring story. He subsequently released two singles from the soundtrack, namely, 'A Boy from Nowhere' which soared to No. 2 in the British chart, and 'I Was Born to Be Me' which didn't. While in Britain promoting this material, 'It's Not Unusual' was reissued by Decca Records, thanks to the (then) European dance influence on the British chart. The single became a Top Twenty hit.

Late in 1988, Jones appeared on the Channel 4 late-night programme *The Last Resort*, hosted by Jonathan Ross, to sing his version of Prince's 'Kiss'. His performance was seen by the instrumental outfit Art of Noise who persuaded Jones to be the vocalist on their version of the track. Released on the China Records label, the single raced into the British Top Five, hitting No. 31 in America. Following this success, the singer had no problem in securing a recording deal with Jive Records.

His first (and only) album under his new contract, titled *At This Moment*, was released in May 1989. A cover version of Phyllis Nelson's 'Move Closer' was lifted as the first single and reached the British Top Fifty. Before the year was out, he recorded the album *After Dark* for Stylus Records which, due to concentrated television advertising, reached the Top Fifty.

Through to the nineties, Tom Jones has continued to record and tour both in Britain and America. He has guested on most of the major televised entertainment shows and performed at numerous charity functions. He is very much established in British music history despite his relocation to America which, many felt, slapped of desertion, because, voice aside, it was the British ladies who in those heady years of his career screamed at, and responded to, his hip swaying, sexual gyrations by throwing panties and telephone numbers at him!

January 1967

THE MONKEES

I'm a Believer

'There was this idea that [a] group was put together, manufactured, to put onto television for the sole purpose of creating hit records . . . We were a very visible part of pop culture, formed by a combination of creative people from movies and television,' Michael Nesmith told Joe Smith.

Davy Jones, born in Manchester on 30 December 1945, was a child actor in Britain starting with *June Evening*, a BBC play. He then moved into ITV's popular soap *Coronation Street* in 1961, playing Colin Lomax, Ena Sharples's grandson, and a year later appeared in the first episode of one of the most popular police series on television, *Z Cars*. Jones then left the small screen for the theatre stage, where he took the role of the Artful Dodger in the British and American productions of *Oliver*. He then returned to television to appear in the American series *Ben Casey*, among others, before appearing with The Beatles on their first performances on *The Ed Sullivan Show*. This led to his first American Top One Hundred hit, titled 'What Are We Going to Do'.

Mickey Dolenz, born George Michael Dolenz Jr in Los Angeles on 8 March 1945, was, like Jones, a child star. He played the lead role of Corky on the American television series *Circus Boy*, before turning to the risque *Peyton Place*, and the racy *Route 66*, both immensely popular television programmes on both sides of the Atlantic. Music-wise, Dolenz performed with Mickey and the One Nighters, later The Missing Links.

Peter Tork, born Peter Thorkelson in Washington DC on 13 February 1944, was an avid member of the folk circuit in and around Los Angeles. He earned a solid reputation by playing with several groups including the Au Go Go Singers.

Mike Nesmith, born Robert Michael Nesmith in Houston, Texas, on 30 December 1942, first entered showbusiness as a follower of the folk circuit in Los Angeles. Under the name Michael Blessing, he recorded for Colpix Records, albeit unsuccessfully.

The four young men met via advertisements for 'Folk and rock musicians-singers for acting roles in a new TV series' placed in *The Hollywood Reporter* and the daily *Variety*, both America trade newspapers. In excess of 400 hopefuls responded, including Paul Williams and Stephen Stills. The advertisement had been placed by producers Bert Schneider and Bob Rafelson who had conceived the idea of the television series based around a vocal group.

In November 1966, the four successful applicants – Davy Jones, Mickey Dolenz, Peter Tork and Mike Nesmith – began filming the pilot show. In January 1966, NBC TV bought the pending series, now titled *The Monkees*. Two months later, while the group members embarked on acting and singing lessons, composers Bobby Hart and Tommy Boyce considered suitable tracks for the group, including 'Last Train to Clarksville'.

By mid-1966, filming started in earnest, with Don Kirshner from Screen Gems in charge of the project, while on the composing front, Gerry Goffin and Carole King, among others, had been hired to work with Hart and Bruce.

A nationwide 'hype' tour was staged prior to the start of *The Monkees* series in September 1966 to ensure maximum viewing from the outset, while the group's debut single, 'Last Train to Clarksville', was issued that November to soar to the top of the American chart. The single bombed in Britain due to the non-appearance (as yet) of the television series. Meanwhile, *The Monkees* shot to No. 1 in the American album chart, where it stayed for thirteen weeks, selling in excess of three million copies.

For the follow-up single in November 1966, the Neil Diamond composition 'I'm a Believer' was chosen. Once again, nothing prevented it from peaking at No. 1 in the American chart, where it stayed for seven weeks. In fact, RCA Records, their American outlet, was hard pushed to cope with its advance order of one million copies, which topped a previous record held by another of their artists, Elvis Presley. In December 1966, The Monkees debuted on stage at Honolulu's International Center Arena, before a staggering 8,000-strong audience. They then toured until the end of the year.

Britain was next to fall under the spell of The Monkees. The hype had crossed the Atlantic and in January 1967, 'I'm a Believer' sold 750,000 copies to become a British chart-topper. The single hung at the top for four weeks, while *The Monkees* was Britain's top-selling album. According to Michael Nesmith, 'Much to everyone's surprise, the thing was an absolute, walkaway, smash hit record. When I say it caught us off-guard, I mean, it blind-sided everybody.'

However, with this unprecedented success came the drawback. The Monkees were conceived as a fictional group of musicians, created by businessmen, and they were now competing against actual musical giants like The Beatles. No one outside showbiz realised The Monkees could not play their instruments! In the studios, musicians were hired for session work, leaving the group to add the vocals. It was true that Mike Nesmith and Peter Tork had musical experience, but Davy Jones and Mickey Dolenz were actors. As Nesmith says, 'We were actors, writers and film makers. None of us had any concept of making records or writing music, or playing in a band. All we knew was that we needed a certain stream of music for the show.'

With the secret leaked, Nesmith and Dolenz visited Britain to impress upon the media that all future recordings would indeed feature all group members as musicians and singers. Meanwhile, their second album, *More of The Monkees*, replaced their debut at the top of the album chart, where it stayed for a staggering eighteen weeks.

During February 1967, 'Last Train to Clarksville' was issued in Britain as the follow-up to their chart-topper 'I'm a Believer'. It was considered a poor seller, peaking in the Top Thirty, and there was more trouble afoot.

Behind the scenes, Don Kirshner resigned from his executive post at Screen Gems, following a confrontation with Mike Nesmith who had demanded that The Monkees be allowed to record their own compositions in future. Publicly, however, Monkeemania continued. 'A Little Bit Me, a Little Bit You' became their third American million-seller, peaking at No. 2 in April 1967, the same month as it reached No. 3 in Britain. The album chart lost *The Sound of Music* from the top spot when *More of The Monkees* was released in May 1967. In America, meantime, their album *Headquarters* – the first on which the group played – replaced The Beatles' chart-dominating *Sgt Pepper's Lonely Hearts Club Band* at the top.

The Monkees continued to play sell-out performances at venues like the Hollywood Bowl, while during June, they performed a trio of concerts at the Empire Pool, Wembley, before standing-room-only audiences. A month on, they embarked upon an extensive American trek with Jimi Hendrix as support act.

'Alternative Title' reached No. 2 in Britain in June 1967, and its follow-up 'Pleasant Valley Sunday' peaked at No. 11 two months later, reaching No. 3 in America. In between the releases, the second series of *The Monkees* started on both sides of the Atlantic.

As their next single, 'Daydream Believer', attained the American top spot, their album *Pisces, Aquarius, Capricorn and Jones Ltd* raced to the top of the British album chart in December 1967. 'Daydream Believer', on the other hand, stalled at No. 5.

As The Monkees started shooting their first full-length movie, *Head*, their television series ended in March 1968 due to tired plots and decreasing viewing figures. A total of fifty-eight episodes had been made. On the recording front, the group collected their tenth gold disc in as many months, while enjoying their sixth million-selling American single with 'Valleri'. The single stalled in the British Top Twenty. With the release of this single, Peter Tork announced his intention to leave the group, tired of the restrictions placed upon the unit. Following the premiere of *Head* in New York during November, he bought himself out of his contract, to form a new group called Release. The remaining

Monkees were likewise eager to disband the group entirely but the financial complications were too enormous for them to consider.

The trio continued recording and performing, but, given falling audiences, they played their last concert in Oakland, California, during November 1969. By 1970, The Monkees were history.

The individual members embarked upon solo careers, until 1975 when, following a lucrative offer from the hamburger giant, McDonald's, to perform in a television commercial, they discussed the possibility of re-forming. Peter Tork, a vegetarian, declined, while Michael Nesmith was uninterested in a one-off proposition. Davy Jones and Mickey Dolenz, on the other hand, recruited Bobby Hart and Tommy Boyce to complete the advertisement, then toured together under the banner 'The Golden Great Hits of The Monkees Show – The Guys Who Wrote 'Em and The Guys Who Sang 'Em'.

During 1977, Mike Nesmith returned to the British Top Thirty with his solo hit 'Rio', and a year later, Jones and Dolenz appeared in the London stage version of *The Point*, written by Harry Nilsson. When the season ended, Dolenz stayed in Britain to work as a freelance director on the television series *Metal Mickey*.

In 1986, The Monkees celebrated their twentieth anniversary in showbusiness, and to celebrate MTV (the American music video channel) screened the group's television series in its entirety, while the group itself re-formed for touring purposes. A year later, they performed in Britain to capitalise on the K-Tel Records' compilation *Hey, Hey, It's The Monkees* which soared into the Top Twenty album chart. At the close of 1986, The Monkees disbanded once more.

Eleven years on, the quartet returned due to public demand. With support act Nancy Boy, The Monkees toured Britain with concerts featuring all their best-known material. To coincide with this 1997 visit, two group videos, containing three episodes of *The Monkees* television series, and a compilation, *The Greatest Hits of The Monkees*, were issued, together with a rerun of the series and the screening of the *Head* movie on Channel Four.

Doubtless they'll be back again!

PETULA CLARK

This Is my Song

From the time she could speak Petula Clark was an entertainer. She had moved from church to radio before she was a teenager; from movies to records before she had reached her twenties. Today she is an international star.

Born on 15 November 1932 in Epsom, Surrey, Petula Clark was encouraged by her father to become a singer. At the age of three she sang in church with her mother, and when she was nine, she auditioned for the BBC Radio programme *It's All Yours*. As a child performer during wartime on radio, Clark was featured in numerous programmes like *The Children's Hour*, while her live performances for the troops earned her the nickname 'The Forces Girl' during 1942.

The following year, Clark joined the Rank Organisation. She appeared in countless movies like *Vice Versa*, *White Corridors*, *Drawn Daggers* and the *Huggett* series with other future stars like Alec Guinness, through the late fifties. Meantime, during 1949 Clark signed her first recording deal with the EMI Records' subsidiary label, Columbia. Her debut single was 'Put your Shoes on Lucy'. A year on, she switched to Polygon Records, later to become Nixa, then Pye Records, where she remained until the early seventies.

Under the guidance of music director Alan Freeman, Clark released the single 'You Are my True Love', and in November 1950 she hosted her first BBC TV show, *Pet's Parlour*, which subsequently ran for three years. Between 1952 and 1954, Clark recorded several children's songs before actually charting at No. 12 with 'Majorca' in 1955. Her second hit of the year was 'Suddenly There's a Valley' which peaked in the Top Ten. During the next two years, a further pair of singles, 'With All my Heart' and 'Alone' reached the Top Twenty in Britain. Early in 1958, 'Baby Lover' became her last hit for nearly three years.

From Britain, the singer turned to France. The president of Vogue Records, the French subsidiary of Nixa, encouraged Clark to record her British hits in French. In turn, this led to her debut French language performance at the Alhambra Theatre in Paris during 1958. Within months, Clark was recording in Paris with Claude Wolff, Vogue

Records' head of promotion. She subsequently signed a recording deal with the French record company and married Wolff in June 1961.

Meanwhile, during February 1961, Clark enjoyed her first No. 1 single in Britain. Titled 'Sailor', and adapted from the German song 'Seeman' by Norman Newell, her version outsold Anne Shelton's which stalled in the Top Ten. The poor-selling 'Something Missing' followed in April, while 'Romeo', released during August, re-established Clark in the Top Ten. Her final single of the year, 'My Friend the Sea', peaked at No. 7 in Britain.

Following Clark's cover version of Lee Dorsey's American R. & B. hit 'Ya Ya Twist' which she sang in French because it was earmarked for the European market, her British career petered out.

However, behind the scenes, Tony Hatch had replaced Alan Freeman as Clark's producer and musical adviser, and it was he who introduced a more commercial slant to her records. The first was 'Downtown', which he had originally written for The Drifters, but in double-quick time, Clark recorded and released the track. It shot to No. 2 in the British chart in November 1964, whereupon Warner Brothers released it in America, where it beat The Beatles to the top of the chart. By selling a million copies during its two-week reign, Clark earned the distinction of being the first British songstress to reach No. 1 in America since Vera Lynn's 'Auf Wiedersehen Sweetheart' in the fifties. 'Downtown' went on to win a Grammy for the Best Rock 'n' Roll Recording of 1964.

Naturally, Clark received television saturation on both sides of the Atlantic. During her first American visit in 1965, she not only sang 'Downtown' on *The Ed Sullivan Show*, but also its follow-up, 'I Know a Place'. Released during April 1965, the single peaked in the Top Twenty in Britain, but in America it soared to No. 3.

While Clark was touring America, 'You'd Better Come Home' was issued in August 1965; it reached No. 44 in Britain and No. 22 in America. She was losing her standing, and as her subsequent singles failed to reach the Top Twenty, she concentrated on stage work, particularly a series of performances at New York's Copacabana. She also made a cameo appearance on the *TNT Award Show* with The Ronettes and Ike and Tina Turner, among others.

Early in 1966, 'My Love' became Clark's second American million-seller; it peaked at No. 4 in Britain. Then once again she suffered a minor setback before 'I Couldn't Live without your Love', penned by Tony Hatch with Jackie Trent, re-established her as a Top Ten artist in both Britain and America. Subsequently, through most of 1966 her time was split between the two countries, as she performed at prestigious venues that included the Savoy Hotel in London, and dates in Las Vegas.

'This Is my Song', written by Charlie Chaplin, was included in his movie, *Countess from Hong Kong*. Clark recorded the track in America with her husband, Claude Wolff, producing. It raced to No. 1 in Britain during February 1967, where it stayed for two weeks, selling half a million copies on the way, holding off another version by ex-Goon Harry Secombe. The single soared to No. 3 in America, and while on a promotional visit there, she performed at the White House for President Johnson.

The chart-topper's follow-up was the catchy 'Don't Sleep in the Subway', a Tony Hatch composition. It faltered outside the British Top Ten during July 1967, while peaking in the Top Five in America. 'The Other Man's Grass (Is Always Greener)' was her first single of 1968. It staggered into the Top Twenty on both sides of the Atlantic, while 'Kiss Me Goodbye' fared much worse that April.

During October 1968, the songstress turned to the big screen to play the role of Sharon McLonergan in the movie *Finian's Rainbow* with Tommy Steele. She had previously rejected a part in *The Valley of the Dolls* and a role in Elvis Presley's *Paradise Hawaiian Style*. A year on, she appeared in her next movie, *Goodbye Mr Chips* with Peter O'Toole.

As remarkable as it seemed, Clark was also the centre of controversy in 1968. During her first American television show, *Petula*, she kissed one of her guests, Harry Belafonte. The programme was sponsored by Chrysler-Plymouth which made its protestations – a white woman doesn't kiss a black man, especially at prime-time viewing – and demanded the kiss be edited. The television network refused, whereupon public outrage ensued.

During the first two years of the seventies, Clark's recording career was relatively dormant but early in 1972 she recorded a version of Tim Rice and Andrew Lloyd Webber's 'I Don't Know How to Love Him' taken from their *Jesus Christ Superstar* musical. The single re-established Clark as a charting artist, albeit in the Top Fifty. In the late seventies, she appeared in the televised musical *Traces of Love* with Paul Jones, before returning to Geneva and her family.

Performances through the eighties included starring as Maria in the London stage version of *The Sound of Music*; appearing in an American Civil War musical titled *Someone Like You* staged at Cambridge, and promoting a remixed dance version of 'Downtown' which crashed into the British Top Ten during December 1988.

Into the nineties and Petula Clark toured Britain for the first time since 1982 before appearing in *Blood Brothers* in New York.

March/April 1967

ENGELBERT HUMPERDINCK

Release Me

With a name like Engelbert Humperdinck one could have been forgiven for thinking he was a comedian. In this instance, the name carved a career for a soloist who had all but given up the music business.

Born Arnold George Dorsey in Madras, India, on 2 May 1936, he was raised in Leicester. His first stab at being a singer was during the fifties when he performed under the name Gerry Dorsey.

Gerry Dorsey was a struggling, all-ambitious soloist when he appeared on the popular television music programme *Oh Boy* following his first attempt at chart success with 'I'll Never Fall in Love Again'. However, manager and composer Gordon Mills came to his rescue by offering to represent him. But by 1963, beat music was strangling Britain and Gerry Dorsey's career was a non-starter.

While coping with further disillusionment. Dorsey fell ill with tuberculosis and watched from the wings as Gordon Mills's latest protégé spiralled up the British chart. Known as Tom Jones, his career escalated almost immediately; his voice was harsh and masculine, while Dorsey's was warm and mature; he was ruggedly attractive, Dorsey was quietly sophisticated. However, instead of Tom Jones leaving his colleague to flounder, he offered a helping hand.

First to go was the name. In its place they chose Engelbert Humperdinck, with obvious assistance from Hansel and Gretel. Next, he was transformed into a balladeer of considerable note. Humperdinck signed a recording contract with Decca Records (also Tom Jones's company), where his first release, 'Dommage Dommage', disappeared without trace. However, the follow-up, a powerful ballad titled 'Release Me', previously recorded by Ray Price during 1954, shot to the top of the British chart in March 1967, two years after Tom Jones's chart-topper 'It's Not Unusual'.

'Release Me' sold in excess of one million copies and dominated the British chart for a staggering five weeks. An album named after the single quickly followed.

To the public, Humperdinck played second fiddle to the established Tom Jones, but Gordon Mills had no intention of producing a Jones's clone. Rather, he wanted to mould Humperdink's image as a middle-of-the-road attraction. He succeeded. Both artists commanded individual followings.

'There Goes my Everything', written by Dallas Frazier, followed the chart-topper to become a No. 2 hit during May 1967. Similar in style to 'Release Me', it proved Engelbert Humperdinck wasn't a one-hit wonder after all.

Also see: 'The Last Waltz', October 1967

May 1967

SANDIE SHAW

Puppet on a String

The Eurovision Song Contest is Europe's premier song competition, and during the years since its inception in 1956 it has either sustained or killed artists' careers. Sandie Shaw was lucky. She lived to sing again.

During the second half of 1966, Sandie Shaw's career began to slowly slide. This was unexpected as she had to date enjoyed two chart-toppers ('(There's) Always Something There to Remind Me' and 'Long Live Love'). However, instead of the decline taking hold, she was fortunate to be chosen to represent Britain in the 1967 Eurovision Song Contest. What did she have to lose? To many, the contest was considered comical. Songs were written with the occasion in mind, and more often than not were banal, uptempo, throwaway tracks. There were exceptions, of course, like Cliff Richard's 'Congratulations' and Abba's 'Waterloo'.

It was the British practice to feature a selection of the songs submitted for consideration on television. When they had all been viewed, usually one per week, votes were taken from the public. In 1967, Sandie Shaw performed the submitted songs on *The Rolf Harris Show* where the winner was 'Puppet on a String' penned by Bill Martin and Phil Coulter. It was typical of the Eurovision standard – a jerky beat, immature lyrics and lightweight in sound.

On 8 April 1967 Shaw represented her country in Vienna, Austria. 'Puppet on a String' won, earning the distinction of being Britain's first winner in five years. Eire's contribution, 'If I Could Choose' by Sean Dunphy, was pushed to second place.

'Puppet on a String' shot to No. 1 in Britain during May 1967, where it stayed for three weeks, selling in excess of half a million copies. World sales would top four million. This was Shaw's third and last chart-topper. Regrettably she was unable to find another song of its ilk, although she released another Martin/Coulter track, 'Tonight in Tokyo'. This stalled outside the Top Twenty, likewise 'Today', her first 1968 release, and her only chart entrant of the year. On the personal front, the singer celebrated her twenty-first birthday on 28 February 1968, and married fashion designer Jeff Banks a month later.

In 1969, her recording career took a healthy turn. 'Monsieur Dupont', issued in April, returned her to the Top Ten, but success was short-lived. After the release of 'Think It All Over', her career nosedived when it stalled in the Top Fifty. This was her last hit for almost fifteen years.

In 1971, her version of Cat Stevens's 'Father and Son' marked the end of her recording career with Pye Records. She subsequently turned to the cabaret circuit in Britain and Europe, only interrupting her schedules to play straight stage roles, in *Hamlet*, among others.

During 1977 she returned to the recording studios under a CBS Records deal to release a pair of unsuccessful singles, and in 1982, alongside other artists who included Tina Turner, sang 'Anyone Who Has a Heart' on Heaven 17's compilation *Music of Quality and Distinction*. Turner's contribution, a copy of The Temptations' classic 'Ball of Confusion' paved the way for her resultant spectacular solo career. Sandie Shaw struggled on.

In the eighties and with her marriage over (she would later marry film producer Nik Powell), Shaw recorded 'Hand in Glove' with The Smiths. It was actually the group's first single, and when issued by their record label, Rough Trade, it returned the barefooted singer to the Top Thirty. This led to her contributing to Carol Aid in 1985. With other artists like Cliff Richard and Lulu, she sang in a carol service held at London's premier gay nightclub, Heaven.

The next year, Shaw signed with Polydor Records to record 'Are You Ready to Be Heartbroken?' which scraped into the Top Seventy. Following other charity recordings, she published her autobiography, *The World at my Feet* in 1991. This gave her much-needed media attention, unlike the unwelcome headlines in October 1991 when she was arrested for not taking a breathalyser test outside her flat in Harley Street, London. Consequently, PC Thomas Nicholls escorted her to Tottenham Court Road police station. When the case came to trial at Marlborough Street magistrates' court a year later, Shaw accused PC Nicholls of sexually assaulting her, but she was still fined £100.

During the sixties Sandie Shaw held her own against immense female competition that included one-hit wonders like Twinkle and Millie, and established names like Cilla Black and Dusty Springfield. When she lost her way during the seventies, retrieving past glory proved impossible. Today, Sandie Shaw is probably best remembered for her bare feet and 'Puppet on a String'. But in what order?

Also see: '(There's) Always Something There to Remind Me', November 1964; 'Long Live Love', June 1965

June 1967

THE TREMELOES

Silence Is Golden

It's unusual for a back-up group to become more successful than its lead singer, but that is exactly what happened when Brian Poole and the Tremeloes split up in 1966. As the group gained momentum, their lead singer returned to his day job.

Formed in Dagenham, Essex, in 1959 by vocalist Brian Poole, The Tremeloes spent at least seven years as a backing band. Eventually comprising saxophonist Alan Howard, born 17 October 1941 in Dagenham; lead guitarist Rick West, born on 7 May 1943, also in Dagenham; rhythm guitarist Alan Blakley, born 1 April 1942 in Bromley, Kent; and drummer Dave Munden, born 12 December 1943, also in Dagenham, the outfit provided musical support for Buddy Holly lookalike Brian Poole, born on 2 November 1941 in Barking, Essex.

Initially, they slogged around local clubs and holiday camps before being booked on BBC Radio's *Saturday Club* in 1961. At the end of the year, they had auditioned for and were signed by Decca Records in preference to The Beatles who likewise auditioned on the same day as Poole and his group.

After a slow start, Brian Poole discarded his Holly glasses, and with a major marketing push from their record company, the group raced into the British Top Five with 'Twist and Shout' in August 1963, a cover version of The Isley Brothers' original, and the first of several during their career. That October, they topped the British chart with a version of The Contours' classic 'Do You Love Me'. Before 'I Can Dance', the chart-topper's clone, was issued, the group had toured Britain with headliner Dusty Springfield and Freddie and the Dreamers.

The hits continued through 1964: 'Candy Man', 'Someone Someone' and 'Twelve Steps to Love'. But by the following year, the chart run had ended with 'I Want Candy' in August. During January 1966 Brian Poole and the Tremeloes disbanded. Alan Howard left to be replaced by Mickie Clarke; Len 'Chip' Hawkes was recruited as their vocalist, while Brian Poole planned a solo career.

During June 1966, The Tremeloes joined CBS Records where their debut was the poor-selling 'Blessed'. The following month 'Good Day Sunshine', a version of The Beatles' *Revolver* album track, was issued. But the group had to wait until March 1967 to taste chart success. With a version of Cat Stevens's 'Here Comes My Baby' they shot to No. 4 in the British chart. The happy-go-lucky tune signified the start of a new career. As The Tremeloes toured Britain with The Hollies and Paul Jones (ex-lead singer with Manfred Mann), CBS Records released Brian Poole's debut solo single, 'That Reminds Me Baby'. His career was a non-starter and he later retired from the music business to return to his family's butcher shop in Dagenham.

For their next single, The Tremeloes flipped The Four Seasons' 'Rag Doll' to record their version of its B-side, titled 'Silence Is Golden'. With the hugging harmonies now perfected by the group the track swept to the top of the British chart in June 1967 where it stayed for three weeks. Instead of basking in its glory, The Tremeloes toured America where 'Here Comes my Baby' had just entered the Top Twenty. 'Silence Is Golden' followed, selling one million copies to reach the top section of the American chart.

Back in Britain, a suitable follow-up had to be found and timing was crucial. Another mid-pacer was chosen, titled 'Even the Bad Times Are Good'. Flavoured with the hit ingredients from 'Here Comes my Baby', this became a No. 4 British hit. The Tremeloes' sound had now been established; close harmonies set against a bouncy beat. So it appeared a strange move when an inferior ballad, 'Be Mine', was released at the end of 1967. It, quite naturally, struggled into the Top Forty. This was a momentary lapse because their familiar sound welcomed in the New Year with the cheery 'Suddenly You Love Me' which returned them to the Top Ten. Still big earners on the touring circuit, The Tremeloes spent much of 1968 on the road in Britain, Israel and North and South America. In between flights, they recorded and released 'Helule Helule' and 'My Little Lady', both Top Twenty British hits. Through 1969 and 1970 their recorded success was maintained with '(Call Me) Number One', one of their biggest sellers; 'By the Way' and 'Me and my Life', Top Forty and Top Five hits respectively.

Like so many groups who enjoyed sixties success and who had ridden the changing styles through the decade, The Tremeloes lost their way during the seventies. 'Hello Buddy' was their last hit in July 1971, and they retreated to allow the glitter and sparkle of the seventies to take over with glam artists like Gary Glitter, Sweet and pop music's elfin Marc Bolan. There was now no room for groups like The Tremeloes.

Thankfully, they had the club circuit to rely on and in spite of personnel changes, The Tremeloes made a lucrative living from touring. In the eighties, the group toured with Brian Poole, treating audiences to sounds from two musical eras, and this continued through to the next decade.

July 1967

PROCOL HARUM

A Whiter Shade of Pale

With inspiration from Bach, Procol Harum eventually found a record company brave enough to put money behind one of the century's most unique singles. However, its success threw the group into sheer panic as it had no permanent line-up and no follow-up.

Robin Trower, born 9 March 1945, Gary Brooker, born 29 May 1945, and Chris Copping were at school together in their home town of Southend. With a couple of friends, drummer Mick Brownlee and singer Bob Scott they formed The Paramounts. They played rock tunes in their local clubs until Gary Brooker replaced the departing Bob Scott as the group's vocalist, and American R. & B. was introduced into the group's repertoire. By 1962 The Paramounts commanded capacity audiences, particularly at Southend's busy Shades Club.

223

Early in 1963, Mick Brownlee left the line-up to be replaced by Barry J. Wilson, born on 18 March 1947, and midway through the year, when Chris Copping left for university life, Diz Derrick stepped in. With this line-up, and on the strength of their demo tape that included 'Poison Ivy', The Paramounts auditioned for EMI Records. They were signed by Ron Richards to EMI's Parlophone label where they debuted with 'Poison Ivy', released in January 1964. It crashed into the British Top Forty. Two months on, the follow-up, 'Little Bitty Pretty One', a cover of Thurston Harris's hit, bombed. Further singles released through to 1965 also flopped.

Towards the close of 1966, The Paramounts disbanded, leaving Trower and Wilson to work together, and Brooker to concentrate on composing with Keith Reid. With compositions stacking up, Reid advertised for musicians in April 1967 as a vehicle for his music. It was at this juncture that the seeds of Procol Harum were planted. Brooker led the outfit, known as The Pinewoods, as singer and keyboardist, while other members included guitarists Ray Royer and Dave Knights (born 28 June 1945), drummer Bobby Harrison and Matthew Fisher (born 7 March 1946) as second keyboardist.

One of their first projects was Brooker's adaptation of one of the movements from Bach's 'Suite No. 3 In D Major', which he retitled 'A Whiter Shade of Pale'. The track was then included in the group's stage act, while its producer, Denny Cordell, sent a tape of it to Radio London, one of the foremost pirate stations. Such was the public response to its airing, that Deram Records, a subsidiary of Decca, rush-released the track. The Pinewoods became Procol Harum (taken from the Latin *procul* – 'far from these things') and within a month 'A Whiter Shade of Pale' burned its way to the top of the British chart, in July 1967. It sold in excess of 600,000 copies and dominated the chart for a staggering six weeks, earning Procol Harum the distinction of being the sixth act to reach No. 1 with their first single. It was also released in America, selling one million copies to peak at No. 6. At the end of its life, 'A Whiter Shade of Pale' had sold an incredible six million copies. It also went on to win the Ivor Novello Award for the International Song of the Year, among other honours.

Unknown to the public at this time, the group had no permanent membership but, more importantly, had no further material available to release. Added to this, Bobby Harrison and Ray Royer left the group to form Freedom, leaving Gary Brooker to call on Robin Trower and Barry J. Wilson (ex-Paramounts' members).

Denny Cordell transferred Procol Harum from Deram to the Regal

Zonophone label, a subsidiary of EMI Records, where the first single was 'Homburg', released in October 1967. In much the same style as the chart-topper, 'Homburg' soared to No. 6 in the British chart and made the Top Forty in America. Their third single, 'Quite Rightly So', released in April 1968, was disappointing, struggling to reach the Top Fifty.

During the closing months of 1968, Procol Harum played belated performances in America, including a date at the Miami Pop Festival. Then once again, the group's line-up changed. When the dust had settled, the membership read the same as 1963's Paramounts. Procol Harum went on to spend the majority of 1969 touring America; first with Ike and Tina Turner, and later with Chuck Berry, Janis Joplin and Creedence Clearwater Revival. In between these dates the album *A Salty Dog* (recorded while Dave Knights and Matthew Foster were still in the line-up) was released. It soared into the American Top Fifty, while its title track reached the British Top Fifty in June 1969, No. 44 on re-entry and No. 44 again on its second re-entry.

Midway through 1971 the group's line-up changed again shortly before a series of Canadian and American tours, and in May 1972 the album *Procol Harum in Concert with the Edmonton Symphony Orchestra* was issued. It sold half a million copies to become the group's biggest-selling album to date. A long-awaited single was issued that August. Titled 'Conquistador', it became a Top Twenty hit on both sides of the Atlantic.

Further personnel changes, lengthy tours and sporadic recordings maintained Procol Harum's public image, and when 'Pandora's Box' was lifted from the album *Procol's Ninth*, it became their last hit. During 1977, following the release of the *Something Magic* album, Procol Harum disbanded.

It was 'A Whiter Shade of Pale' that brought Procol Harum fame and recognition. And this was remembered when in October 1977 the single was named joint winner of Best British Pop Single 1952–77 at the British Record Industry's Britannia Awards ceremony held in Wembley, Middlesex. The other single winner was Queen's 'Bohemian Rhapsody'. Both were musical milestones and both used classic composers for inspiration.

THE BEATLES

All You Need Is Love

During the year of 1967 the world was introduced to *Sgt Pepper's Lonely Hearts Club Band*. The album started life as *Dr Pepper's Lonely Hearts Club Band* until The Beatles realised Dr Pepper was the name of an American drink. When 'Penny Lane'/'Strawberry Fields Forever' (the follow-up single to 'Yellow Submarine'/'Eleanor Rigby') stalled at No. 2 in the British chart – their first official single not to reach No. 1 – the group was in a quandary. The tracks they were recording for their pending album bore little resemblance to each other; there was no overall theme, no concept, and certainly no single potential.

For starters, they had recorded the album's title song, 'Sgt Pepper's Lonely Hearts Club Band', influenced by the craze for Victorian militaria being sold in a host of London shops, but as The Beatles were now regular users of LSD, their music tended to move from one musical pitch to another. With 'Lucy in the Sky with Diamonds' (which many believed dealt with the LSD drug), 'A Day in the Life' (subsequently banned by BBC radio because of its reputed drug implications) and 'With a Little Help from my Friends' (courtesy of Ringo Starr's mundane vocals), the whole album appeared to be a pot-pourri of drug-induced music.

The album took four months to record at an exorbitant cost and was later recognised as the climax of the group's career. The Beatles had turned music inside out, and had changed the face of British pop beyond recognition. It was without question a slice of musical history, a monstrous masterpiece which others desperately attempted to emulate. The album's colourful double cover was designed by Peter Blake, where The Beatles were dressed in satin uniforms amidst a group of characters like Diana Dors, Laurel and Hardy, and several wax figures. EMI Records were fearful of legal action from some of the artists featured on the sleeve, so eventually The Beatles indemnified the record company against any possible action. However, what the legal beavers omitted to notice were the pots of marijuana plants at the feet of Sgt Pepper's band.

Sgt Pepper's Lonely Hearts Club Band was rush-released in June 1967 and soared to the top of most countries' album charts. At the Grammy Awards ceremony in 1968, it won several categories, including Album of the Year, Best Contemporary Album and Best Album Cover.

When The Beatles were asked to appear as Britain's representatives in the BBC TV's *Our World* spectacular, which would form part of the Canadian Expo 1967, they decided to be filmed recording at Abbey Road Studios. The track they chose was one written during May 1967 titled 'All You Need Is Love', and two Beatles abandoned their familiar instruments to introduce a different sound, befitting what they hoped would be a universal song. George Harrison played violin, while Paul McCartney played bass with a bow on the single's initial backing track. On top of this the group then dubbed their usual instruments, creating a much heavier sound.

Their producer, George Martin, played piano and was responsible for the strains of the French national anthem at the beginning of the track, together with the slice of 'In the Mood' taken from Glenn Miller catalogue. Snippets of 'She Loves You' and 'Greensleeves' were included by the group.

As well as the thirteen musicians accompanying The Beatles, friends like Marianne Faithfull, Mick Jagger, Jane Asher and Eric Clapton attended the session. The studio was crammed to bursting with bodies. When 'All You Need Is Love' was performed during the six-hour *Our World* programme, 400 million people in 26 countries viewed via satellite.

The single shot to No. 1 in the British chart during August 1967, and within days attained the same position in America. The potential of the song was obvious and EMI Records were hard pushed to satisfy the public's demand.

Also see: 'From Me to You', May/June 1963; 'She Loves You', October 1963; 'I Want to Hold your Hand', December 1963; 'Can't Buy Me Love', April 1964; 'A Hard Day's Night', August 1964; 'I Feel Fine', January 1965; 'Ticket to Ride', May 1965; 'Help!', August 1965; 'We Can Work It Out'/'Day Tripper', January 1966; 'Paperback Writer', July 1966; 'Yellow Submarine'/'Eleanor Rigby', September 1966; 'Hello Goodbye', January 1968; 'Lady Madonna', April 1968; 'Get Back', May 1969; 'The Ballad of John and Yoko', July 1969

SCOTT McKENZIE

San Francisco (Be Sure to Wear Some Flowers in your Hair)

Kaftans, the tinkle of Indian bells, multi-coloured beads adorning necks and arms, flowers being stuck into rifle butts, love-ins, acid dropping and a whole new language. That was the scenario depicted by Scott McKenzie, a young man whose aura was one of peace and love. 'San Francisco (Be Sure to Wear Some Flowers in your Hair)' was the anthem of 1967, but like the flowers he sung about, McKenzie's success lasted as long as a summer bloom.

For the time being, though, flowers and drugs were plenteous, and so was the music inspired by them. It was sight and sound largely induced by the so-called revolutionary drug LSD. The hallucinatory experiences it induced opened musicians' minds to reach for the unattainable in music, and San Francisco was the forerunner. The city gave birth to this new musical society where drop-outs hung out in their own clubs and theatres, devising an 'alternative society' which would be adopted internationally. During the year's long hot summer they very nearly convinced the world that love was the answer.

This was the environment in which Scott McKenzie found gold with his gently persuasive 'San Francisco' because it reflected the hippie element of this American dream. And through the song's lyrics he urged people to visit and experience San Francisco's new society. Many followed his appeal.

Scott McKenzie was born Philip Blondheim on 1 October 1944 in Arlington, Virginia. He started performing in the folk group The Journeymen which also included John Phillips, born 30 August 1935 in South Carolina, and who went on to form The Mamas and The Papas. During a low-key American tour when The Journeymen took top billing, another folk outfit, The Halifax Three, headed by Dennis Doherty, was support act. The ensuing intertwining of groups and associates with John Sebastian (later of Lovin' Spoonful) and Barry McGuire ('Eve of Destruction' in 1965) finally led to the line-up of The Mamas and The Papas, namely Phillips and Doherty, plus Ellen Naomi Cohen (Cass Elliott) and Holly Michelle Gilliam. 'California

228

Dreamin" and 'Monday Monday' were both million-sellers from them in 1966. Their career lasted for approximately two years.

When The Journeymen split up Scott McKenzie performed as a soloist until he met John Phillips again. Together they worked on the folk song 'No No No No No' which McKenzie recorded. It flopped. Next, Phillips wrote 'San Francisco (Be Sure to Wear Some Flowers in your Hair)'. It slotted in perfectly with the Flower Generation and shot to the top of the American chart, reaching the top in Britain during September 1967. This success was repeated across Europe where factions of Flower People adopted it as their anthem. An album, *The Voice of Scott McKenzie*, followed.

McKenzie released two further singles, 'Like an Old Time Movie' and 'Holy Man' but neither enjoyed chart status. Following the release of his second album, *Stained Glass Morning*, in 1970, Scott McKenzie dropped from the public eye. During the eighties he returned briefly to perform with John Phillips in The 'new' Mamas and The Papas.

October 1967

ENGELBERT HUMPERDINCK

The Last Waltz

With the No. 1 single 'Release Me' under his belt, a loyal following of screaming females drooled over Engelbert Humperdinck's sultry handsome features, seductive eyes and mellow voice. He was one of Britain's top male stars. Regrettably, that star twinkled only for a while.

'The Last Waltz' was the first in a run of singles to be written by Les Reed and Barry Mason. Reed had already penned 'It's Not Unusual' for Tom Jones, so it seemed natural he would also write for Gordon Mills's second protégé. One of the sixties' most prolific composers, Les Reed teamed up with Barry Mason to produce numerous million-sellers, notably for Mills's boys.

In October 1967, 'The Last Waltz' topped the British chart. The evergreen track was aimed at the middle-of-the-road audience. Remarkably, it was Engelbert Humperdinck's second and last chart-topper.

'Am I That Easy to Forget' followed, to climb to No. 3 early in 1968, the first of three singles during the year. 'A Man without Love' and 'Les Bicyclettes de Belsize', both Top Five singles, were the others.

The relaxed manner adopted by the singer on stage – no gyrating or hip swaying for Hump! – was refreshing. It also distanced him from Tom Jones, whose frenetic antics on stage regularly provoked women to throw items of underwear in his direction.

After the trio of Top Ten singles, Engelbert Humperdinck had to content himself with Top Twenty hits in 1969. 'The Way It Used to Be,' 'I'm a Better Man' and 'Winter World of Love', all significant releases, were all powerless to overcome the competition.

At the start of 1970, the struggle was on once more. 'My Marie' stalled outside the Top Thirty, while 'Sweetheart' reached No. 22 in September, and upon re-entry a month later, peaked in the Top Fifty. It was evident that public taste was changing, the balladeers were losing ground, being shunted on to the cabaret circuit.

Nonetheless, one single charted in 1972, namely 'Too Beautiful to Last', which, remarkably, reached the Top Twenty, aptly titled because it was Humperdinck's last to rise so high. By November 1973, his selling power had more or less crumbled when 'Love Is All' limped into the Top Fifty.

As Humperdinck's career petered out in Britain, he found a niche waiting for him in America, particularly on the lavish and extremely lucrative Las Vegas circuit. He quickly became a regular and successful performer, following in the footsteps of his musical colleague Tom Jones in elite cabaret. So rewarding was Humperdinck's American career that, like Jones, he took up residence there.

During 1976 Humperdinck returned to the American chart with a surprise Top Ten single, 'After the Lovin'', and in 1987 RCA Records issued his first album in a decade, titled *Remember I Love You*, which included a duet with seventies' disco diva Gloria Gaynor. His comeback passed unnoticed except by his stalwart fans.

Also see: 'Release Me', March/April 1967

November 1967

THE BEE GEES

Massachusetts

The brothers' success story has spanned almost three decades, yet few people believe there was life before *Saturday Night Fever*. In fact, many of their finer compositions belonged to the sixties or early seventies when melody and lyric were the all-important factors.

Barry Gibb was born on 1 September 1947, and his twin brothers Maurice and Robin were born on 22 December two years later, all in Douglas, Isle of Man. Their mother, Barbara, was a singer, while their father, Hughie, was the leader of his own orchestra on the Mecca circuit. The family moved to Lancashire before emigrating to Australia where Andy, the fourth son, was born. Before leaving Britain, the brothers had already performed before an audience, usually at the Manchester Gaumont's Saturday picture shows, where, known as The Rattlesnakes, they sang the then current songs.

Once settled in Australia the brothers, still using the name The Rattlesnakes, befriended Bill Good, organiser of the Speedway Circus in Brisbane, where they performed between races, and 4KQ Radio's DJ, Bill Gates, who played their taped material on air. In fact, the brothers took their name from Bill Gates and Bill Good's initials to become The BGs.

Their first television appearance on *Anything Goes* in 1960 led to other one-off performances before they secured a residency at Brisbane's Beachcomber Hotel. Two years on, they moved to Sydney where one of their first performances was supporting Chubby Checker at the city's stadium. They also started flexing their composing hand to write 'Let Me Love You', followed by 'Starlight of Love', which was recorded by the Australian vocalist Col Joyce.

Most of 1963 was taken up with a residency at a Queensland nightclub but between performances the Bee Gees signed a recording deal with Festival Records. Their debut was 'Three Kisses of Love', while 'Wine and Women' became their first hit two years later. Switching to Spin Records, they recorded a series of minor Australian hits until 'Spicks and Specks', released late in 1966, became their first Australian chart-topper.

Early in 1967, The BGs decided they wanted to return to Britain. Despite their parents' initial reluctance, Hughie Gibb posted copies of his sons' Australian album to numerous notable British management companies, including NEMS Enterprises, once owned by Brian Epstein, now controlled by Robert Stigwood. Stigwood agreed to audition The BGs upon their arrival; this in turn led to a recording contract with Polydor Records.

'New York Mining Disaster 1941' was The (renamed) Bee Gees' debut British single – and the first to be recorded outside Australia – released during May 1967. It also marked two additions to the brothers' line-up – guitarist Vince Melouney and drummer Colin Peterson, both Australians. The three-part vocalising on 'New York Mining Disaster 1941' pushed the single to No. 12 in the British chart and No. 14 in America. During its life the disc sold in excess of one million copies. While The Bee Gees were in America midway through 1967 to promote 'New York Mining Disaster 1941', they wrote a song for Otis Redding. However, instead of giving it to him, they opted to record it themselves. Titled 'To Love Somebody', it peaked at No. 41 in Britain and No. 17 in America, but more importantly, it became one of the most covered Bee Gees' songs. Nina Simone, Janis Joplin, Jimmy Somerville and Michael Bolton, among others, re-recorded it.

Another track penned during their first American trip was 'Massachusetts', and when released it became The Bee Gees' first British No. 1 single during November 1967. It soared into the American Top Twenty. Once more, it was the superb three-part harmonising that made the song so compelling, and it was this that would sustain the trio's popularity for years to come. It was often a point of ridicule by impressionists – but who laughed all the way to the bank? Before the end of 1967, The Bee Gees' fourth single, 'World', was a Top Ten British hit, establishing them among the biggest-selling acts of the year.

The brothers' first live appearance of 1968 was at the Convention Centre, California, while their first single of the year was 'Words', a No. 8 British hit in the February; No. 15 in America a month later. This charting coincided with their first appearance on *The Ed Sullivan Show*. Once back in Britain, the brothers embarked upon an extensive tour with Dave Dee, Dozy, Beaky, Mitch and Tich.

This was just the beginning of a spectacular career for The Bee Gees, who would enjoy megastar status three decades later. However, their success took its toll; the future was blighted by disappointment and tragedy.

Also see: 'I've Gotta Get a Message to You', September 1968

Also a No. 1 single in November 1967: 'Baby Now That I've Found You' by The Foundations

LONG JOHN BALDRY

Let the Heartaches Begin

As 1967 closed, album sales outweighed singles for the first time, leading to the decline in those artists who relied on forty-fives for a career. Albums were becoming more intense and adventurous, new acts sprang to life, yet it was still The Beatles who led the way, notably with *Sgt Pepper's Lonely Hearts Club Band*. In this daring and drug-inspired decade, saturated with mismatching music that was often indecipherable, it was, ironically, usually a ballad of sorts that topped the charts.

'Let the Heartaches Begin' was a powerful performance from Long John Baldry, a British artist whose leanings were towards R. & B. Tom Jones was possibly his nearest rival in voice and style, having started the year with 'Green Green Grass of Home', although, of course, he moved on to superstardom, whereas Long John Baldry simply enjoyed a taste of success. Standing six foot seven – hence 'Long' John Baldry – the singer didn't fit into the mould of a pop star at all. He appeared ill at ease on stage, making his height a disadvantage. Yet his mature, gritty voice made him instantly attractive to the middle-of-the-road audience who invariably purchased singles in sufficient numbers to push an artist to the top of the chart.

Baldry, born on 12 January 1941 in London, was a regular performer from the age of sixteen. He tackled various types of music – folk, jazz and pure blues – before deciding to settle with R. & B. Alexis Korner invited him to join his Blues Incorporated, one of the most influential outfits on the London circuit. Baldry's strong, emotional voice amply suited the R. & B. mode as can be heard on the 1962 album *R. & B. from the Marquee with Korner*. From Korner's group, Baldry toured the USAF bases in Germany, before returning to London at the end of 1962 to join Cyril Davies's R. & B. All Stars. Early in 1963 Pye Records signed the group and they recorded two singles of note, 'Country Line Special' and 'Preachin' the Blues'. When Cyril Davies died a year later, Baldry used members of the All Stars to form a new band, The Hoochie Coochie Men, which featured, among others, future singing star Rod Stewart.

233

United Artists Records signed this new group to release the 'Up above my Head' single and *Long John's Blues* album. Both flopped, despite critical acclaim. With no recorded success and income from club work their only means of survival, The Hoochie Coochie Men decided to disband during October 1965, leaving Baldry and Rod Stewart to join Julie Driscoll and Brian Auger in Steampacket. Within a year, that too had split up, whereupon Baldry joined another influential band, Bluesology, this time featuring Reg Dwight, later to become Elton John, on keyboards.

With commercial success constantly evading him, Baldry opted to try a solo career and became a Pye Records artist in 1967. He abandoned his roots to record the ballad produced and penned by Tony Macaulay and John McLeod, 'Let the Heartaches Begin'. Baldry likewise discarded his casual, well-worn stage gear for sharp, tailored suits and an acceptable, short hairstyle, befitting his new 'pop' image.

'Let the Heartaches Begin' stormed to No. 1 in December 1967 where it stayed for two weeks, later becoming a minor American hit. Everyone wanted this new, lanky discovery, but found it difficult to believe he'd spent his musical upbringing entrenched in R. & B.

Another ballad, 'When the Sun Comes Shinin' Through', followed in September 1968, but stalled in the Top Thirty. The third release fared better, and rightly so, because it was 'Mexico', the theme to the BBC TV coverage of the Olympic Games. But the public was fickle and by 1969 Baldry enjoyed his last hit, 'It's Too Late Now'.

Accepting that his pop career was dead, the singer dumped his sharp suits and trimmed haircut to grow a beard and don stage clothes more befitting an audience outside pop. But he didn't abandon recording. With the production expertise of his two friends Rod Stewart and Elton John, Baldry joined Warner Brothers to record the album *It Ain't Easy*. It bombed in Britain, but became a hit in America, whereupon he undertook his first tour there. This was the start of a new career, albeit short-lived, after which the singer was admitted into a mental institution.

By 1980, Long John Baldry was confined to small-time performances in Canada and America, his British career long forgotten. Yet in 1988, a compilation album was issued, *Let the Heartaches Begin – The Best of Long John Baldry*, so someone somewhere must have remembered the six foot seven pop star who really didn't fit the mould.

THE BEATLES

Hello Goodbye

Prior to the release of The Beatles' next single in 1968, several changes occurred which affected the group both personally and professionally. They were still heavily into LSD, appeared in an uninspiring and poorly organised film and sought solace in the teachings of Maharishi Mahesh Yogi. But first they suffered the biggest blow to their career.

On 27 August 1967 their manager and mentor, 32-year-old Brian Epstein, was found dead in his bed at 24 Chapel Street, London. He had committed suicide, the last of several attempts which began in 1966. The Beatles were, naturally enough, devastated by the senseless loss but when the media exposed Epstein's private life, their burden trebled. In music business circles it was well known that Brian Epstein was gay and that he was besotted by John Lennon. Indeed, this infatuation led to several arguments within the Beatle camp. However, what wasn't generally known was Epstein's reputed masochistic nature which often led to his disappearing for lengths of time only to return bruised and battered. Gary Herman in his book *Rock 'n' Roll Babylon* even suggested that his preferences and final death had more to do with rubber mask suffocation than a pill overdose. However, many felt that the fact that The Beatles weren't as reliant on him as they had been in the past, preferring to go their separate ways, seemed the most likely cause of his suicide.

The news of Epstein's death was broken to Paul McCartney who, with the other group members, was in Bangor, North Wales, searching for universal answers with the Maharishi Mahesh Yogi. They instantly returned to London. Brian Epstein's funeral was held on 29 August 1967, with only family in attendance. The Beatles would attend his memorial service held at the New London Synagogue in London on 17 October.

Professionally speaking, the group's two composers, Lennon and McCartney, went their separate ways. Paul McCartney, who was due to announce his engagement to Jane Asher, was the more adventurous of the two when he began formulating ideas for a Beatles movie titled

Magical Mystery Tour. His plans became reality when, during September 1967, forty-three people including a midget, a fat lady, a few journalists, extras and the group sat in a coach advertising *Magical Mystery Tour.* The coach left London, hit Banbury and later Devon and Brighton, causing the most unimaginable disruption on its journey. With Brian Epstein's passing, The Beatles were more or less left to their own devices, and without his guidance and support, the tour was a total disaster. Originally the movie was to have been filmed at certain locations (wherever the coach stopped, basically) and completed at Shepperton Film Studios. The final film was one befitting that of an amateur cameraman, although sections were memorable like 'I Am the Walrus' and 'Fool on the Hill' performed by Lennon and McCartney respectively, and The Beatles, dressed in white tie and tails, embarking on a Busby Berkeley routine with ballroom dancers, while singing 'Your Mother Should Know'.

Magical Mystery Tour should never have left home base because it was confusing, cluttered and disappointing. It was the first time The Beatles had bombed, and they had no one to protect them from the printed onslaught that followed. In retrospect, Brian Epstein would probably have vetoed the project before it had been formulated, thus saving the public embarrassment and the wasted money. During December 1967 BBC TV premiered *Magical Mystery Tour* and plans to screen it in America were dropped in view of the poor British reaction. It would eventually be aired a year later, and indeed would be screened twice more by the BBC in colour during January 1968 and December 1979. During the eighties the film would attract a cult following, who hailed it as adventurous, innovative but premature.

John Lennon, on the other hand, had in 1966 accepted the part of Private Gripweed in the Richard Lester movie *How I Won the War.* He had flown to West Germany for the start of the filming, and while in Celle had agreed to have his hair shorn and to wear 'National Health' glasses. He needed to wear them anyhow, but to date vanity had prevented him from doing so in public. In future, it was rarely that Lennon and his 'granny glasses' were separated. From Celle, the filming moved to Spain, where Lennon stayed with his wife Cynthia between shooting. The premiere of *How I Won the War* was held at the London Pavilion cinema during October 1967. All the Beatles attended. Ringo Starr then followed in Lennon's footsteps to accept a role in *Candy*, being filmed in Rome.

In 1967 The Beatles opened their own boutique, Apple, in London's Baker Street. It was an elegant and fashionable establishment, designed by The Fool, and swamped with young customers who preferred to swipe rather than buy. Nonetheless, it was 'the' place for the beautiful people of the sixties.

It was on the back of this professional mayhem that 'Hello Goodbye' was released in January 1968. The track was recorded during the filming of *Magical Mystery Tour* but wasn't intended to be included on the soundtrack, unlike the B-side, 'I Am the Walrus'. Lennon was inspired to write this track after reading the poem 'The Walrus and the Carpenter' from Lewis Carroll's *Alice in Wonderland*. The lyrics, though, were far-reaching; certainly not designed for children's ears. Nonetheless, Lennon believed Carroll had referred to capitalism, and good and evil, with the two main characters. Session musicians were used on the backing track, alongside the (unlikely) Michael Sammes Singers who contributed 'oompah oompah, stick it up your jumper'. BBC Radio, as was expected, banned the song, not because of Lennon's interpretation of the poem but because the lyrics contained the word 'knickers'! Lewis Carroll would probably have turned in his grave at the very idea.

'Hello Goodbye' shot to the top of the British chart where it stayed for seven weeks, matching 'From Me to You' as the longest stay at the top by The Beatles. The promotional film for the single couldn't be screened by BBC TV due to the Musicians Union banning lip-synching (miming) to songs. Several alternatives were proposed by the television company but none was sanctioned by the Union. When 'Hello Goodbye' was eventually promoted on television, snippets from their movie *A Hard Day's Night* were used. The single became the group's fifteenth American chart-topper after a four-week climb, while the soundtrack of *Magical Mystery Tour* topped the album chart. In Britain, released as a double EP, it peaked at No. 2.

This was also the year when The Beatles' discontent reached new heights: when the police would hound them in pursuit of drugs and when it looked as if the cracks in their relationships would finally break open.

Also see: 'From Me to You', May/June 1963; 'She Loves You', October 1963; 'I Want to Hold your Hand', December 1963; 'Can't Buy Me Love', April 1964; 'A Hard Day's Night', August 1964; 'I Feel Fine', January 1965; 'Ticket to Ride', May 1965; 'Help!', August 1965; 'We Can Work It Out'/'Day Tripper', January 1966; 'Paperback Writer', July 1966; 'Yellow Submarine'/'Eleanor Rigby', September 1966; 'All You Need Is Love', August 1967; 'Lady Madonna', April 1968;

'Get Back', May 1969; 'The Ballad of John and Yoko', July 1969

Also a No. 1 single in January 1968: 'The Ballad of Bonnie and Clyde' by Georgie Fame

February 1968

LOVE AFFAIR

Everlasting Love

A two-year career and five Top Twenty singles sum up Love Affair's contribution to British music during the late sixties. Their music was undiluted commercial pop, and one single in particular can still be found on jukeboxes.

Comprising little Steve Ellis as vocalist, fronting guitarists Mick Jackson and Rex Brayley, drummer Maurice Bacon and keyboardist Morgan Fisher, the group was born in London during 1966.

Despite Steve Ellis being under age, the quintet was a regular act in the London clubs. When CBS Records signed them their first single featured only Steve Ellis backed by session musicians, thus indicating the band members were not as proficient in the studio as they were on stage.

That first single was 'Everlasting Love', a version of soul singer Robert Knight's classic. A quick-paced dance number, it was more brash than the original, and shot to the top of the British chart in February 1968, much to the surprise of CBS Records.

Managed by Maurice Bacon's father, the group was cushioned somewhat from the exploitative side of the music business, but by the same token didn't take advantage of the No. 1 single. Instead of the obligatory touring schedules, Love Affair saturated the teenage magazines; their young good looks, particularly those of Steve Ellis, elevated them into teen pin-ups rather than a music group to be reckoned with.

The follow-up to the chart-topper was the equally impressive 'Rainbow Valley', a Top Five British hit in April 1968. The third of the year was another Top Ten hit, 'A Day without Love'.

Love Affair's lowest-selling single, 'One Road', was the first of 1969 when it stalled at No. 16, while their 'Bringing on Back the Good Times' fared much better at No. 9. This was their last chart single.

The hit run over, Love Affair wandered musically until Steve Ellis left the group to start another band called Ellis. Maurice Bacon retired into the background to concentrate on music publishing, while Morgan Fisher joined Mott The Hoople who, in 1972, enjoyed a No. 3 single with 'All the Young Dudes' and later a Top Ten hit with 'Roll Away the Stone', among others.

During the mid-eighties, Love Affair's *Greatest Hits* album was issued, leaving the group's name to be used by all and sundry for touring purposes.

March 1968

ESTHER AND ABI OFARIM

Cinderella Rockafella

Novelty records have always had a place in the British chart, usually because of impulse-buying. More often than not, the songs are extremely catchy, often repetitive, and pure nonsense, but people love them. Singles from the Continent tend to have a tough time breaking through the sales barrier, especially those in a foreign tongue. Naturally there are exceptions, like Jane Birkin and Serge Gainsbourg's 'Je t'aime moi non plus' in 1969 (and later during 1974). However, they are few and far between these days. 'Cinderella Rockafella' was one of those irritating, surprise, runaway hits, sung in English, which fell into the novelty category.

The couple responsible were Esther Ofarim, born Esther Zaled on 13 June 1943 in Safed, Israel, and Abraham Reichstadt born on 5 October 1939 in Tel Aviv, Israel.

Prior to the release of 'Cinderalla Rockafella', the husband and wife team were among the top-selling acts in their home country. Their ambition was to go international and when the chance came to represent Switzerland in the 1963 Eurovision Song Contest they grabbed it. (They lost to the Danish entry, Grethe and Jorgen Ingman with 'Dansevise'.) Nonetheless, Esther and Abi Ofarim had penetrated the Continental market, and following the release of numerous foreign language records, decided Britain was next.

Called a 'novelty love duet' by Eamonn Andrews when he announced the duo on his high-rating television show, the single's

239

British fate was sealed. From that one appearance the public swooped in droves on record stores to buy it. Written by Mason Williams and picked up by the Philips label for release, 'Cinderalla Rockafella' topped the chart for three weeks and stayed within them for thirteen, thus indicating it didn't want to die.

Despite general opinion, Esther and Abi Ofarim were not one-hit wonders because the follow-up, 'One More Dance', had a good showing at No. 13 in June 1968. Two albums were also issued, *2 in 3* in 1968 and *Ofarim Concert Live* a year later.

However, the two singles mentioned above marked the extent of their British career. Esther and Abi Ofarim continued to work in Europe until the partnership broke up when they divorced.

Also a No. 1 single in March 1968: 'The Legend of Xanadu' by Dave Dee, Dozy, Beaky, Mick and Tich

April 1968

THE BEATLES

Lady Madonna

A month prior to the release of their next single, The Beatles once more showed their devotion to Maharishi Mahesh Yogi by travelling to Rishikesh, India, to receive tuition in transcendental meditation. Their stay was shorter than intended. Firstly, Ringo Starr and his wife returned to London claiming the retreat was like a Butlin's holiday camp. He was soon to be followed by the remaining Beatles when the Maharishi allegedly assaulted Mia Farrow. The Beatles denounced him within the year.

At the beginning of 1968 The Beatles opened and spearheaded their own group of companies under the parent name, Apple Corps Ltd, with offices at 3 Savile Row, London. This operation included their own record label, Apple, which would be licensed to and distributed by EMI Records. All future Beatles discs would carry the Apple label instead of Parlophone. Apart from the group itself, the label's artists would include Grapefruit, and later, Mary Hopkin, Billy Preston and Doris Troy, among others.

Following the premiere of its promotional film on the BBC TV programme *All Systems Freeman*, 'Lady Madonna' shot to the top of the British chart during April 1968. Remarkably it stalled at No. 4 in America.

But it was The Beatles' private lives that attracted more attention than their music, in particular John Lennon and his relationship with Yoko Ono. They had first met in November 1966 at a private preview of an art exhibition, 'Unfinished Paintings and Objects', in London. Yoko Ono was the artist. In June 1968 the couple appeared in public for the first time, at the opening of Apple's second boutique in London's King's Road. They later planted an acorn together at Coventry Cathedral, and attended the opening of the National Theatre's production of Lennon's book *In his Own Write* at the Old Vic Theatre, London.

While the romance between John and Yoko blossomed, Jane Asher announced on the television programme *Dee Time* that her engagement to Paul McCartney was over. McCartney had met his future wife, Linda Eastman. Meanwhile, Lennon's wife Cynthia sued her husband for divorce, citing adultery with Yoko Ono. It was at this point that the future of The Beatles became uncertain – when Yoko Ono stepped in, the remaining Beatles threatened to walk out. They claimed the influence she had on Lennon would eventually destroy the group; in retrospect they were right. The long-term view, though, would be different.

Before 1968 closed, John and Yoko were remanded on bail following a police raid on an apartment (owned by Ringo Starr) where they had been staying. The police discovered grains of cannabis resin. Lennon pleaded guilty to the charge of possession (to protect Yoko since she wasn't a British citizen and could have been deported) in November 1968 before Marylebone Magistrates' Court. This conviction later contributed to Lennon being denied a resident's permit when he decided to settle in America with Yoko.

However, this glaring headline news was quickly replaced by the announcement that the happy couple were expecting their first child. Unhappily, Yoko Ono later miscarried. While this news was fading in print, they released their controversial album *Two Virgins*, where both John and Yoko posed nude on the front cover. When the album was released in New Jersey, America, it was banned immediately on the grounds of being pornographic. And while Cynthia Lennon's divorce was granted, her ex-husband and Yoko Ono appeared within a white bag at the Royal Albert Hall as their contribution to an art movement's Christmas party.

On the recording front, Paul McCartney wrote 'Hey Jude', The

Beatles' next single, for Lennon's son, Julian. It was the longest track the group had recorded, with a running time of seven minutes plus, and raced to the top of the British chart. Almost immediately, *The Beatles*, the group's 'white album', so called because the packaging was entirely white and free from lettering, was issued. This album was significant because it represented a division in recording techniques. Instead of working together as usual, The Beatles recorded separately on several occasions, signalling the ensuing breakdown in communication that would lead to the final decision – should The Beatles continue as a recording unit? It was a marvel in itself that the public remained oblivious to the dramas behind the scenes, and that the group recorded the album at all.

With the intervention of Allen Klein, their new business manager, the future got tougher.

Also see: 'From Me to You', May/June 1963; 'She Loves You', October 1963; 'I Want to Hold your Hand', December 1963; 'Can't Buy Me Love', April 1964; 'A Hard Day's Night', August 1964; 'I Feel Fine', January 1965; 'Ticket to Ride', May 1965; 'Help!', August 1965; 'We Can Work It Out'/'Day Tripper', January 1966; 'Paperback Writer', July 1966; 'Yellow Submarine'/'Eleanor Rigby', September 1966; 'All You Need Is Love', August 1967; 'Hello Goodbye', January 1968; 'Get Back', May 1969; 'The Ballad of John and Yoko', July 1969

May 1968

LOUIS ARMSTRONG

What a Wonderful World

'I always loved music and it didn't matter what the instrument was or who played it, so long as the playing was good.' – Louis Armstrong

Born Louis Daniel Armstrong on 4 July 1900 to Mary Ann and Willie in New Orleans, Louisiana, Armstrong was raised in the Storyville district. As a youngster he used his wits to provide for his family, roaming an area of brothels, theatres and churches where to hustle was the only means of survival.

On New Year's Eve 1913, Armstrong swiped his father's handgun and fired it in the street. The reason wasn't explained. However, this act led to him being arrested and placed in the Waifs' Home for Boys. It was this period of incarceration that secured his future. He first sang in the home's group before being taught by music teacher Peter Davis to play the cornet. This led to him being nicknamed 'Satchmo', abbreviated from 'satchel mouth'.

In 1917 Armstrong left the home to play on borrowed cornets in numerous jazz bands, while working at manual jobs during the day. Armstrong: 'I kept on driving my coal cart. Outside the cornet, the coal cart was the only job I enjoyed working.' Over a period of time, his musical reputation spread because he transformed New Orleans jazz into a personal and more mainstream music. It was this that brought him to the attention of New Orleans' premier cornetist, Joe 'King' Oliver. Armstrong went to work with the King until such time as he actually replaced him in the Kid Ory Band. (King had been asked to relocate with a new band of musicians in Chicago.) Armstrong: 'The first night I played with The Ory Band the boys were so surprised they could hardly play their instruments for listening to me blowing up a storm. But I wasn't frightened one bit. I was doing everything exactly the way I'd heard "King" Oliver do it. I even put a big towel around my neck 'cos that was the first thing Joe Oliver always did – he'd put a bath towel around his neck and pin up his collar underneath so's he could blow free and easy.'

Oliver and Armstrong were reunited in Chicago during 1922, despite the latter's reluctance to leave his home state. For two years the two musicians played together, garnering tremendous audience support. At this point, Lillian Hardin, a pianist, entered Armstrong's life. She encouraged him to concentrate on his own career by leaving Oliver. In 1924, Armstrong and Hardin married and moved to New York where he joined Fletcher Henderson's band. Once again, Armstrong was an outstanding success due to his solo spots in the act. New York punters soon elevated him into a headline attraction on the theatre circuit. In 1925 he returned to Chicago at his wife's request to perform with her band. Needless to say, he was welcomed as the conquering hero.

During the following three years, Armstrong recorded with numerous acts including Clara Smith and Bessie Smith, made countless radio broadcasts as leader of the Hot Five and, later, the Hot Seven, before recording his first single under his own name for Okeh Records. Titled 'My Heart', it was the first of approximately sixty tracks recorded, including 'Melancholy Blues' and 'Fireworks'. He went on to work with Carroll Dickerson's band, and later with Erskine

Tate, before opening a jazz club with Zutty Singleton and Earl Hines. By the end of the twenties, Louis Armstrong was in demand across America, particularly Washington DC and Los Angeles.

By 1930, Armstrong had abandoned the cornet for the trumpet and worked with several orchestras, including Chick Webb's and Les Hite's, with whom he also recorded. During 1933, he visited Europe for the first time where audiences flocked to hear him play. Two years later, he joined Luis Russell's orchestra, outshining Henry Allen, the band's own trumpeter.

On the personal front, Armstrong divorced Lillian Hardin to marry Alpha Smith in 1938. Four years later he married for the third time.

During the thirties he moved from music into the movie world to appear in (among others) *Pennies from Heaven* and *High Society*.

With the gradual demise of the big band era, and the passing of the swing fad, Louis Armstrong found himself isolated, unable to find a niche for his art. Early in 1940, his style was considered old-fashioned and his audiences subsequently dropped. At this juncture, he met Joe Glaser, a hard-nosed businessman, and instead of allowing the trumpeter's career to slide further, Glaser replaced Armstrong's band members with younger musicians, reduced the size of the band and renamed them The All Stars. The ploy worked, re-establishing Armstrong as a top audience-puller. Eventually, Louis Armstrong and the All Stars became the highest-paid group of its size, touring the world playing their own brand of traditional jazz.

However, through constant use of the trumpet, Armstrong's cheek muscles began weakening. Undeterred, he started singing, and it was his lazy delivery, and his deep growling voice that fronted his biggest-selling singles. He was, incidentally, one of the first artists to sing scat, introduced by accident during a recording session when he forgot the lyrics to a song!

Armstrong's first hit single in Britain was 'Takes Two to Tango' in December 1952. The single, released on the Brunswick label, soared to No. 6 in the chart. Four years later, and now signed to Philips Records, 'Theme from the Threepenny Opera' re-established him in the Top Ten. Armstrong went on to enjoy two further British hits that year – 'Take It Satch' and 'The Faithful Hussar'.

By now, Louis Armstrong was classed as an entertainer; his performances were spiced with humour, and his antics, like rolling his eyes, were condemned by the Civil Rights Movement because he was seen to be poking fun at his own race. Armstrong ignored the criticism, claiming he was above and beyond any political organisations, having lived most of his life without protection from white persecution.

In November 1959 he once more entered the British chart with 'Mack the Knife' which became a Top Thirty hit. There came a further hiatus until 1964 when 'Hello Dolly' was issued on the London label to soar to No. 4.

'What a Wonderful World' backed with 'Cabaret' was first issued during 1968, when in May it soared to the top of the British chart, giving Armstrong his first and only No. 1 single. It was re-issued in April 1988 when it stalled in the British Top Sixty.

'Sunshine of Love' was the follow-up to 1968's 'What a Wonderful World' in the June when it staggered into the Top Forty. A year later Armstrong's 'We Have All the Time in the World', written by Hal David and John Barry, was included in the James Bond movie *On Her Majesty's Secret Service*.

In between recording sessions, and despite health problems which had dogged him since 1959, when he suffered his first heart attack, and major problems with his lip which affected his trumpet playing, Armstrong was a tireless performer. In fact, just weeks before his death, he was on the road. Following heart and kidney failure, Louis Armstrong died in his sleep shortly before his seventy-first birthday in July 1971. He once said, 'I'm not afraid of dying but, like all of us, I don't want to go before I have to . . . life's fun!'

Every so often that 'Satchmo' voice or face reappears, usually via television advertisements. As recently as 1996 the building society, Abbey National, used his image in full-page newspaper advertisements.

A showman beyond equal, he is as popular in death as he was in life.

June 1968

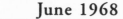

GARY PUCKETT AND THE UNION GAP

Young Girl

Much of Gary Puckett and the Union Gap's success was attributed to cavalier lyrics with sharp, commercial music backdrops. Puckett's distinctive voice told a believable tale, usually of love, lost and found. Unfortunately, their career was short-lived. Did love go out of vogue?

Vocalist Gary Puckett, born in Hibbing, Minnesota, on 17 October

1942, headed the Union Gap which comprised drummer Paul Whitbread, born on 8 February 1946, Gary Witham, keyboardist, born on 22 August 1946, saxophonist Dwight Benett, born on 1 December 1945, all in San Diego, California, and Kerry Chater, born on 7 August 1945 in Canada.

Originally calling themselves The Outcasts, they enjoyed popularity on the club circuit, before renaming themselves the Union Gap during early 1967. As the name suggested, they did wear American Civil War uniforms on stage.

With help from Jerry Fuller, a noted composer/producer, Gary Puckett and the Union Gap released a string of top-selling singles. Their first to crack Britain was in fact 'Young Girl', released by CBS Records. Remarkably, the single soared to the top of the chart in June 1968, as it told its tale of an older man's love for a much younger girl. It was a vividly strong storyline, but then this was the sixties. 'Young Girl' likewise hit the top of the American chart. The single was also re-issued in Britain during 1974 when it became a Top Ten hit.

All together the group enjoyed four British hits; 'Young Girl' counted as two. The next was 'Lady Willpower', released during August 1968, when it reached the British Top Five. Again it was a powerfully-worded track.

Finally, a single first issued in America during 1967, when it sold a million copies, was released in Britain. Titled 'Woman Woman', it sold badly, limping into the Top Fifty during August 1968.

When the run of hits finished, Gary Puckett and the Union Gap disbanded. This prompted Puckett to pursue a solo career, releasing one album of significance, *The Gary Puckett Album*, during 1971.

Despite their brief appearance in the music business, the group did forge an indelible mark with 'Young Girl' whose lyrics are as vital three decades later as they were the first time around.

July 1968

THE EQUALS

Baby Come Back

A multi-racial group, The Equals embodied the phrase 'blue-eyed soul'. Their music was a combination of rock and soul, spliced with

R. & B., and gave birth to a significant solo contributor in the development of reggae in Britain.

Formed by twin brothers, Lincoln and Derv Gordon, born on 29 June 1948 in Jamaica, The Equals comprised drummer John Hall, born 25 October 1947, and guitarist Patrick Lloyd, born 17 March 1948, both in Holloway, London, and Eddy Grant, lead guitarist, born 5 March 1948 in Guyana. These musicians complemented the twins – Derv, who played rhythm guitar, and Lincoln, the group's vocalist.

From 1965 The Equals played in and around North London, before recording for President Records two years later. Their first single, 'I Won't Be There', bombed despite being heavily supported by the pirate radio stations. Their debut album, *Unequalled Equals*, released during December 1967, was promoted as the 'party' album by pirate stations which pushed it into the Top Ten of the British album chart. This was followed by *Equals Explosion* a year later. Neither spawned hit singles, except 'I Get So Excited', which reached the British Top Forty during February 1968. With recorded work to their credit, The Equals toured Europe for six months where they commanded a loyal following, particularly in Belgium, Germany and Holland.

Written by Eddy Grant, 'Baby Come Back' was actually recorded as a flipside to 'Hold Me Closer' during 1966, which, when first released as a single in March 1968, became a Top Forty British hit. As a topside, 'Baby Come Back' was first issued on the Continent to soar up the German chart, before topping several other European listings. It earned The Equals a gold disc for sales in excess of one million copies. Inspired by this extensive success, President Records in Britain re-issued 'Baby Come Back', this time as an A-side, and watched it reach the top of the British chart in July 1968.

'Laurel and Hardy' was the follow-up but its chart achievement was disastrous as it struggled into the Top Forty in August 1968. Ironically, it was The Equals' only American hit, reaching the Top Forty. The next release, 'Softly Softly', fared worse.

To start 1969 the strangely titled 'Michael and the Slipper Tree' managed a British Top Thirty placing, but with the next, 'Viva Bobby Joe', in July 1969, the magic of the 1968 chart-topper returned to re-establish The Equals as Top Ten artists. The track, incidentally, was later adopted by football supporters under the title 'Viva Bobby Moore'! The last of the year was the poor-selling 'Rub a Dub Dub'.

The Equals' final hit was a year later in 1970 with 'Black Skin Blue Eyed Boys' which reached the British Top Ten. The group had released their tried and tested musical formula for the last time.

With no hits, The Equals underwent countless line-up changes until they settled on the nightclub circuits in Britain and Europe. During 1972, their songwriter, Eddy Grant, left to pursue solo projects, including developing his own recording label, Ice Records, based in Guyana and London. In 1977 he issued his debut album, *Message Man*, and two years later leased his material via his Ice label to Ensign Records in Britain. 'Living on the Front Line', released in July 1979, reached the British Top Twenty. This was the first of several British hits through to the mid-eighties when he composed music for *Romancing the Stone*, an adventure movie starring Michael Douglas and Kathleen Turner.

Eddy Grant is still recording in the nineties, although the whereabouts of The Equals is less certain.

Also a No. 1 single in July 1968: 'I Pretend' by Des O'Connor

August 1968

TOMMY JAMES AND THE SHONDELLS

Mony Mony

Critics dictate that music should be placed in categories. 'Mony Mony' could fall into several – bubblegum, blue-eyed soul, pure pop. But at the end of the day, everyone had to agree it was good singalong dance music, and the fact that the track is remembered three decades later proves that . . . 'here she comes now' . . .

Tommy James, born Thomas Jackson in Dayton, Ohio, on 29 April 1947, was given his first record player and a handful of discs when he was two years old. At three, he had mastered the ukulele; by nine he had conquered the guitar. When his family moved to Michigan, James formed his first group, The Tornadoes. He was eleven years old.

In 1962 the youngster persuaded guitarists Larry Wright and Larry Coverdale, drummer Jim Payne and keyboardist Craig Villeneuve to join him to record 'Long Pony Tail'. Tommy James was fifteen years old. Local DJ Jack Douglas showed interest in the song and requested more. Tommy James suggested 'Hanky Panky', a song he'd heard a few times, written by Jeff Barry and Ellie Greenwich and recorded by The Raindrops in 1963. James's version, however, was ad-libbed rather than sung because he didn't know all the lyrics. Nonetheless, it was released on the Snap label to become a local hit in and around Illinois, Indiana and Michigan.

During 1965, James graduated from high school, and with no job pending, flew to Pittsburgh in response to a request from radio DJ Bob Mack who had regularly played 'Hanky Panky' since its release date. To promote the single James needed a pick-up group so, while in Pittsburgh, he formed The Shondells from members of a local group called The Raconteurs – Mike Vale, bassist; Ronnie Rosman, organist; and, later on, Peter Lucia, drummer, and Eddie Gray, guitarist.

Midway through 1966, 'Hanky Panky' was once again issued; this time by the New York-based Roulette Records. It sold in excess of one million copies to dominate the top of the American chart. It also peaked at No. 38 in Britain during July 1966. Two months later, the 'Hanky Panky' album was issued to reach the American Top Fifty.

For their next single, Tommy James and the Shondells chose an R. & B. track previously recorded by Jimmy Gilmer and the Fireballs. Titled 'What I Am', it became a Top Twenty American hit, but bombed in Britain.

A significant musical change occurred in late 1966, when the group worked with composer/producer Richie Cordell and Bo Gentry. Their first collaboration, 'It's Only Love', reached the Top Forty, but was another non-starter in Britain. Through 1967 the group was rarely out of the American listing with singles that included 'I Think We're Alone Now' (No. 4), 'I Like the Way' (No. 25) and 'Out of the Blue' (No. 43).

Following a hesitant start in 1968 with 'Get Out Now' which struggled into the American Top Fifty, Tommy James and the Shondells quickly re-established themselves in the upper echelon. Richie Cordell and Bo Gentry wrote 'Mony Mony', a title pinched from a store sign hanging outside Tommy James's apartment. It was a nerveless, impetuous dance track with a compulsive hookline that many believed pre-empted the 'garage' sound. It soared into the American Top Three, and for the first time the group made a serious inroad into the British chart. 'Mony Mony' became the summer hit of 1968 when it soared to No. 1 during August 1968, a position it held for three weeks.

Before the end of the year, 'Somebody Cares' was issued as the follow-up. It stalled in the American Top Sixty, while the next, 'Do Something to Me', struggled into the Top Forty. The latter was the follow-up to the British release of 'Mony Mony', but had depressing sales, plummeting Tommy James and the Shondells into the one-hit wonder category.

From 1969 to mid-1970, the group remained consistent sellers in America thanks to Tommy James masterminding their entire musical output with gems like 'Crimson and Clover' (a chart-topper which went on to sell in excess of five million copies), 'Crystal Blue Persuasion' and 'Ball of Fire', among others. During June 1970, following the release of 'Come to Me', Tommy James collapsed during a concert in Alabama. Following his hospitalisation and while he recuperated, The Shondells disbanded to form the Hog Heaven.

By August 1970 James was sufficiently recovered to embark upon a solo career. Originally he was to have released 'Tighter and Tighter' as his debut, but produced it instead for the group called Alive and Kicking. The following month 'Ball and Chain' was released as James's first solo effort, to reach the American Top Fifty. His biggest-selling single was 'Draggin' the Line', a No. 4 hit, in August 1971.

Tommy James continued to record through to the eighties, although his singles stumbled around the lower regions of the American chart. That is until he joined Millennium Records to release the million-selling, Top Twenty hit 'Three Times in Love' in March 1980.

Early in 1991, with his recording career over, James recognised the potential in the 'oldies but goldies' concerts and toured America with other artists who had enjoyed success during the sixties.

Also No. 1 singles in August 1968: 'Fire' by The Crazy World of Arthur Brown; 'Do It Again' by The Beach Boys

September 1968

THE BEE GEES

I've Gotta Get a Message to You

For a trio to survive fame's downside to rise again to recapture former success took guts and an unwavering talent. The Bee Gees did just that and inadvertently created the dance phenomenon *Saturday Night Fever*.

The Bee Gees' sixties success spiralled them into the top league of artists within months and the pressures that went hand-in-hand with such elevation were beginning to show by 1968. Minor disagreements within the group were usually disposed of but when Barry Gibb announced he wanted to leave the line-up to concentrate on a movie career, the remaining brothers knew his vacancy could not be filled. When Robin Gibb collapsed from exhaustion during a British tour to be admitted to a London nursing home, they realised their lifestyle needed to be modified. Robin's illness made them postpone their pending American tour for a month until August 1968 which, in turn, meant they would not be able to properly promote their next British single, 'I've Gotta Get a Message to You'. The track told a chilling tale of a man on death row whose only future was the electric chair. The public loved it and pushed it to No. 1 in September 1968; it peaked at No. 8 across the Atlantic. This was to have been the last single to feature Barry. However, before he could fulfil his movie ambitions, events overtook them.

During November, midway through a German and Austrian tour, Robin and Barry Gibb were taken ill and ordered to rest. Hence their remaining dates were cancelled. Then their musicians Vince Melouney and Colin Peterson announced their intention to leave, though they would remain until May 1969. And the disagreements within the trio worsened, probably heightened by their excessive drinking binges.

'It Started as a Joke' was the brothers' first single of 1969, a No. 6 British and American hit, and was the last to feature Melouney and Peterson. It also marked the final single for Robin Gibb who, tired of constant arguments with Maurice, left the trio. Robin did, however, forget his differences to be best man at Maurice's wedding to Scottish singer Lulu in April 1969.

As a duo, Maurice and Barry Gibb became involved in the *Cucumber Castle* project, a film starring Frankie Howerd, Spike Milligan and Lulu, among others. 'Don't Forget to Remember', lifted from the soundtrack, was issued during September 1969 to reach No. 2 in Britain, but in America sales were abysmally low as the single floundered in the Top Eighty. Following a period where each brother became involved in his own ventures, The Bee Gees re-formed late in 1970 at Robin's instigation. 'If we hadn't been related, we would probably never have gotten back together,' he said. The British were slow to support them this time, as reflected by their first single, titled 'Lonely Days', which stalled in the Top Forty. The Americans, on the other hand, pushed it to No. 3.

From 1971 to 1974 The Bee Gees toured the world and released Top Twenty singles on both sides of the Atlantic. But music was changing; the public wanted to dance. The seventies were slowly being strangled by disco music, and artists not previously associated with dance were cashing in, many losing credibility on the way. Nonetheless, disco was booming, and new acts were becoming big-sellers as the beat dictated. The Bee Gees were responsible for changing, or, as many believed at the time, destroying the good of the dance.

In August 1975, the brothers released 'Jive Talkin'", a fiery, stuttered dance track. It soared into the British Top Five and topped the American chart. The song was lifted from the brothers' recently finished album, *Main Course*, recorded in New York and Miami with producer Arif Mardin. A second track, 'Nights on Broadway', was lifted to become a Top Ten American hit during December 1975.

A year later 'You Should Be Dancing' smashed into the world's charts, peaking at No. 5 in Britain, while topping the American chart, giving The Bee Gees their third No. 1 single there. Indeed, the brothers had returned to the music business with a vengeance, but there was more to come.

During February and March 1977, Robert Stigwood, now owner of his own RSO Records, was producing the dance movie *Saturday Night Fever*, starring John Travolta. He approached The Bee Gees for songs to be included in the film's soundtrack. In total, they provided 'Jive Talkin'", 'How Deep Is your Love', 'Stayin' Alive', 'Night Fever' and 'You Should Be Dancing'. They also wrote 'More Than a Woman' for The Tavares, and 'If I Can't Have You' for Yvonne Elliman, both later million-sellers.

Saturday Night Fever was premiered in New York during December 1977 and thanks to The Bee Gees' music (certainly not the movie's storyline) disco music would never be the same. The soundtrack album went on to sell a staggering thirty million copies worldwide to top charts in most countries. At the time of writing, it remains the top-selling soundtrack album of all time. The Bee Gees themselves enjoyed handsome spin-off successes with 'How Deep Is Your Love', a No. 3 British hit in December 1977, and a million-selling chart-topper in America. 'Stayin' Alive' soared into the British Top Five, while the Americans pushed it to the top, a position it would hold for four weeks.

Saturday Night Fever was an absolute monster, from the music to the army of John Travolta lookalikes who donned white suits and perfected solo dance routines. They could be spotted on nightclub dancefloors, strutting their Travolta stuff, right arm raised in the air, finger pointing, body jerking, oblivious to the hidden smiles from other dancers. And the lookalikes lived into the nineties – very sad.

Once the furore had died, predictably killing disco music, The Bee Gees turned their talents elsewhere. During 1980 they wrote and produced Barbra Streisand's *Guilty* album, and in 1985 did the same for Diana Ross with *Eaten Alive*. Both singers enjoyed instant British chart-toppers; Streisand with 'Woman in Love', Ross with 'Chain Reaction'. Yet, amidst the unprecedented and phenomenal success that was now associated with the brothers, others fell by the wayside. Maurice and Lulu's marriage ended in divorce (he went on to marry Yvonne Spencely), and brother Andy, who had enjoyed considerable American success including three chart-toppers that included 'Shadow Dancing', died at the age of thirty from an inflammatory heart virus in 1988.

Through the eighties and into the nineties, The Bee Gees shrugged off setbacks to re-emerge as the megastars they are. A series of charting singles like 'You Win Again' (1987), 'Ordinary Lives' (1989), 'Secret Love' (1991) and 'For Whom the Bell Tolls' in 1993 ensured their continued high profile.

The Bee Gees are among the finest composers and performers known to British music and there's no reason why they shouldn't continue.

Also see: 'Massachusetts', November 1967

October 1968

MARY HOPKIN

Those Were the Days

The young, blonde-haired Welsh folk singer was another performer to benefit from the talents (and generosity) of The Beatles. Paul McCartney took Mary Hopkin under his wing to present her with a No. 1 single.

Born in Pontardawe, Wales, on 3 May 1950, Mary Hopkin started singing at the age of four in her local church choir. While at school she became interested in folk music, and this, in turn, led to appearances on Welsh television. In 1967, she recorded Welsh language material on the Cambrian label that included her debut 'Llais Swynol Mary Hopkin'. She then appeared on *Opportunity Knocks*, a television talent show hosted by Hughie Green. Twiggy saw Hopkin's act and recommended her to Paul McCartney. Equally impressed, he signed the young Welsh singer to Apple, The Beatles' own record label, during 1968.

McCartney took Hopkin into the studios to record a handful of tracks including the Gene Raskin composition, 'Those Were the Days', a traditional Russian song titled 'Darogoi Dlmmoyo'. Produced by McCartney, the track was not only Mary Hopkin's debut release, but the first single bearing the Apple label. The haunting melody against Hopkin's soft voice sold in excess of 750,000 copies to soar to No. 1 in the British chart during October 1968. 'Those Were the Days' also became an American hit, and when the singer promoted it on *The Ed Sullivan Show*, she pushed its sales past the one million mark to reach No. 2. Later recordings, in different languages including Italian, Spanish and French, ensured hits in those countries. Before the song died entirely, worldwide sales were in excess of six million copies.

Early in 1969, Hopkin's first album, *Post Card*, was issued. Produced by Paul McCartney, it became a Top Three hit in the album chart. To capitalise on this achievement, she embarked upon her first British tour in March, supporting Engelbert Humperdinck.

The follow-up to 'Those Were the Days' was 'Goodbye', this time written and produced by John Lennon and Paul McCartney. The single raced to No. 2 in the British chart, while across the Atlantic it reached the Top Twenty. At the end of the year, Mary Hopkin followed the route of other successful artists to appear in pantomime – co-starring with Tommy Steele in *Cinderella*.

During March 1970, Hopkin's next single marked a change of producer to Mickie Most. Titled 'Temma Harbour' it returned her to the British Top Ten, reaching No. 39 in America. Mary Hopkin was then chosen to sing a selection of songs earmarked for the forthcoming Eurovision Song Contest. 'Knock Knock Who's There', written by John Carter and Geoff Stevens, was selected by the public to represent Britain in the Song Contest. Despite being tailor-made for the occasion, 'Knock Knock Who's There' was runner-up to Dana's 'All Kinds of Everything', submitted by Eire. Nonetheless, Hopkin took her song to No. 2 in the British chart, while Dana soared to the top.

Errol Brown (lead singer from Hot Chocolate) wrote the Welsh girl's next release. Titled 'Think about your Children', it stalled in the British Top Twenty during November 1970. Then Hopkin took an eight-month hiatus before issuing 'Let my Name Be Sorrow', which reached No. 46 in Britain. By December 1971, 'Water, Paper and Clay' became her final single on the Apple label. Regrettably, it was also her last hit. Fortunately, the personal front painted a happier picture, because after working with producer Tony Visconti, Mary Hopkin married him at the close of 1971.

Following another absence when she worked as back-up vocalist for countless acts that included David Bowie, Hopkin signed a recording deal with Bell Records to release 'Summertime Summertime' under the pseudonym Hobby Horse. She then joined EMI Records' Regal Zonophone label to issue 'Mary Had a Baby' in time for the 1972 Christmas market.

There was a further four-year gap before Hopkin recorded again, this time for her husband's label Good Earth, where she issued a cover version of Edith Piaf's 'If You Love Me' which re-established her in the British Top Forty. 'Wrap Me in your Arms' followed – and bombed – before she returned to her roots to record the album *The Welsh World of Mary Hopkin*, issued by Decca Records. After this, Hopkin retired from the music business to devote herself to her family.

During 1980, Mike D'Albuquerque and ex-Springfield Mike Hurst persuaded Hopkin to record once more. Under a recording deal with Bronze Records, the trio, known as Sundance, released 'What's Love' during 1981. After a relatively short stay, Hopkin left the trio. Her marriage was also dissolved.

Four years on, the pull of music brought Mary Hopkin back to the recording studio. As lead singer for Oasis, which also included Julian Lloyd Webber and Peter Skellern, she recorded one eponymous album. Ill health forced her to retire. Then, once more, she was encouraged to return to her music. This time producer George Martin asked her to contribute to his *Under Milk Wood* compilation released during 1988, and a year on, she made another attempt to establish herself by recording the *Spirit* album. She failed. Mary Hopkin may have disappeared from the public eye once again, but she will always be remembered for the perennial 'Those Were the Days', whether she likes it or not.

November 1968

JOE COCKER

With a Little Help from my Friends

Joe Cocker is one of Britain's finest soul singers. His career, though, has had more dips and rises than most. So he now claims to be a survivor: 'I get called a fossil, which is okay when I start thinking of some of the musicians I've known who are dead . . . I'm sure I've been talked about as the next potential dead candidate.'

Born John Cocker in Sheffield, South Yorkshire, on 20 May 1944, he left school to join the Gas Board as a fitter. By night, he sang in his brother Victor's group before being relegated into The Cavaliers as a drummer and singer. Cocker told Joe Smith: 'Trying to sing and drum was difficult. I remember the band saying, "You have to do one or the other, and we'd prefer it if you drum because we'll never find another drummer."'

In 1963, after The Cavaliers became Vance Arnold and the Avengers, they worked as support act for numerous professional touring groups. By now, Cocker was known as Joe, and he had abandoned his drums to become the group's lead singer.

Following an audition for record producer Mike Leander, Joe Cocker signed a recording contract with Decca Records. Moonlighting from the Gas Board, he travelled to London to record his first Lennon/McCartney track, 'I'll Cry Instead', at Decca's studios. It bombed, whereupon Cocker teamed up with The Big Blues to tour Britain with The Hollies.

Decca Records dropped him so he returned, albeit reluctantly, to his fitter's job, confining his musical activities with The Avengers to the evenings. With only the occasional booking to support them, the group decided to disband, leaving Cocker to team up with Chris Stainton to form The Grease Band during 1964. For two years the outfit played on the Northern club circuit. Cocker: 'We'd go to these pubs every night after our day jobs and drink a lot of beer and play until the pubs closed . . . We weren't in that big a hurry to be successful.'

In 1968, after sending a demo tape of their act to producer Denny Cordell, Joe Cocker, solo, issued 'Marjorine' (written by the singer and Stainton) on EMI Records' Regal Zonophone label. It became his first Top Fifty hit, and he spent most of the year touring, establishing himself with the public, as support act to The Who, among others.

For his next single Cocker returned to Lennon/McCartney to record a version of their 'With a Little Help from my Friends'. The single shot to the top of the British chart to stay one week during November 1968, the same month as John Lennon and Yoko Ono released their controversial *Two Virgins* album. The Beatles were so delighted with Cocker's throat-wrenching, white soul interpretation that they bought music press space to congratulate him. Across the Atlantic, the disc stalled just outside the Top Sixty. Twenty years later, the group Wet Wet Wet took their version of the single to the top of the British chart, where it stayed for four weeks.

Joe Cocker had never hidden the fact that he had been a heavy drinker since his teens. He later turned to marijuana. In December 1968, he was busted for possession of the drug. His girlfriend at the time told the police the drugs were hers and the charges against Cocker were dropped. Cocker: 'I never smoked pot when I was young. I sort of made up for it after. I always swore I'd be a drinker to the end. But then, when someone turned me on to some black hash, musically speaking, it was such an opening to the ears and senses.'

The surprise success of 'With a Little Help from my Friends' escalated Cocker into the mainstream league, his audience expanding from a few hundred club drinkers to a nationwide following. His stage act which had been accepted in the dimly lit, smoky atmospheres, was now questionable because many believed he was mimicking a disabled person. He stalked through a song, his arms twitching, while his body and facial features became distorted with the music. Cocker said he was unaware of this, but stressed his hand movements were a subconscious act of directing the music.

During 1969, Cocker and The Grease Band toured Britain before embarking upon a lengthy American tour. While there, they contributed to the Newport '69 Festival and, of course, the Woodstock Music and Art Fair, later affectionately known as *Woodstock* on film and album. He then performed at the Isle of Wight Festival of Music, before returning to play a stint at Fillmore West in San Francisco.

In 1969, Cocker released 'Delta Lady' as the follow-up to his 1968 chart-topper. Penned by Leon Russell, whom he met at Woodstock, it soared into the British Top Ten. As Cocker now wanted to concentrate on a solo career, The Grease Band disbanded, although Chris Stainton continued to work with the singer.

Early in 1970 Cocker once more turned to The Beatles to record 'She Came in through the Bathroom Window'. It was a Top Thirty American hit. To capitalise on his growing popularity there, he formed a further band known as Mad Dogs and Englishmen for a thirteen-week tour. Sections of that tour were recorded and filmed. In his absence, 'The Letter', a cover version of The Box Tops' hit, was issued in May 1970 to become a Top Forty British hit. It reached No. 7 in America.

During the early seventies. Cocker's heroin addiction controlled his life. He was incapable of working, but thankfully material had been previously canned to ensure records could be released at respectable intervals. Following the release in 1972 of the album *Joe Cocker/With a Little Help from my Friends*, and a performance at Crystal Palace, London, with The Beach Boys, Cocker embarked upon an Australian tour. He and members of his entourage were convicted of drugs possession and assault, and were deported. In 1973, he was arrested for possession of marijuana while visiting his family in Sheffield (of all places!) and, four years later, was deported from America on the grounds of illegal entry. Trouble certainly followed Cocker's every move.

Even though his British recording career was stagnant, Cocker continued to chart in America. He worked with several producers and record companies, and recorded poor-selling material as a result. 'I'm So Glad I'm Still Standing' with The Crusaders in February 1982 was a good example. That same month, Cocker signed a serious recording contract with Island Records. His luck changed. The chance came to duet with Jennifer Warnes on 'Up Where We Belong' for the movie soundtrack of *An Officer and a Gentleman*. The song raced to No. 7 in the British chart during January 1983, and to the top in America where it stayed for three weeks. The song also won several Grammy Awards, and Joe Cocker a recording contract with Capitol Records. Two poor-selling singles followed, namely 'Unchain my Heart' in November 1987, and 'When the Night Comes' over two years later.

Much of the singer's career was American-based, yet, like the proverbial bad penny, he rose again in Britain during 1991 to contribute 'Sorry Seems to Be the Hardest Word' on the compilation *Two Rooms: Celebrating the Songs of Elton John and Bernie Taupin*, and again in the spring of 1992 with '(All I Know) Feels Like Forever', lifted from the movie *The Cutting Edge*. It became a Top Thirty British hit. He also duetted with Sass Jordan on 'Trust in Me' which was included on the soundtrack of Whitney Houston's first film, *The Bodyguard*.

During 1992, Cocker enjoyed three British hit singles with 'Now that the Magic Has Gone' (Top Thirty), and re-releases of 'Unchain my Heart' (Top Twenty) and 'When the Night Comes' (Top Seventy). His trips to Britain are now rare, but up to 1993 he still sustained a healthy career as a touring act in America.

Thanks to his new manager Roger Davies, who elevated Tina Turner to solo superstardom, Cocker, with his alcohol and drug addiction in check, has recreated a lucrative career for himself. So much so that for the first time in his life he is finally reaping financial rewards. His albums are once again selling in healthy quantities and European concerts, in particular, are high-earners, with audiences in excess of 5,000. Cocker told journalist Anna Treacher in a 1997 *Hello!* magazine interview: 'It seems strange to think of a 60-year-old rock 'n' roller ... I find the road gets harder as you get older because you take knocks a bit harder. But there's always enough reason to get up and continue.'

Also a No. 1 single in November 1968: 'The Good, the Bad and the Ugly' by Hugo Montenegro and his Orchestra and Chorus

December 1968

SCAFFOLD

Lily the Pink

If ever there was the perfect party song 'Lily the Pink' was it. The lyrics, foolish as they are, could be sung with the greatest of ease when alcohol flowed. And it was all thanks to Scaffold, a trio of humorists, who didn't, like their fellow Liverpudlians, rely on the Merseybeat explosion for success.

This trio of unlikelies comprised Mike McGear, younger brother of Paul McCartney, born 7 January 1944; John Gorman, born 4 January 1937 and Roger McGough, born 9 November 1937. Despite being formed in Liverpool, the outfit wasn't musically inclined; their forte was satire. Featured on the late-night television programme *Gazteet*, they later performed their act at the Establishment Club in London. Regular spots at Edinburgh venues ensured their growing popularity among theatre-goers.

In 1967, Scaffold were encouraged to record their satire by EMI Records, who released their first single, 'Thank U Very Much', on its Parlophone label. The novelty element pushed the single into the British Top Four, and although the public was aware that Mike McGear was related to Paul McCartney, he had no hand in Scaffold's success.

The follow-up, 'Do You Remember', staggered into the Top Forty during March 1968, before the trio pulled the rabbit from the hat – 'Lily the Pink'. Like their debut release, this offered absurd lyrics which attracted the record-buying public. It was released during the Christmas period of 1968, and the trio watched it soar to No. 1 with amazement. The *Lily the Pink* album followed shortly, but instead of being much of the same inaneness, it offered diversification from humorist John Gorman and poet Roger McGough.

A year on from their chart-topper, Scaffold issued 'Gin Gan Goolie', usually associated with the Scouts and schoolboy banter. It first entered the British chart at No. 38, then during January 1970, re-entered to reach the Top Fifty.

By now, though, a larger conglomerate of Liverpool satirists had been formed. Known as Grimm, it eventually swallowed up Scaffold. With no group to front, Mike McGear recorded the solo single 'Woman', which bombed. He then re-formed Scaffold to perform with members of the Average White Band and Zoot Money to combine their humour with rock music.

During 1977, Scaffold once more enjoyed unexpected chart status with 'Liverpool Lou'. Released by Warner Brothers (EMI Records having dropped the trio) the single soared to No. 7 in the British chart. Warner Brothers also issued a further solo number from McGear that October. Titled 'Leave It', the disc became a Top Forty hit.

After the trio's last album, *Sold Out*, the members pursued individual careers. John Gorman moved into television to appear on *Tizwas* and actually became a recording artist again in 1980 when 'The Bucket of Water Song', released by CBS Records, reached the Top Thirty in May. Gorman wasn't alone; he had Chris Tarrant, Lenny Henry and Sally James to assist.

Roger McGough returned to poetry, his first love, leaving Mike McGear to continue as a soloist until his recording contract with Warner Brothers expired.

January 1969

MARMALADE

Ob-La-Di Ob-La-Da

Before Marmalade enjoyed nationwide chart success, they were Scotland's foremost group. When they became a top-selling act with a little help from Lennon and McCartney, they practically ruined their lives with backstage antics.

Ex-clarinet player Junior Campbell, born Wullie Campbell Jr on 31 May 1947 in Glasgow, and Patrick Fairley, born on 14 April 1946, also in Glasgow, formed the nucleus of the group during 1961. The couple recruited Dean Ford, born Thomas McAleese on 5 September 1946 in Coatbridge, Scotland, whom they had seen perform in The Monarchs (after The Tonebeats) and who was a Ford Motors apprentice plater by trade.

A short time afterwards, Raymond Duffy joined as drummer, while training as a chef during the day. Finally, in 1964, Graham Knight, born on 8 December 1946 in Glasgow, answered an advertisement for a bass guitarist in a local newspaper to complete the line-up. Known as The Gaylords, the group swiped material from Cliff Richard and The Shadows for the basis of their stage act. By 1964 they were voted Scotland's top act.

As the group's popularity spread during 1965, their repertoire expanded to include American R. & B. songs. This moved the group into the American Air Force bases in Britain.

In time their reputation attracted EMI Records' Norrie Paramor who at the time headed its subsidiary label, Columbia. Paramor signed the group and they released their first single, 'Twenty Miles', a version of the Chubby Checker track which they had included in their act for some time. The single was a big seller in Scotland but on a national basis it bombed. The follow-up 'Mr Heartbreak's Here Instead' also died.

During 1966, 'He's a Good Face, but He's Down and Out' became their next flop, whereupon they were dropped from the Columbia label's artist roster. Determined not to give up, The Gaylords decided to move to London, leaving Raymond Duffy behind in Scotland. Alan Whitehead, born 24 July 1946 in Oswestry, Shropshire, replaced him. (Raymond Duffy would later join Matthews Southern Comfort.) The group renamed itself Marmalade (Ford and Campbell, lead singers; Knight, bass guitar and vocals; Fairley, guitar; Whitehead, drums).

By 1967 Marmalade were still without a record company but were building up a healthy reputation among London clubs, notably the Marquee. A change of musical direction seemed to be the only answer. So shrugging off their American repertoire, they headed for commerciality. The move worked. CBS Records signed them and their first single was 'It's All Leading up to a Saturday Night'.

Before the end of 1967 they issued 'I See the Rain' which was voted the top single of the year. Unfortunately, the voters weren't in Britain but Holland where the single peaked in the Top Thirty. The tide was soon to turn when in 1968 they issued 'Lovin' Things', a version of The Grass Roots' track. This became their first British hit, reaching

No. 6 during May 1968. 'Wait for Me Marianne' followed that October to falter in the Top Thirty. Nevertheless, Marmalade was no longer a no-hit outfit.

After hearing The Beatles' white album, Marmalade wasted no time in lifting and recording a track for immediate release, titled 'Ob-La-Di Ob-La-Da'. This happy sound gave the group their first (and only) British chart-topper in January 1969. It dominated the chart for three weeks. Another version of the song recorded by The Bedrocks managed to reach the Top Twenty before disappearing altogether.

That all-important follow-up was issued midway through 1969. Titled 'Baby Make It Soon', it reached No. 9 and marked their last single for CBS Records because competitor Decca Records had lured them away with a recording deal that included freedom to record without interference from company executives. This meant Marmalade's underrated composing duo Junior Campbell and Dean Ford could flex their writing muscles. Consequently, the group's debut single for Decca was their own composition, 'Reflections of my Life', which went on to sell in excess of two million copies. Not only did the disc race to No. 3 in Britain but also reached the American Top Ten.

Marmalade's second Decca single, 'Rainbow', also became a Top Three hit in Britain during July 1970, while across the Atlantic it stalled in the Top Sixty. Following this release, Junior Campbell expressed his wish to leave the group. When 'My Little One' had peaked at No. 15 in Britain during March 1971, he quit the group, leaving it without its most prolific songwriter. Ex-Poets member Hugh Nicolson replaced him. A short time afterwards, Alan Whitehead likewise left Marmalade; Dougie Henderson, another from The Poets, stepped in.

With the new line-up settled, Hughie Nicolson penned 'Cousin Norman', which reached the British Top Ten during October 1971. The following month, the group suffered a further upheaval when Patrick Fairley retired from the public spotlight. He first concentrated on the group's various companies before becoming general manager for the Robert Stigwood Organisation. Marmalade did not replace him.

Before 1971 had ended, they released 'Back on the Road' which stalled at No. 35, their lowest chart position to date. As if that wasn't enough to contend with, a Sunday tabloid exposed Marmalade's sexual antics with girl groupies. Almost overnight their touring schedules were halved. Perhaps if they had concentrated more on their music Marmalade might not have started the downward slide so quickly. As it was, in May 1972, they enjoyed a reprieve when 'Radancer' re-established them in the British Top Ten. It was a much-needed hit because within three months, ex-Marmalade member Junior Campbell released his first solo outing, 'Hallelujah Freedom', on Decca Records' subsidiary label Deram. This crashed into the British Top Ten, while its follow-up, 'Sweet Illusion', reached the Top Twenty.

Meanwhile, Marmalade was on the move once again, and by 1976 the only original group members were Alan Whitehead and Graham Knight. They recruited further members to re-establish Marmalade as a recording entity. During 1977 they were fortunate to sign a recording deal with Target Records, owned by Tony McCauley. There they released the aptly named single 'Falling Apart at the Seams'. It reached No. 6 in the British chart, and was their last hit.

During the eighties, Marmalade, with further line-up changes, concentrated on the cabaret circuit, and with the expanding public interest in nostalgia concert tours, they are still performing today.

February 1969

FLEETWOOD MAC

Albatross

Fleetwood Mac were an international group sprung from a blues-based outfit. Yet to the general public they'll be remembered for a handful of mainstream singles including 'Albatross', which was alien to their 'root' sound.

Mick Fleetwood, born in London on 24 June 1942, after working in bands that included The Bo Street Runners and Shotgun Express, became a member of The Bluesbreakers, headed by John Mayall, in 1967. Other Bluesbreakers members included Peter Green, born Peter Greenbaum in London on 29 October 1946, and John McVie, also born in London, on 26 November 1945. The quartet recorded together, the members gelling with their ideas, but within a few weeks both Green and Fleetwood were sacked.

In time the couple met Bob Brunning and Jeremy Spencer, both experienced guitarists, and formed the blues group, Fleetwood Mac. Their most regular performing site was in Fulham's Black Bull public house until August 1967 when they performed at the Windsor Jazz and Blues Festival in Berkshire. This led to gigs at London's Marquee Club, among other niteries. At this point, Brunning left the line-up to be replaced by ex-Bluesbreaker John McVie, and during November 1967 the group debuted on record with 'I Believe my Time Ain't Long' on the Blue Horizon label, owned by Mike Vernon.

Early in 1968, the album *Fleetwood Mac* was issued to reach No. 4 in the British album chart, while 'Black Magic Woman' peaked at No. 37 in the singles chart. 'Need your Love So Bad', a cover version of Little Willie John's original, was released as the group's next single during July. As it peaked in the British Top Thirty, the group toured America for the first time, stopping off in Detroit, San Francisco and Los Angeles. This was followed by a lengthy British tour, and Danny Kirwan joined the line-up.

During September, with Chicken Shack member Christine Perfect (born 12 July 1943 in Birmingham) on piano, 'Mr Wonderful' was issued to soar into the Top Ten. Not a group to sit on its laurels, Fleetwood Mac returned to America to join Marvin Gaye and others at the Miami Pop Festival in Florida.

Early in 1969, Fleetwood Mac changed musical direction. They moved away from the confinement of the blues to experiment with an instrumental that was so compulsive, it still lives on three decades later. Titled 'Albatross' and written by Peter Green, it flew to the top of the British chart during February 1969. The single subsequently repeated its success throughout Europe, leaving the group little option but to undertake an extensive tour there, occasionally teaming up with B.B. King. 'Albatross' rose again in June 1973 when it was re-issued and reached No. 2 in the British chart.

Fleetwood Mac's recording contract with Blue Horizon ended in May 1969. Keen to extract itself from the label, the group moved to Immediate Records, owned by Andrew Loog Oldman, then manager of The Rolling Stones. Their debut single was 'Man of the World', another Peter Green composition, which reached No. 2 in the British chart. Much of 1969 was spent touring America, so Blue Horizon re-released 'Need your Love So Bad', which reached the British Top Forty. At the end of the year, Fleetwood Mac joined Reprise Records, and narrowly missed their second chart-topper with 'Oh Well', penned by Green, which highlighted his rejection of the Jewish faith for Christianity, and which peaked at No. 2. In America the sales were poor by comparison, as the single stalled in the Top Sixty.

The group suffered a major upheaval during 1970 when Peter Green left the line-up for no apparent reason, except that he was unable to cope with the stresses of his career. His decision was taken midway through a European tour in April but he agreed to complete the itinerary for fear of being financially penalised. His final single with Fleetwood Mac was the unusually titled 'The Green Manalishi (with the Two-Pronged Crown)' which revealed his confused mental state. As the single became a Top Ten British hit, the group arranged a further tour of America. It was at this juncture that Christine Perfect officially joined Fleetwood Mac's line-up. Later, she married John McVie and used his surname. Before 1970 ended, Peter Green issued *The End of the Game*, his first solo album, while Fleetwood Mac, desperate to prove they didn't miss his talent, released *Kiln House* which peaked in the Top Forty and Top Seventy in Britain and America respectively.

The next year, 1971, also placed Fleetwood Mac in turmoil. During February, Jeremy Spencer 'disappeared' during an American trek to join the American cult, the Children of God. It later transpired that Spencer suffered the same pressures as Green and was unable to cope with his current lifestyle. However, it was Peter Green who stepped in to replace Jeremy Spencer to complete the tour.

Now minus their main composers, Fleetwood Mac floundered until Bob Welch, ex-member of the American pick-up group, Seven Souls, joined in April to replace Spencer, and to record a new album. Of the three issued before the end of 1971, *Future Games* was by far the most successful. Another change of membership occurred in 1972. Bob Weston from Long John Baldry's back-up group replaced the sacked Danny Kirwan, while ex-Savoy Brown member Dave Walker was also recruited. It was this line-up that recorded the album *Penguin*, issued in May 1973.

From 1974 through to 1977, Fleetwood Mac suffered professionally and personally. A legal fight ensued between them and their manager, when an American tour wasn't fulfilled. The manager formed a 'fake' Fleetwood Mac line-up but that soon dissolved. There was a further personnel change; Christine and John McVie divorced, and Stevie Nicks, born on 26 May 1948 in Phoenix, Arizona, and her boyfriend, Lindsay Buckingham, born on 3 October 1947 in Palo Alto, California, joined the group. Meanwhile, Peter Green entered a mental hospital. Despite this turmoil, Fleetwood Mac managed to complete an American tour and, now signed to Warner Brothers, recorded the highly-acclaimed *Rumours* album, released during February 1977 to top both the British and American charts. It went on to sell in excess of 15 million copies and is the second best-selling album of all time. (Michael Jackson's *Thriller* holds the top position.) The group was also re-established on the singles front with 'Go your Own Way' and 'Don't Stop', both Top Forty British hits.

Individual members of Fleetwood Mac worked on their own musical projects through the late seventies and early eighties, but re-formed the group to tour, especially on the American circuits where they were much in demand, and to record the follow-up album to *Rumours*. Issued during 1979, the double album *Tusk* was classed as an ambitious release that was too self-opinionated for comfort. The album's title track was released as a single and reached the Top Six during October 1979.

During 1982 two British singles charted – 'Gypsy' in the Top Fifty, and 'Oh Diane' in the Top Ten. In 1987 two others stalled in the Top Sixty, namely 'Seven Wonders' and 'Family Man', and another pair hit the Top Ten – 'Big Love' and 'Little Lies'. A year later, 'Everywhere' soared to No. 4, while 'Isn't It Midnight' staggered into the Top Sixty.

With another line-up upheaval, Fleetwood Mac released a further chart-topping album during 1990. Titled *Behind the Mask*, it spearheaded a lengthy nationwide tour before capacity audiences, and spawned two singles, 'Save Me' and 'In the Back of my Mind', both only reaching the British Top Sixty.

The group then lost Christine McVie and Stevie Nicks, which culminated in another unsettling period when the band disintegrated. They re-formed in 1993 to perform 'Don't Stop' at President Bill Clinton's Inaugural Concert at the Capitol Centre. For a group that underwent so many personnel changes it really was a remarkable feat to maintain such a high standard in music. 'Albatross' formed such a tiny part of their overall success, yet it was the only one to reach the top. Doubtless, Fleetwood Mac will rise again.

Also No. 1 singles in February 1969: 'Blackberry Way' by The Move; '(If Paradise Is) Half as Nice' by Amen Corner; 'Where Do You Go to my Lovely' by Peter Sarstedt

MARVIN GAYE

I Heard It through the Grapevine

' "I Heard It through the Grapevine" was recorded at an early stage of my career when I wasn't into myself as an artist.' – Marvin Gaye

Marvin Gaye's version of 'I Heard It through the Grapevine', written and produced by Barrett Strong and Norman Whitfield, was one of at least six versions recorded by his fellow Motown artists. The Miracles were first, recording it as a track for their 1968 album *Special Occasion*, followed by The Isley Brothers. Although Gladys Knight and the Pips recorded their version (which sold in excess of two million copies) after Gaye, they enjoyed the single release first because Gaye and Motown founder, Berry Gordy, were at loggerheads, Years on, The Temptations and The Undisputed Truth (both produced by Norman Whitfield) recorded it, together with a host of non-Motown acts including Elton John and Ike and Tina Turner.

Gaye's version could have remained lost for years without the integrity of Norman Whitfield, who sneaked the track on to an album listing, and the enthusiasm of WVON Radio's Rodney Jones, who acquired a copy of that listing which formed the basis of Gaye's pending *In the Groove* album. Jones saturated the airwaves with this one track and the effect was phenomenal; listeners blocked the radio station's switchboard, demanding the album track be released as a single. Motown sprung into action and 'I Heard It through the Grapevine' became one of its biggest-selling singles of all time.

Behind the scenes, Gaye was sceptical about issuing his version on the back of Gladys Knight and the Pips' success, but due to his moody, haunting and hypnotic interpretation, the worry was unfounded. In America alone the single sold two and a half million, topping the charts for seven weeks, fending off fellow Motowners Stevie Wonder with 'For Once in my Life' and Diana Ross and the Supremes with The Temptations' 'I'm Gonna Make You Love Me'. Across the Atlantic, he enjoyed his first and only British chart-topper, while scoring high marks in twenty-six other countries.

Marvin Pentz Gay was the much-wanted first son of Alberta and Marvin Gay Snr, born on 2 April 1939 in Washington DC. He spent his first seventeen years living in a slum area he called 'Simple City' on 1617 1st Street. When their home was demolished in the mid-fifties, the family moved to 10 Sixtieth Street in the East Capitol Dwellings. Gay lived there with his parents, two sisters and younger brother.

Raised on fear and religion, the boy's deepest ambition was to sing, although performing for neighbours and relatives wasn't exactly what he had in mind. At school, though, he joined a handful of groups, and played hookey at the Howard Theater, watching artists like Jackie Wilson and James Brown. Studying came third in his list of priorities. Adhering to his father's demands, Gay joined the Air Force where he rebelled against authority until he was granted an honourable discharge. According to him, 'It was a horrible experience, and the worst thing I have ever done. I hated the discipline and was always getting into trouble because I was a frustrated member of the ground staff. I was never taught to fly – I peeled potatoes!'

With music still coursing through his veins, he drifted into the remains of his pre-force group, The Rainbows, before settling into The Marquees, who were working as studio session musicians for Okah, a Chess/Checker label. A chance meeting with writer/producer/performer Harvey Fuqua took Gay nearer his musical goals, although an instant recording contract wasn't in the offing. Instead, Fuqua took the youngster under his wing, and taught him the rudimentaries of the music business, before recruiting him as a member of the newly formed Moonglows, as the original group, led by Fuqua, had disbanded some while earlier.

It was inevitable that in time this outfit would likewise flounder, and during 1960 Fuqua persuaded Gay to join him at Anna Records, headed by Billy Davis and Berry Gordy's sister, Gwen. The lack of business expertise meant that Anna Records soon lost money, while, across town in Detroit, Berry Gordy's Tamla Motown label was gaining momentum. In 1961 when Anna folded, Harvey Fuqua opened the Tri Phi and Harvey labels as replacements, again transferring Gay. Once more, his role was not one of artist but of session musician, playing the piano and drums. In time, any success enjoyed by Tri Phi and Harvey was overshadowed by the growth of Tamla Motown. Instead of competing, Harvey Fuqua opted to join forces with Berry Gordy; hence Marvin Gay became a Motown artist almost by default.

Yet again, the young man was confined to the back room simply because Berry Gordy had no idea how to present him on vinyl.

Together they regularly experimented with various types of music, before recording a selection of songs for an album. *The Soulful Moods of Marvin Gaye* was the end result, issued in 1961. As expected, it bombed, as did the lifted single 'Let your Conscience Be your Guide'. Gaye admits, 'It was a real disaster . . . and must have been one of the few lemons Berry had. He's a fine writer, so it must have been my performance.' The single signified a change in the singer's name – Gay became Gaye, a move he had wanted to make for some time because 'I was tired of being teased that I was gay'.

Eventually the musical mix gelled with 'Stubborn Kind of Fellow', co-written by Marvin, Berry Gordy and Mickey Stevenson. Released in July 1962, this uptempo slice of commercial soul soared into the American chart, thus beginning Gaye's conveyor belt of dance hits that included 'Hitch Hike' in 1962, 'Pride and Joy' and 'Can I Get a Witness' a year later.

Following the release of Mary Wells's American chart-topper 'My Guy', Berry Gordy decided to team her with Gaye on record. They recorded one album, titled *Together*, from which 'Once upon a Time' was lifted as a single to become their debut British hit, peaking in the Top Fifty during July 1964. Gaye: 'Mickey Stevenson [producer] cut this album of us duetting but there weren't that many strong songs [on it]. The whole thing seemed to be a watered-down version of my style and her style.'

Watered-down or not, the singing combination was successful, and in turn led to Gaye recording with a further Motown songstress, Kim Weston. Although sufficient tracks were recorded for an album, only two singles were issued, namely 'What Good Am I without You' in 1964, and 'It Takes Two' during 1966. Both were minor hits. Nonetheless, this did not prevent a further duetting career with Tammi Terrell when their debut single, 'Ain't No Mountain High Enough', written by Valerie Simpson and Nickolas Ashford, was the first in a run of hit singles in 1967. Gaye: 'I had no idea that [Tammi] was as good a singer as she turned out to be.' Record buyers were entranced by Gaye and Terrell's uncomplicated image. When she commanded, he obeyed; when she seduced him, he responded. Their phrasing was magical.

Although Ashford and Simpson engineered the Gaye/Terrell success story, they were unprepared for the finale. For some time, Terrell had been suffering from blinding headaches, and in mid-1967 as she and Gaye finished singing at the Hampton-Sydney College in Virginia, she collapsed into his arms. Doctors diagnosed a brain tumour. The singer's health deteriorated drastically as she lost weight and became partially paralysed. During a respite in her illness, Terrell had started recording a third album with Gaye (the previous two being *United* in 1967 and *You're All I Need* in 1968). The sessions were short-lived, as her health deteriorated once again and only half of the album was completed. Valerie Simpson added her vocals to Marvin's to complete the album *Easy*, due to be issued in 1969. On 16 March 1970 Tammi Terrell lost her two-year battle against a brain tumour, despite seven attempts by surgeons to eradicate it. Gaye: 'I was hurt because such a talented and beautiful human being died so young.'

He was more than hurt; the death of his singing partner had repercussions that placed his career in jeopardy. The intensity of his mourning startled his friends as they attempted to pluck him from his gloomy depths and back to reality. However, what Gaye did not realise at the time was that his period of self-imposed exile would give him the strength and inspiration to produce his finest and most controversial work ever.

When the horrors of the Vietnam War were related to him by his younger brother Frankie, so intense were Gaye's feelings that he wanted to tell the world. This he did with the stunning *What's Going On*, issued in May 1971. The album floundered in the British chart, but soared to the top in America. Music from the soul for the soul, a work dictated by human conscience. It lifted Motown out of the age of the suppressed artist, ensuring the seventies would not be bogged down by memories of the sixties.

Marvin Gaye's prolific career with Motown continued until the early eighties when his drug abuse escalated uncontrollably to interfere with his career and personal life. Recorded work was by now sporadic, yet what Marvin did release – *Let's Get It On* in 1973, and *I Want You* in 1976, both sexually explicit – sold in excess of one million copies each to become America's top-selling albums. Once again, British chart placings were poor. In between these two releases, Gaye teamed up with Diana Ross on record. It was a disastrous liaison for both artists, but produced the magnificent *Diana and Marvin* album in 1973.

Gaye's reluctance to record new material for Motown became apparent when what was to become his last album for the label comprised rehashed material. Titled *In our Lifetime* and released during 1981, it portrayed a fallen genius; sales were abysmal, leaving its creator devastated.

Freedom from Motown was his only means of recapturing his creativity, he believed, so he demanded Berry Gordy release him from his recording contract. This was done quickly and quietly at which point Gaye struck a deal with CBS (Sony) to record the album *Midnight Love*. 'Sexual Healing' was the first single, released during 1982, and when it became a worldwide hit, Gaye was consumed by a renewed confidence. He reclaimed his Soul Man crown and took his career seriously. On the downside, drugs still dominated his life, leaving him irrational and uncontrollable, while his colleagues and peers were powerless to stop the self-destruction happening before them.

Marvin Gaye's artistry was channelled into many new musical avenues, but his final musical destination was never established, nor could be. On 1 April 1984, the day before his forty-fifth birthday, following a violent argument at his family home in Los Angeles, Marvin Gaye was shot dead by his father. From information garnered following the tragedy, it appeared the singer might have lived if the paramedics had been able to enter the family home upon their arrival.

'Let's put it this way, I didn't dislike Marvin.' – Gay Snr

'I would like to be remembered as one of, if not the greatest, artist to have walked the face of the earth. I would like to be remembered as one of the twelve music disciples, and as a man who was aware and conscious of his environment, and as a person who was full of sensuality, erotic, profound. A person who has depth, feeling and concern for the needs of others. A man who tried to create music, a whole individual . . . I thank God for my wonderful life.' – Marvin Gaye

April 1969

DESMOND DEKKER AND THE ACES

The Israelites

'*Get up in the morning, slaving for bread, sir, so that every mouth could be fed . . . oooh ooh, the Is-rae-lites.*' This song enabled Desmond Dekker and the Aces to open the door in Britain for further Jamaican acts like The Pioneers. Dekker was only toppled from his Jamaican pedestal when Bob Marley's international reign began.

Born Desmond Dacres in Kingston, Jamaica, on 16 July 1941, he was orphaned as a child. He lived in Seaforth, St Thomas, before returning to his birthplace to work as a welder. He then turned to music. Joining The Aces, Dekker recorded his debut single, 'Honour your Mother and Father', on the Yabba label; in Britain it was issued via Island Records. The group continued to release further Jamaican hits like 'Generosity' in 1964, '007 (Shanty Town)' and 'Jezebel', both in 1966. In total they enjoyed twenty Jamaican chart-toppers.

However, late in 1966, Desmond Dekker and the Aces started working with producer Leslie Kong. Influenced by James Bond and the current rock steady trend, '007 (Shanty Town)', the former Jamaican chart-topper, infiltrated the cult clubs in America before going overground to reach the Top Forty. Pyramid Records issued the single in Britain during August 1967 when it became a Top Twenty hit, while Dekker was runner-up in the prestigious Jamaican Song Festival.

There was a two-year gap as the singer concentrated on his lucrative and successful recording career in Jamaica before 'The Israelites'. Penned by Dekker with Leslie Kong, it climbed to the top of the British chart in April 1969. This chart-topper gave the group the distinction of becoming the first Jamaican act to reach No. 1 in Britain with a rock steady single. In America it soared into the Top Ten in June 1969, transforming Desmond Dekker into an international reggae artist almost overnight.

The follow-up single, 'It Miek', written by Dekker, became a Top Ten British hit in July 1969, as *This Is Desmond Dekker* reached the Top Thirty in the album chart. Before the close of 1969, Desmond Dekker and the Aces performed, alongside Jimmy Cliff, Max Romeo and others, in the first Caribbean Music Festival staged in Wembley, Middlesex.

The next year, 1970, started badly for Dekker with the poor-selling 'Pickney Gal', a temporary set-back because 'You Can Get It If You Really Want', released during October, stormed to No. 2 in the British chart. The song was, incidentally, written by Jimmy Cliff for the movie *The Harder They Come*.

As reggae was now making healthy inroads into mainstream British music, due to the more commercially slanted artists like Jimmy Cliff and the acceptance of Bob Marley and the Wailers, Desmond Dekker moved to London during 1971.

Despite being onsite to promote his career, there was a further low spot until 1975 when the reggae label Cactus re-issued 'The Israelites'. It reached the British Top Ten in June. Three months later, 'Sing a Little Song' peaked at No. 16, pushing Dekker once more into the public eye.

With the start of the eighties, Two-Tone Music was making its presence felt. In the hope of capitalising on this new wave sound, Dekker recorded an album with Rumour Records titled *Black and Dekker*. It bombed. In a last-ditch attempt to regain past success, Stiff Records signed him to record and release the album *Compass Point*. That too bombed.

Sporadic recording sessions and the occasional concert performance sustained Desmond Dekker's career up to 1985 when he was declared bankrupt by a British court due to a financial breakdown between him and his management.

Then, in 1990, for the third time, 'The Israelites' grew legs. Not as a hit song but as the theme to the television commercial for Maxell tapes.

What an ending for a symbol of reggae music!

May 1969

THE BEATLES

Get Back

The year of 1969 was the last The Beatles would have together as a group. For some time it had been clear each member wanted to expand his music but within the confines of the quartet it was impossible. It was the year when the group would record their last music as The Beatles and when they would star in their last movie. Newly appointed business manager Allen Klein was the instigator of the split, hired by John Lennon to untangle the business knot they had created. From the outset, Klein's appointment alienated Paul McCartney who insisted his business affairs be represented by the New York company, Eastman and Eastman. Besides, he was to marry the boss's daughter, Linda.

It was John Lennon's decision that The Beatles' next album should be recorded with the sophistication of studio wizardry, overdubs, backward playing tapes and other musical toys. He wanted to revert to the sound of their early recordings, where music was easy and free. He also intended to film the group as they worked, as a final memento of The Beatles.

Under the working title *Get Back*, filming began in January 1969 at Twickenham Film Studios. Before the shoot was a week old, George

Harrison walked off the set, claiming he was tired of McCartney constantly 'getting at him'. He returned some time later, with his friend Billy Preston, whom he had met in 1962 when Preston appeared with Little Richard in Liverpool. He invited the keyboard player to join in the recording sessions, which included 'Get Back'. (Preston would be the second person to share a record label with The Beatles: the first was Tony Sheridan.)

Before 'Get Back' was issued as a single, Lennon and Yoko Ono married in Gibraltar on 20 March 1969. They then flew to Amsterdam to begin a seven-day-long 'bed in' for world peace at the Hilton Hotel. The media ridiculed the couple unmercifully but nothing could persuade them to abandon their bed. From Amsterdam, they travelled to Vienna, Austria, to conduct a press conference from inside a white sack. Back in Britain, meantime, George Harrison and his wife Patti were arrested for possession of cannabis on 12 March 1969, the day Paul McCartney married Linda Eastman at Marylebone Registry Office.

Following initial radio play of 'Get Back' The Beatles withdrew it because they wanted to remix it. This move built up an extraordinary public demand resulting in 'Get Back' debuting in the British chart at No. 1 in May 1969. As part of the film project, The Beatles were filmed performing the single on the roof of their Savile Row offices. Such was the commotion from fans at street level, and complaints of noise from representatives of the nearby Royal Bank of Scotland, that the police halted the filming.

The *Get Back* album was also withdrawn from sale because, once again, The Beatles were unhappy with the result. More importantly, though, they were totally uninterested in the project altogether. In the end, Phil Spector was asked to produce it, a move which caused considerable controversy because it was felt George Martin should have been at the controls. John Lennon's original concept of a 'free and easy' album had grown into a mixer's dream.

With Phil Spector working on the *Get Back* album, due to be retitled *Let It Be*, The Beatles started recording a further album. During August 1969, they were photographed walking across a zebra crossing in Abbey Road, London. The picture was destined for the sleeve of the aptly titled *Abbey Road* album. This photograph later instigated 'Paul is dead' rumours in America simply because he was the only Beatle not wearing shoes. It was rumoured he had been killed in a car accident in Scotland. In truth, it was John Lennon and his son Julian with Yoko Ono and her daughter Kyoko (from her previous marriage) who were hospitalised following a car crash in Golspie, Scotland. No amount of denial could persuade the Americans otherwise.

Amidst the professional mayhem, the movie *Let It Be* was finally ready for release. The world premiere was held on 13 May 1970 in New York, followed seven days later by simultaneous premieres at the London Pavilion and the Liverpool Gaumont. The Beatles attended none of the events.

The 'Let It Be' single, packaged in cardboard, prompting one music critic to write it was a 'cardboard tombstone', shot to No. 2 in the British chart during March 1970. The album was issued alongside Paul McCartney's solo eponymous album. With Ringo Starr due to record his own *Sentimental Journey* album, and Lennon working with Yoko Ono and the newly formed Plastic Ono Band, the demise of The Beatles was predicted as imminent.

When, in December 1970, Paul McCartney successfully filed a lawsuit against the remaining Beatles to dissolve their relationship and in turn prevent Allen Klein from managing his affairs, the end of a musical era was confirmed.

Also see: 'From Me to You', May/June 1963; 'She Loves You', October 1963; 'I Want to Hold your Hand', December 1963; 'Can't Buy Me Love', April 1964; 'A Hard Day's Night', August 1964; 'I Feel Fine', January 1965; 'Ticket to Ride', May 1965; 'Help!', August 1965; 'We Can Work It Out'/'Day Tripper', January 1966; 'Paperback Writer', July 1966; 'Yellow Submarine'/'Eleanor Rigby', September 1966; 'All You Need Is Love', August 1967; 'Hello Goodbye', January 1968; 'Lady Madonna', April 1968; 'The Ballad of John and Yoko', July 1969

June 1969

TOMMY ROE

Dizzy

It's not often a teenager composes a song that, in time, sells in excess of one million copies. But it happened to Tommy Roe with 'Sheila'. His inspiration came from Buddy Holly, the artist who was emulated by so many young artists, but not often successfully.

Born on 9 May 1942 in Atlanta, Georgia, Tommy Roe attended the Brown High School where he formed his first group, The Satins. He also started writing songs and was a mere fourteen-year-old when he penned 'Sheila'. Two years later, he signed a recording contract with Judd Records, a local company. During 1960, Roe released his beloved 'Sheila' as a single, but without national coverage, it bombed. So Roe returned to his group to play local gigs.

It was during this period that he met DJ Paul Drew, who in turn introduced him to Felton Jarvis. Roe gave Jarvis his collection of compositions; Jarvis gave Roe a recording deal with ABC Paramount Records. 'Sheila', naturally, was his debut single in June 1962.

By this time, Roe had left school and worked for General Electric where he soldered wires for $70 per week. As the single climbed the American chart, the singer was required to promote it. Roe was reluctant to do this because he didn't want to resign from his day job where he was in line for promotion. However, when ABC Paramount waved a $6,000 cheque in his direction, Tommy Roe hit the road.

'Sheila' soared to the top of the American chart, selling one million copies. In October 1962, HMV Records released it in Britain, where it soared to No. 2. 'Susie Darling', Roe's cover version of Robin Luke's original, was the follow-up during November – a Top Forty hit in America and Britain.

To coincide with the singer's first British tour with Chris Montez, as support acts to The Beatles, HMV Records released his version of Merle Kilgore's 'The Folk Singer' which soared to No. 4, but was a poor seller Stateside, barely reaching the Top Eighty.

A sluggish few months followed until Roe released 'Everybody', a track he had written after returning to America from his first British tour. Unlike his previous singles, 'Everybody' was issued in Britain first to crash into the Top Ten in time for his next tour with Brian Poole and the Tremeloes, among others. In America, the single became his second million-seller, peaking at No. 3.

Just as Roe had returned to big-selling status, his career was frozen. National Service beckoned and he was drafted into the Army. When he was discharged in 1966 the music business had changed: the British had invaded America. It was to Britain he turned once more to embark upon a national tour with acts like Cilla Black and P.J. Proby. Then, during July 1966, he returned to the American chart with his third million-seller, 'Sweet Pea'. Although he enjoyed further Stateside hits, it wasn't until June 1969 that he returned to the British chart with a vengeance.

After working with P.F. Sloan, composer Steve Barri branched out on his own to work primarily with ABC Paramount artists. Tommy

Roe was assigned to him, where Barri's first aim was to move the singer from the 'bubblegum' mould into mainstream music. To this end he produced three tracks with him, but they both chose 'Dizzy', written by the singer and Freddy Weller (from Paul Revere and the Raiders) which was reminiscent of the sound he wanted to escape from. Barri gave the track to Jimmie Haskell, who added a string arrangement, bringing the song alive, making it sound slightly different to the 'bubblegum' style.

'Dizzy' topped the American chart for four weeks to become Roe's biggest-selling disc ever, selling in excess of two million copies. In June 1969, the single likewise dominated the British chart, replacing The Beatles' 'Get Back'.

According to Tommy Roe, 'All artists want to outdo themselves but how did I top "Dizzy" which sold six million copies?' He didn't bother. Moving into a Malibu dream home brought him unhappiness, so he abandoned his career to return to Georgia, his home state. His recording deal with ABC Paramount by now had ended, so he was under no further pressure to record. Subsequently, Roe remained there for approximately four years and recorded for MGM South, an Atlanta-based record company. One single, 'Working Class Hero', released in May 1973, actually reached the American Top One Hundred. It was his last chart entry.

Three years on, Tommy Roe returned to Los Angeles to record a pair of albums, *Energy* and *Full Bloom* for Monument Records. Both bombed. More recently, during the nineties, the album *The Best of Tommy Roe: Yesterday, Today and Tomorrow* was released in Britain. It did little to rejuvenate his flagging career, which is now confined to nightclubs and cabaret venues.

July 1969

THE BEATLES

The Ballad of John and Yoko

While The Beatles' saga continued, their break up confirmed, the individual group members extracted themselves from the daily trauma. John Lennon and Yoko Ono planned their move to the newly-purchased Tittenhurst Park, Sunninghill, Berkshire; Paul and Linda McCartney holidayed in Corfu, and Ringo and Maureen Starr sailed from Southampton to New York on the *Queen Elizabeth II*.

In May 1969 John and Yoko had flown to the Bahamas to hold another 'bed in' for peace. They had intended to do this in New York but the American authorities refused Lennon a visitor's visa, reputedly because of his drug conviction in 1968. The Bahamas proved too hot for lying in bed, so the couple moved to Montreal, Canada, where they stayed bed-bound for eight days in the Queen Elizabeth Hotel. During their stay, John and Yoko and their guests recorded 'Give Peace a Chance', a future single.

Meantime, 'The Ballad of John and Yoko' was issued, featuring only Lennon (who wrote it) and McCartney (who played drums) because George Harrison and Ringo Starr were outside Britain. The track (The Beatles' first in stereo) chronicled the marriage of the Lennons on 20 March 1969 in Gibraltar. It peaked at No. 8 in America. This low placing was due to spasmodic radio play; the lyrics contained the liberal use of the word 'Christ'. The British, on the other hand, held no such qualms. 'The Ballad of John and Yoko' shot to the top of the chart during July 1969, and was The Beatles' last release to achieve this.

On the business front, The Beatles had relinquished all ties with NEMS Enterprises Ltd, the company formed by Brian Epstein. And their newly appointed manager, Allen Klein, had renegotiated their recording contract with EMI Records. Apart from securing a higher royalty rate, Klein released The Beatles' back catalogue for repackaging. He also took over as manager of Bag Productions, a company recently opened by John and Yoko.

'Give Peace a Chance' was released as the follow-up to 'The Ballad of John and Yoko', but the name on the record label was The Plastic Ono Band. The single soared to No. 2 in the British chart; No. 14 in America. The track went on to become the universal anthem for any cause connected with world peace. During September 1969 Lennon was asked to perform at an open-air 'Rock 'n' Roll Revival Show' in Toronto. He quickly recruited musicians to form The Plastic Ono Band, notably Eric Clapton and Klaus Voorman to play alongside himself and Yoko Ono. They rehearsed on the flight and performed a shaky rock 'n' roll set the following evening.

In November, as The Plastic Ono Band's next single, 'Cold Turkey', detailing the agonies of drug withdrawal, peaked at No. 14 in the British chart (No. 30 in America), John Lennon returned his MBE to the Queen. The accompanying letter explained why: 'In protest against Britain's involvement in the Nigeria–Biafra thing, against our support of America in Vietnam, and against "Cold Turkey" slipping down the charts . . .'

At the close of 1969, Lennon made his last British appearance at the UNICEF 'Peace for Christmas' benefit concert held in London. His name refused to leave the headlines. Early in 1970 a London exhibition of his lithographs portraying him and Yoko in various sexual positions was raided by police who removed some, claiming them to be indecent. Indeed, some were!

On the recording front, 'Instant Karma', written and recorded in one day was issued during February 1970 to reach No. 5 in Britain and No. 3 in America. Also featured on the 'noisy' track were the regulars of Hatchetts nightclub. Following the release of its follow-up, 'Power to the People', a No. 7 British hit; No. 11 in America, John Lennon flew to New York.

He would never return to Britain. The date was 13 August 1971.

Also see: 'From Me to You', May/June 1963; 'She Loves You', October 1963; 'I Want to Hold your Hand', December 1963; 'Can't Buy Me Love', April 1964; 'A Hard Day's Night', August 1964; 'I Feel Fine', January 1965; 'Ticket to Ride', May 1965; 'Help!', August 1965; 'We Can Work It Out'/'Day Tripper', January 1966; 'Paperback Writer', July 1966; 'Yellow Submarine'/'Eleanor Rigby', September 1966; 'All You Need Is Love', August 1967; 'Hello Goodbye', January 1968; 'Lady Madonna', April 1968; 'Get Back', May 1969

Also a No. 1 single in July 1969: 'Something in the Air' by Thunderclap Newman

August 1969

THE ROLLING STONES

Honky Tonk Women

The Rolling Stones were big business, multi-million dollar league. But with every achievement came the knock-back, sometimes at their own instigation. In a word: 'drugs'. Yet they learned to survive. However, what wasn't expected was the tragedy that befell them.

During the previous two years Brian Jones's health deteriorated, his drug intake increased and his insecurities led him to believe that Mick

Jagger and Keith Richard were conspiring against him. He wasn't wrong. In June 1969 it was announced that Jones was leaving the group to be replaced by guitarist Mick Taylor, from John Mayall's band, born in Welwyn Garden City, Herts, on 17 January 1948.

On 3 July 1969 Brian Jones was dead. He was found in his swimming pool at his home at Cotchford Farm in Sussex, once owned by A.A. Milne, creator of Christopher Robin. During the day Jones and his girlfriend Ann Wohlin had drunk alcohol excessively, and towards the evening he had also taken 'downers'. At midnight, after sleeping, Jones got out of bed and went for a swim. Wohlin found him lying face down on the bottom of the swimming pool. The Who's Pete Townsend said, 'It's a normal day for Brian. He died every day.'

At the inquest, the coroner heard the results of the post mortem. Blood and urine samples had shown vast quantities of alcohol and amphetamine substances, and Jones's liver was twice its normal size, in an advanced state of fatty degeneration. His heart was also distended. The verdict therefore was given as death from drowning, although many believe (to this day) that he was murdered. Journalists and authors alike have since published varying reports of Jones's final hours, but it remains to be proven how he met his death.

Two days after the tragedy, The Stones played a free concert in Hyde Park, London. Jagger, dressed in a white Greek-style tunic dress, paid tribute to Brian Jones by reciting Shelley's 'Adonais' before releasing 3,000 butterflies. For added security at this concert, the group hired British Hell's Angels, a tactic which, when repeated in America, would have disastrous effects. This free concert marked Mick Taylor's debut as a Stone.

The next day, 6 July, Jagger flew to Australia to start work on the movie *Ned Kelly*. Marianne Faithfull travelled with him, but when Jagger told her their affair was finished, she attempted suicide and was comatose for eight days. Meanwhile, back in Britain, Brian Jones's funeral was held at the Hatherley Road Parish Church in Cheltenham before his body was buried in the Priory Road Cemetery. Jones had written his own epitaph: 'Please don't judge me too harshly.'

Within days of the funeral, The Stones' next single, 'Honky Tonk Women', was issued and became a British chart-topper in August 1969. It dominated the chart for five weeks, and when issued in America shot to the top where it stayed for four weeks. During November 1969, the group celebrated their American success by touring there for the sixth time. A month into the tour, they intended to repeat their Hyde Park success by giving a free concert at the

Altamont Speedway in Livermore, California. Regrettably, plans went astray. For security, the group employed the American equivalent of Hell's Angels who, under the influence of alcohol and drugs, provoked angry scenes which culminated in a teenager, Meredith Hunter, being knifed to death while The Stones played 'Sympathy for the Devil'. As total confusion followed, the group rushed through their programme to escape in a helicopter. It was the end of peace in the rock world.

While *Ned Kelly* was premiered in Australia, Jagger was cited in Marianne Faithfull's divorce proceedings against her husband John Dunbar. In September Jagger met his future wife, Bianca Rose Perez Moreno de Macias, in Paris. On the business front, the group had sacked Allen Klein and recruited Prince Rupert Loewenstein as their financial adviser.

In March 1971, The Stones embarked upon a British tour, following which they decided to live as tax exiles in the south of France. Now split from Decca Records, they opened their own label, Rolling Stones Records, which was distributed on a worldwide basis by the Kinney group via Atlantic Records. The group's first single in two years and under the new deal was 'Brown Sugar', issued during May 1971, the same month as Jagger and Bianca married. Jade, their daughter, was born during October. 'Brown Sugar' soared to No. 2 in the British chart, while topping the American listing.

Law suits, drug busts and harassment became part of the group's life for the next two years. Jagger and Richard were arrested following an altercation with photographers during an American tour; Richard and his girlfriend Anita Pallenberg had arrest warrants issued against them in Paris, and an entry ban on a member of the group was issued prior to the start of their Australian tour. The ban was eventually lifted, but the list was endless.

Then the Stones suffered another personnel upheaval when Mick Taylor left in December 1974, suffering from exhaustion. He was quickly replaced by Faces' guitarist Ron Wood, born in Hillingdon, London, on 1 June 1947.

Throughout the seventies and eighties The Stones continued to dominate the headlines either with marriages or drug busts. Their tours, particularly those in Britain, still attracted mob scenes, even though their record sales had slackened off. The individual group members became involved in their own projects and due to Richard's inability (on occasion) to compose with Jagger, record sleeves carried the credit 'The Glimmer Twins'.

Albums released during the two decades included *Black and Blue*,

Love You Live, Some Girls, Emotional Rescue, Undercover and *Dirty Work* – all were exceptional sellers. While a run of singles entered the British chart, including 'Fool to Cry', No. 6; 'Respectable', No. 23; 'Start Me Up', No. 7 and 'Waiting on a Friend', No. 50. The Stones also passed through several record companies, with their financial advances becoming more spectacular with each move. The companies realised the group's selling power had diminished but from the prestige viewpoint The Stones were the premier group, who never lacked media coverage. For example, Jagger's personal life once more made headline news when he divorced Bianca, eventually marrying top model Jerry Hall in November 1990.

Through the nineties, Bill Wyman left the group and divorced Mandy Smith (whom he married in June 1989) to marry fashion designer Suzanne Accosta in April 1993. Jagger and Hall had a daughter, while his first daughter, Jade, made him a grandfather. Charlie Watts remained happily married to his first wife, while Keith Richard settled into a calmer lifestyle.

The Stones were now a far cry from the arrogant, anti-Establishment (in fact 'anti' everything), hard-nosed blues musicians of the sixties. But no matter their age, The Rolling Stones still hold the title of 'the greatest rock 'n' roll band in the world'.

Also see: 'Little Red Rooster', December 1964; 'The Last Time', April 1965; 'Get off my Cloud', November 1965

September 1969

ZAGER AND EVANS

In the Year 2525 (Exordium and Terminus)

This single can't be classed as a novelty throwaway because it was, many believed, a work of sixties art. The decade that brought change, self-belief and disregard for establishment rules, also provoked self-analysis and prognostication. Anything went, and usually did! The lyrics of 'In the Year 2525 (Exordium and Terminus)' reflected one young man's feelings, which gave an insight into the world's future, albeit from a pessimistic viewpoint. It was also one of the biggest-selling singles of 1969.

Zager and Evans did, however, fall into the category of one-hit wonders but by choice. Denny Zager decided the music business wasn't for him and left the duo shortly after the single had peaked.

Denny Zager was born in 1944 in Wymore, Nebraska, while Rick Evans was born a year earlier in Lincoln, Nebraska. During 1961 and while at high school, Zager formed a quintet, The Eccentrics. Evans filled the vacancy for guitarist after Zager saw him perform at Wesleyan University (where The Highwaymen also studied).

While a member of The Eccentrics, in 1964, it took Evans thirty minutes to compose 'In the Year 2525 (Exordium and Terminus)', and he fully intended to record it with them. But events overtook them when Zager left to join The Devilles, an outfit that lasted until 1968. By now, both Zager and Evans had become disillusioned with their respective groups and believed they'd work better together as a duo.

'In the Year 2525 (Exordium and Terminus)' was among the pile of material the two were assessing for inclusion in their stage act, and as they were both ballad singers, Denny Zager rewrote the song's arrangement to suit them. In time, this song became a regular in their act and prompted audience requests, and it was this response alone that made them record it.

Using a studio in Odessa, Texas, Zager and Evans cut the song for approximately $500, pressed one thousand copies on Truth Records, their own newly-formed label, and distributed them to radio stations and record stores. The demand staggered them. When 'In the Year 2525 (Exordium and Terminus)' topped the local charts, a representative of Management III signed the couple to a management deal and arranged for RCA Records to press and distribute the single.

The revolutionary disc further surprised Zager and Evans when it soared to the top of the American chart, a position it dominated for six weeks. When issued in Britain during September 1969, the success was repeated for a three-week stay. Five million copies were eventually sold worldwide. Not bad for a song that took thirty minutes to write and $500 to record!

Denny Zager turned his back on music, returning to private life while Rick Evans performed as a soloist.

CREEDENCE CLEARWATER REVIVAL

Bad Moon Rising

'We were four guys from a small town called El Cerrito, totally outside the mainstream of the record business . . . [But] during our time when we were at our peak, I don't think anyone could top us,' John Fogerty told Joe Smith.

Multi-instrumentalist John Fogerty, born in Berkeley, California, on 28 May 1945, formed his first group while at Portola Junior High in El Cerrito. He recruited Doug Clifford, born in Palo Alto on 24 April 1945; Stu Cook, born in Oakland on 25 April 1945, and later his brother Tom, likewise born in Berkeley, on 9 November 1941. After extensive rehearsals they became a regular attraction on the local circuit by 1959.

In 1963 the quartet left school behind them and known as Tommy Fogerty and the Blue Velvets played in and around El Cerrito. They even recorded the single 'Bonita' for a local label. Meantime, Fantasy Records, based in the brothers' home town, was making its presence felt, so Tom Fogerty secured a job there as a shipping clerk. In time, the group auditioned for the record company and was signed by Hy Weiss. They changed their name to The Visions but in view of the British invasion of America, Weiss was keen to give the impression they too were British so called them The Golliwogs. It was under this name that 'Don't Tell Me No Lies' was issued during November 1964.

Early in 1966 The Golliwogs relocated to Fantasy's new teenage label, Scorpio, where 'Brown-Eyed Girl' became a minor local hit. It was also issued in Britain on Vocalion Records. As the group's next single, 'Fight Fire', was issued, Doug Clifford and John Fogerty were drafted into National Service. 'Walking on the Water' was released in their absence and happily (for them) was the last to be issued using the name The Golliwogs.

Midway through 1967, Clifford and Fogerty were reunited with the group, whereupon their music changed from the pseudo-British style to American rock. They rechristened themselves Creedence Clearwater Revival. Incidentally, on the day Fogerty was discharged he wrote 'Proud Mary' (the name of a Mississippi steamboat) but it would be some time before the monster track was unleashed for public consumption.

After releasing the single 'Porterville' late in 1967, Creedence Clearwater Revival concentrated on live performances to establish their new musical style with the public. In between gigs they recorded Dale Hawkins's 'Suzie Q', which marked the switch from Scorpio to Fantasy's premier label. 'Suzie Q', split over two sides of the single, became Creedence Clearwater Revival's first American Top Twenty hit in October 1968. This track and 'Porterville' were included on their eponymous debut album.

By now the group had performed at some of America's most influential events, including several dates at Fillmore West in San Francisco. It was during this time that 'Proud Mary' was recorded: a fiery, fast few minutes which when released in March 1969 raced to No. 2 in the American chart, their first million-selling single. A month on, it peaked in the British chart at No. 8. 'Proud Mary' grew legs, and with Phil Spector's powerhouse production it became another hit for Sonny Charles and the Checkmates, and a million-seller for Ike and Tina Turner. Even Elvis Presley couldn't resist the challenge to record it as an album track.

John Fogerty: 'Creedence was . . . different from others musically. My roots were in Memphis. My idols were Howlin' Wolf, Elvis, Jimmie Rodgers, all in a way traditionally America.' He called Creedence's music 'swamp rock' and when the group's 'Bayou Country' was issued in 1969 it emphasised Fogerty's creativity in this field. It also sold in excess of one million copies.

Following further dates at Fillmore West, the group appeared at the Newport '69 Pop Festival in Northridge, California, with acts like Jimi Hendrix, and at the Woodstock Music and Art Fair alongside other high-ranking acts. Meantime the follow-up to 'Proud Mary' was issued in June 1969. Titled 'Bad Moon Rising' it was classed as 'hillbilly soul' (!) and soared to No. 2 in America, but when issued in Britain it became the group's first chart-topper, during October 1969, a position it held for three weeks. While 'Bad Moon Rising' dominated the British chart, 'Green River' was released in America to become their third million-seller. 'Green River' reached the British Top Twenty in December 1969.

According to Fogerty, 'When you hear "Proud Mary" and "Bad Moon Rising" they sound all-American. People forget that they came out right in the middle of the acid period . . . That's what was all

285

around us, and yet I was preserving my own vision of what I thought rock 'n' roll should be.'

Creedence Clearwater Revival's next British hit, 'Down on the Corner', stalled in the Top Forty in February 1970, while their next album, *Willy and the Poorboys* (so named from a line in 'Down on the Corner') became a further million-seller in America.

In April 1970 the group performed at London's Royal Albert Hall as part of a lengthy European tour. This added impetus to their current single, 'Travellin' Band', by re-establishing them as a Top Ten act. 'Up round the Bend' followed in July to soar to No. 3, beating its American placing by one position. But when Creedence's album *Cosmo's Factory* was issued in August, it notched up a staggering three million sales; the album also topped the British chart for one week.

Before 1970 ended, 'Long As I Can See the Light' reached the Top Twenty in Britain and peaked at No. 2 (the group's favourite position) in America. Two further British hits were enjoyed during 1971, namely, 'Have You Ever Seen the Rain' in March, and 'Sweet Hitch-Hiker' in July. But across the Atlantic, Tom Fogerty had left the group to concentrate on solo projects, following continuing disagreements with his brother. By October 1972, after the release of the disappointing *Mardi Gras* album, the group disbanded entirely. According to John Fogerty, 'Success became a nightmare, a wonderful love affair gone sour. Looking back now, I wish we'd had an outside manager instead of me . . . The end of Creedence was like what Will Rogers said about real estate: "They ain't making it any more."' He also admitted that by the time he reached thirty, his creativity and enthusiasm had dried up. He had no more hit records within him, so instead of trying to compete against his contemporaries he 'retired'. Nonetheless, he continued to record, while Creedence Clearwater Revival album tracks and compilations were issued through to the eighties.

In 1985, Fogerty rose again with the chart-topping album *Centrefield*, issued by Warner Brothers, and could be seen performing as a soloist at charity functions. One such occasion was during February 1990 when he appeared at a benefit concert for the late Roy Orbison held in California. Seven months after this performance Fogerty's brother Tom died from tuberculosis.

Three years later, in 1993, John and the remaining members of Creedence Clearwater Revival were inducted into the Rock and Roll Hall of Fame. A spectacular career had been honoured.

Also No. 1 singles in October 1969: 'Je t'aime moi non plus' by Jane Birkin and Serge Gainsbourg; 'I'll Never Fall in Love Again' by Bobbie Gentry

November/December 1969

THE ARCHIES

Sugar Sugar

Without Don Kirshner and Ron Dante, The Archies might never have existed. And there are a lot of people who wish they hadn't! In actual fact, The Archies never existed; they were the alter-egos of John L. Goldwater's American cartoon characters like Jughead, Betty and, of course, Archie. Yet despite their non-existence, 'Sugar Sugar' was real enough to sell in excess of six million copies worldwide.

Don Kirshner and Ron Dante worked together as teenagers for Aldon Music whose roster of writers included Neil Sedaka and Howard Greenfield, Gerry Goffin and Carole King. After singing on their demo recordings, Dante started writing songs in his own right, and when Kirshner first began thinking of a group in The Archies mould, he remembered the demo singer and asked him to sing on the sessions. Jeff Barry, the power behind The Monkees, another fictitious group at one point, was recruited as producer.

From the outset this trio was responsible for The Archies' sound, from the debut single 'Bang-Shang-a-Lang' in September 1968 which became a Top Thirty entrant in America. For some reason, its follow-up, 'Feelin' So Good (Skooby-Doo)', failed abysmally. Both singles featured Ron Dante on lead vocal so when the next single, 'Sugar Sugar' (written by Jeff Barry and Andy Kim, later a singer in his own right whose 'Rock Me Gently' became a No. 2 British hit in 1974), was planned there seemed no reason to change the vocalist. In actual fact, despite the record's 'group' sound, there were only two main singers, Dante and Toni Wine. All the other voices were multi-tracked by both singers.

'Sugar Sugar' – the very title suggested the twee, sweet, simple song that it turned out to be – was one of a series of 'bubblegum' singles, a musical trend that enjoyed a successful though relatively short life. Staying at the top of the American chart for eight weeks, 'Sugar Sugar' sold three million copies. Despite the cartoon characters being unknown in Britain, the song was likewise a chart-topper from November 1969 for eight weeks. It was also the biggest selling single of 1969 and was The Archies' only British hit. Although certain sections of the public believe this to be one of the worst singles ever produced, it was fun. More remarkably, other artists thought so too, as it was re-recorded several times, most notably by American soul artist Wilson Pickett in 1970, and Britain's most colourful of artists, Jonathan King, under the name Sakkarin, one of his several pseudonyms. Indeed, Ron Dante himself recorded an updated version during the seventies – and used his real name!

Recording novelty discs is similar to walking on thin ice. Once is enough. Nonetheless, Kirshner and Dante felt confident enough to record two further singles, 'Jingle Jangle', which sold one million copies, and 'Who's your Baby', which didn't, heralding The Archies' last Top Forty single in America.

The ice had broken, and The Archies had sunk.

Prior to creating The Archies' vocal sound, Ron Dante was the voice behind another fictitious group, The Detergents, who had enjoyed an American hit with 'Leader of the Laundromat', a humorous take-off of The Shangri-Las' 'Leader of the Pack'. When The Archies' project was finished, Dante moved to Decca Records to record 'Tracy', again using another name, The Cuff Links. In time, Ron Dante moved into radio and television commercials before producing 'Mandy' for Barry Manilow, himself involved in the jingles field before moving into superstardom.

Irrespective of people's negative comments, 'Sugar Sugar' refused to die. As recently as 1987, the original version resurfaced as a nightclub hit to scrape into the British Top One Hundred.